YALE PUBLICATIONS IN RELIGION, 16

JAMES F. CHILDRESS

CIVIL DISOBEDIENCE AND POLITICAL OBLIGATION

A STUDY IN CHRISTIAN SOCIAL ETHICS

NEW HAVEN AND LONDON, YALE UNIVERSITY PRESS, 1971

Published with assistance from
the foundation established in memory of
Amasa Stone Mather of the Class of 1907, Yale College.

Library of Congress catalog card number: 75–158137
International standard book number: 0–300–01493–7

Designed by Sally Sullivan
and set in Linotype Baskerville type.
Printed in the United States of America by
The Carl Purington Rollins Printing-Office
of the Yale University Press

Distributed in Great Britain, Europe, and Africa by
Yale University Press, Ltd., London; in Canada by
McGill-Queen's University Press, Montreal; in
Latin America by Kaiman & Polon, Inc.,
New York City; in Australasia by
Australia and New Zealand Book Co., Pty., Ltd.,
Artarmon, New South Wales; in India by UBS Publishers'
Distributors Pvt., Ltd., Delhi; in Japan by John
Weatherhill, Inc., Tokyo.

For my parents, Roscoe and Zella,
and my wife Georgia

CONTENTS

PREFACE

Few conflicts are more dramatic than the confrontation between the claims of conscience and the claims of the state. From Antigone's defiance of Creon's edict to the actions against war and racism in the United States in the 1960s, this conflict has provoked complex moral questions. Civil disobedience has been offered as a solution to it, as "a new answer to the question of how to divide our duties to Caesar and God"[1]; it has been interpreted and defended by such "classic" theorists as Thoreau and Tolstoy, Gandhi and King; but in the last decade it has been subjected to closer scrutiny from a variety of perspectives, including moral evaluation. It is surprising that there has been so little theological-ethical reflection on this phenomenon, in view of the activities of clergy and laity alike in such protest. With only a few exceptions, such as Paul Ramsey and Daniel Stevick, Christian ethicists have not given the careful, critical attention to civil disobedience that political, legal, and moral philosophers have.[2]

Of course, resistance in totalitarian regimes has been treated

1. Harris Wofford, Jr., "Non-Violence and the Law: The Law Needs Help," in Bedau, *CD*, p. 68.
2. Paul Ramsey, *Christian Ethics and the Sit-In* (New York: Association Press, 1961) and Daniel Stevick, *Civil Disobedience and the Christian* (New York: Seabury, 1969). It is interesting that Stevick gives no attention to Ramsey's book.

almost exhaustively, particularly by German theologians since World War II. Even more recently, theologians have focused on violence and revolution, although often quite uncritically.[3] Perhaps in the light of a conviction that revolution is necessary and desirable, civil disobedience appears to be trivial or, at the very least, unproductive of significant moral issues. At any rate, it has been treated most often as an afterthought, if at all, and only rarely in nonrevolutionary and nontotalitarian contexts, specifically in a relatively just constitutional democracy.

Other factors have also converged to limit theological reflection on civil disobedience. First, widespread agreement with the goals of much contemporary civil disobedience has obscured the need to ask difficult questions about the justification of such action. Second, several theologians may have been overwhelmed by the sentiment which Hugo Bedau expresses:

> the insufficiency of a law for obedience (and of conscientious scruples for disobedience) forces one to look elsewhere if one is to specify a principle that would identify the sufficient and necessary conditions, applicable in all situations, under which one's obedience (or disobedience) is justified. Unfortunately, I do not see how any such principle could be produced, or that it would be of any use once it was available.[4]

But it is certainly possible to affirm Bedau's point and yet to stress the importance of theological-ethical reflection on civil

3. See, among other works, Martin Marty and Dean Peerman, eds. *New Theology No. 6* (New York: Macmillan, 1969) and the writings of Richard Shaull, including "Revolutionary Change in Theological Perspective," *Christian Social Ethics in a Changing World: An Ecumenical Theological Inquiry,* ed. John Bennett (New York: Association Press, 1966), pp. 23–43.

4. Hugo Bedau, "On Civil Disobedience," *The Journal of Philosophy* 58, no. 21 (October 12, 1961): 663.

disobedience, so long as one has not already assumed that
situation ethics is the final word. After all, situation ethics has
been less liberating and helpful in social and political ethics
than in interpersonal relations.

Undoubtedly the current emphasis in religious rhetoric on
action rather than intellectual reflection has also limited
theological-ethical inquiry into this problem, but thought and
action should not be separated. The clarification of the principles and procedures for determining when civil disobedience is justified may be a substantial contribution that the
ethicist can make to continuing moral-political debate and
action.[5] He can aid in the construction of a framework for
the discussion and justification of civil disobedience—a framework which will include, as a fundamental and indispensable
element, a theory of political obligation which is especially
applicable to a relatively just constitutional democracy. This
study attempts to delineate such a framework for a relatively
just democratic order rather than for all civil contexts.

Demonstrating that this can be done and even doing it are
not equivalent to showing that it ought to be done, for many
would say that civil disobedience belongs to an earlier, lost
age and that now, in an era of violence and revolution, it is
irrelevant and obsolescent. I do not deny the central importance of theological-ethical examination of violence and revolution, but nonviolent and nonrevolutionary civil disobedience raises some important moral questions that cannot be
evaded. Furthermore, it is questionable that civil disobedience is a relic of the past, soon to be of interest only to the political antiquarian, for there are grounds for thinking that it
will persist as an important political option in a mass democratic society. Christian Bay, a political philosopher, indicates

5. For one of the best statements of the role of the ethicist, see Ralph
Potter, *War and Moral Discourse* (Richmond, Va.: John Knox Press,
1969), especially the preface and chapter 1.

"the likelihood of a progressively expanding role for civil disobedience in the political life of modern democracies."[6] His
prognosis is based on several features of contemporary life:
the increasing understanding of political behavior and democratic political institutions, the heightened sense of individual
responsibility, which was evidenced by the Nuremberg ver-
dicts and the Eichmann case, and the high premium placed on
the independent conscience. This study, then, is not an au-
topsy but an exploratory examination of a living phenomenon in the light of theological-ethical reasoning.

J.F.C.

Charlottesville, Va.
1971

6. Christian Bay, "Civil Disobedience," *International Encyclopedia of
the Social Sciences,* vol. 2, ed. David L. Sills (New York: Macmillan and
Free Press, 1968), p. 483.

ACKNOWLEDGMENTS

From its inception as a Ph.D. dissertation (Yale University, 1968) through its evolution to its present form, this study has benefited from the critical scrutiny of many teachers, friends, and students. They have contributed to its development in numerous and often unspecifiable ways. James Gustafson offered many helpful suggestions, especially at the outset, and influenced the study in other ways as well. David Little, dissertation adviser and now colleague, found time in a hectic schedule to evaluate the material and to offer many valuable criticisms and words of encouragement. David Harned has been both faithful friend and critic for the last three years; his labors as chairman of the Department of Religious Studies at the University of Virginia have helped to provide an exciting context for teaching and research. Other friends read portions or all of the manuscript, but they will not feel slighted if I mention only four: Stanley Hauerwas, who continues to serve as an intellectual gadfly, Charles Reynolds, Paul Ramsey and Wendell Dietrich. My indebtedness to these persons is, of course, coupled with the recognition that I alone bear responsibility for the study's inadequacies.

Institutional support was indispensable for the completion of this project, and I appreciate the aid of a Kent Fellowship, a Rockefeller Doctoral Fellowship, and two faculty fellowships for summer research in the humanities and social sciences at the University of Virginia. With patience and great efficiency, Mrs. Doris Mays typed and retyped different versions of the manuscript. Editor Wayland Schmitt and other members of the Yale University Press were always helpful, even beyond the call of duty.

Finally, I owe much to my parents, Roscoe and Zella Childress, for their unfailing support in numerous ways over the years, and to my wife Georgia, whose inexhaustible patience, understanding, and encouragement contributed so much to this project. Georgia and our twin sons, Fred and Frank, form my immediate sustaining community, with its rich tapestry of human experiences, so essential for life and work.

LIST OF ABBREVIATIONS

Bedau, *CD*

Hugo Bedau, ed., *Civil Disobedience: Theory and Practice* (New York: Pegasus, 1968).

Hook, *L&P*

Sidney Hook, ed., *Law and Philosophy* (New York: New York University Press, 1964).

Ramsey, *Deeds and Rules*

Paul Ramsey, *Deeds and Rules in Christian Ethics* (New York: Scribner's, 1967).

Wolf, "Die Königsherrschaft Christi"

Ernst Wolf, "Die Königsherrschaft Christi und der Staat," in W. Schmauch and E. Wolf, *Königsherrschaft Christi*, Theologische Existenz heute, n.s. 64 (Munich: Chr. Kaiser Verlag, 1958).

Wolf, "Politischer Gottesdienst"

Ernst Wolf, "Politischer Gottesdienst: Theologische Bemerkungen zu Röm. 13," in *Ecclesia und Res Publica*, ed. Georg Kretschmar and Bernhard Lohse, Festschrift für K. D. Schmidt (Göttingen: Vandenhoeck and Ruprecht, 1961).

Zinn, *Disobedience and Democracy*

Howard Zinn, *Disobedience and Democracy: Nine Fallacies of Law and Order* (New York: Vintage, 1968).

I

THE CONCEPT OF CIVIL DISOBEDIENCE

PROBLEMS OF DEFINITION

The moral discussion of civil disobedience often flounders because of a lack of conceptual clarity. Examples of confusion are plentiful. Mark MacGuigan writes, "among the forms civil disobedience has taken have been revolution, regicide, 'underground' resistance, riots, strikes, picketing, refusal to obey superior orders, boycotts of commodities, hunger strikes, freedom rides, marches, sit-ins, protest meetings, and simply non-compliance."[1] Other commentators, such as Paul Weiss and Jonathan Weiss, insist that civil disobedience includes "acts of violence and destruction that occurred in the riots of long hot summers of civil rights."[2] Still others, such as Martin Luther King, would circumscribe the concept, limiting its use to public, nonviolent, submissive violation of law.[3] Many of the features of the latter definition, which I shall defend

1. Mark R. MacGuigan, "Civil Disobedience and Natural Law," *Catholic Lawyer* 11 (1965): 120.
2. Paul Weiss and Jonathan Weiss, *Right and Wrong* (New York: Basic Books, 1967), p. 119.
3. This is the definition of civil disobedience used in this study. Cf. Martin Luther King, Jr., "Letter from Birmingham Jail," *Why We Can't Wait* (New York: New American Library, Signet Edition, 1964), pp. 83–84.

and utilize in this study, are present in the classical tradition of civil disobedience (e.g. Thoreau and Gandhi) as well as contemporary approaches.

Both supporters and opponents of civil disobedience have contributed to the conceptual muddle. But theologians, as a rule, have produced less discriminating examinations than their philosophical and juristic counterparts. These rare theological explorations have usually suffered seriously from a failure to make precise distinctions. One article, for example, uses civil disobedience, civil resistance, and revolution interchangeably.[4] Its assumption apparently is that to evaluate one form of resistance is to evaluate all. Such an assumption is unwarranted, for, as I shall contend, the various forms of resistance to the state raise somewhat different moral questions. A failure to make the necessary distinctions can only obscure the moral complexity of resistance.[5]

Conceptual clarification is absolutely indispensable for a constructive discussion of the moral issues. It is one thing to identify an act of civil disobedience, and another to justify it. There is thus a distinction between the criteria of the concept of civil disobedience and the criteria of the justification of the act. But these criteria are not totally unrelated. The definition suggests certain essential conditions for the identification of acts of civil disobedience. Some of these conditions, for example, nonviolence, will be salient in any description of the act and, therefore, will significantly affect the question of justifi-

4. Robert Meyners, "Theology and Civil Disobedience," *The Chicago Theological Seminary Register* 57, no. 6 (May 1968): 7–17.

5. There are a few exceptions to this trend. One example is Martin Rock's *Widerstand gegen die Staatsgewalt: Sozialethische Erörterung* (Munster: Regensberg, 1966), which uses distinctions that are important in philosophical and legal analysis of resistance, although it finally falls short, especially in the examination of what I am calling civil disobedience (see especially pp. 117–36). Cf. also his more recent work, *Christ und Revolution* (Augsburg: Verlag Winifried-Werk, 1968), vol. 2 of Christliches Leben heute.

cation even though they may not be sufficient for justification.[6]

Several approaches to the definition of civil disobedience are possible. The definition can be reportive, in that it summarizes common usage in a coherent picture. On the other hand, a stipulative definition will demarcate the area of discussion for purposes of a particular analysis. Or a definition can serve primarily as a proposal about the proper way of using the phrase. None of these approaches is free of difficulties.

A reportive definition must contend with a wide variety of uses in speeches and lectures, articles and books; ultimately, indeed, it seems to break apart on the rocks of diverse usage. The second line of attack—a stipulative definition—is more promising. Indeed, there are no major obstacles in the way of specifying a particular definition and then confining discussion to it. Of course, even such a definition will be judged in terms of its usefulness to the particular study. Some definitions simply restrict rather than facilitate discussion. The value of the discussion largely determines the value of the definition.

Anyone who wishes to claim more for his analysis of the concept of civil disobedience must move beyond both reportive and stipulative approaches and make a general recommendation about the use of the term. The arguments supporting such a proposal can be illustrated with reference to my claim that civil disobedience should be understood as non-violent, public, submissive violation of law as an act of protest. The general unanimity among the major theoreticians of civil disobedience about the use of the term is significant. But the fact that Thoreau, Gandhi, King, and others concur in the fundamental criteria for its use does not provide a suffi-

6. For Howard Zinn's confusion of descriptive or definitional and evaluative questions, see *Disobedience and Democracy*, p. 43.

cient foundation for a particular definition. Other considerations are necessary. How clear is the concept? Does it clarify the phenomena being discussed? How does it relate to other concepts and similar phenomena (e.g. revolution)? While the reportive, stipulative, and reformative approaches to the concept of civil disobedience are analytically distinct, they are often combined. My proposal about the use of the phrase *civil disobedience* is reformative and thus depends in part on a summary of usage by major theoreticians and in part on formal analysis, but I hasten to emphasize that my argument will not be weakened if the reader takes the definition as a stipulation rather than as a recommendation of proper usage.

Evident in much contemporary discussion of *civil disobedience* is confusion about whether it is a generic or specific term. But none of the attempts to make it a generic label covering all forms of direct-action protest, all resistance to the state, and all violations of law have been satisfactory. Civil disobedience is best understood as a particular species of disobedience to law and resistance to the state. An overly broad definition—like Howard Zinn's "the deliberate violation of law for a vital social purpose"[7]—obfuscates the further distinctions that are necessary if moral discourse is to proceed. Regardless of the terminology, some illegal acts have features (nonviolence, openness, submission) which so obviously set them apart that they cannot simply be equated with all other forms of disobedience to law (e.g. theft) and resistance to the state (e.g. rebellion). Because of the peculiarly significant questions of political obligation and resistance raised by civil disobedience, a broad definition must at some point distinguish between public and clandestine, nonviolent and violent, submissive and evasive forms of lawbreaking. Arguments about justification will differ accordingly. But the essential question

7. Ibid., p. 39.

remains: what conditions must be present for an act to be labeled civil disobedience?

First, the phrase *civil disobedience* suggests that a law of the state, the *civitas,* is broken. This criterion is rather obvious, but one is surprised to discover just how often it is overlooked. For example, MacGuigan's statement brought together under the one rubric of civil disobedience such diverse phenomena as hunger strikes, marches, protest meetings, and other forms of direct action. It is very difficult to find the thread that binds them together, unless it is protest. But then the term *protest* would seem to be more appropriate than *civil disobedience,* since such acts are not necessarily illegal.

The criterion of illegality raises several problems. Does the law have to be valid? What if one is testing the law in the courts? I shall return to these problems later. For the moment it is sufficient to emphasize, with Christian Bay, that the requirement of illegality means only that the actor understands the act to be "illegal or of contested legality." Bay continues, "the act of disobedience must be illegal, or at least be deemed illegal by powerful adversaries, and the actor must know this if it is to be considered an act of civil disobedience."[8]

As this quotation suggests, the violation of law must be intentional if the act is to be counted as civil disobedience. A group marching to the center of a town to protest the failure of local officials to carry through some proposed projects will not be engaged in civil disobedience if they are unaware of a local ordinance which prohibits parading without a permit. They technically violate the law, but it is part of the description of the act of civil disobedience that the agent know and *intend* the illegality of his act.

8. Christian Bay, "Civil Disobedience," *International Encyclopedia of the Social Sciences,* vol. 2, p. 473. Cf. also Christian Bay, "Civil Disobedience: Prerequisite for Democracy in Mass Society," *Political Theory and Social Change,* ed. David Spitz (New York: Atherton Press, 1967), which has some of the same material.

Intentional violation of law was absent from the Montgomery bus boycott, although Martin Luther King and several members of the Montgomery Improvement Association were arrested. At the outset they were not aware of a law prohibiting boycotts, nor did the opposition apply this old state law until violence failed to throttle the boycott. Having decided to eliminate segregation on the buses, King and the Montgomery Improvement Association might have committed civil disobedience by breaking the ordinance requiring segregation, but they chose instead to stay away from the buses. That they were arrested does not make their action civil disobedience, since the violation was incidental rather than deliberate and intentional.[9]

It is essential to understand that the adjective *civil* in the phrase *civil disobedience* does not stand in contrast to *criminal*. The actor in civil disobedience may well be charged with criminal behavior, although there is no crime of civil disobedience as such. Stuart Brown points out that the crime with which the civilly disobedient person is charged is "a punishable breach of a rule of law, each crime being defined by such a rule."[10] For example, the charge in a case involving a violation of a town ordinance against marching without a permit is not that the participants were engaged in an expression of conscientiously held ideals or a protest against the present social order, but that they violated the ordinance. Particular crimes can be committed, of course, without being acts of civil disobedience. The refusal to pay a portion of one's income taxes is not *without further specification* an act of civil disobedience.

9. See Martin Luther King, Jr., *Stride Toward Freedom* (New York: Harper and Row, Perennial Library, 1964), pp. 122 ff. Cf. Rex Martin's analysis, "Civil Disobedience," *Ethics* 80, no. 2 (Jan. 1970): 124.

10. Stuart Brown, "Civil Disobedience," *The Journal of Philosophy* 58, no. 22 (Oct. 26, 1961): 671.

Other connotations of *civil* are quite important in outlining what is involved in civil disobedience. One commentator has given an excellent summary of Gandhi's use of the term, explaining that the disobedient act is called

> "civil" because it is non-violent resistance by people who are ordinarily law-abiding citizens; also because the laws which they choose to disobey are not moral laws but only such as are harmful to the people. It is civil also in the sense that those who break the law are to observe the greatest courtesy and gentleness in regard to those who enforce the law. They are even to seek not to embarrass the opponent if possible.[11]

Gandhi writes, "We must therefore give its full and therefore greater value to the adjective 'civil' than to 'disobedience.' Disobedience without civility, discipline, discrimination, nonviolence is certain destruction."[12] The question of whether embarrassment and coercion are excluded from civil disobedience, as Gandhi sometimes seems to require, will be examined later. At this point I can only indicate that I reject Gandhi's proposal to exclude, almost by definition, coercion from civil disobedience, for reasons which will also be given later.

Even if civility can include coercion, Gandhi's statement suggests other components that require careful attention, although he was more concerned with moral guidance than with conceptual analysis. To Gandhi the word *civil* suggests that the act of disobedience must be public. This criterion may appear ambiguous, but, at the very least, it indicates that civil disobedience does not involve evasion of arrest and pun-

11. Bharatan Kumarappa, Editor's Note, in M. K. Gandhi, *Non-Violent Resistance,* ed. Bharatan Kumarappa (New York: Schocken Books, 1961), p. iv.
12. Ibid., p. 173.

ishment by secrecy or concealment. As Bedau points out, it would be odd for a policeman to report that he had surprised several people in the act of civil disobedience.[13] While there are, of course, varying degrees of openness and publicity, the main point is clear. A person who refuses to pay part of his income tax to protest the nuclear armament system can hardly be said to be engaged in protest if he fails to make his motives public—that is, known to the proper officials. A person may withhold from the Internal Revenue Service the same amount as the protestor but conceal his action; he also violates the law but he does not commit civil disobedience.

It is important to stress again that this conceptual exercise does not prejudge the possibility of justifying other forms of disobedience or resistance. According to my analysis, those conducting the Underground Railroad were not engaged in civil disobedience, for their purposes could not be accomplished without secrecy and concealment. But to say that these illegal acts were not civil disobedience is not to prejudge or determine their justifiability. This point holds also for the surreptitious violations of law by physicians who perform abortions.

Another necessary element in civil disobedience is nonviolence. Gandhi, who was committed to nonviolence as a way of life, saw civil disobedience as a specification of nonviolence in the political sphere. Other protestors do not embrace nonviolence as a way of life, although they advocate nonviolent, civil disobedience on different grounds. For example, one might argue that while violence is not intrinsically evil, it cannot be conjoined with the appropriate respect for the prevailing order. Another consideration which is often decisive is expediency: a group which simply cannot muster sufficient force to make violence effective may temporarily

13. "On Civil Disobedience," p. 655.

adopt nonviolent disobedience as a tactic. Thoreau, in contrast to Gandhi and King, was not committed to nonviolence
as a way of life, as his enthusiastic response to John Brown's
raid at Harper's Ferry indicates. Thoreau's refusal to pay his
poll tax has been more significant than his rhetoric for the
theory of civil disobedience.

Regardless of the grounds on which it is justified, nonviolence is an essential feature of civil disobedience. But since it
is perhaps the most disputed criterion, it requires further discussion. Violence can be defined as "willful application of
force in such a way that it is physically or psychologically in-
jurious to the person or group against whom it is applied."[14]
The boundaries are not absolutely clear, but certainly such
acts as assassination or regicide could not be regarded as civil
disobedience, although they might conceivably be committed
openly and with submission to arrest. In other words, there
are certain human rights which cannot be infringed in an act
of *civil* disobedience. Hence, in effect, not every law (e.g. the
legal prohibition of murder) can be violated civilly.

Any discussion of this question is complicated by the contemporary political rhetoric of violence. Radicals tend to reject various policies of the established social order as "violent," although it is often much easier to argue that the
policies are immoral or unjust. But the other side is no less
ready to brandish the term against all threats to the established order. For example, one judge describes civil disobedience as a "form of violence with all the risks and dangers that
such acts imply and generate."[15]

Beyond these persuasive uses of the term *violence,* difficult
questions are raised by borderline cases. What about the

14. Theodore Paullin, *Introduction to Non-Violence* (Philadelphia:
Pacifist Research Bureau, 1944), p. 6.
15. William T. Sweigert, "Moral Preemption: Part III: Claims of
'Right' under the Positive Law," *The Hastings Law Journal* 17 (March
1966): 470.

provocation to violence? What about an act which ignites the
tensions of a community so that it bursts into violence? What
about damage of property instead of persons? It is very difficult to classify these actions, and good arguments can be ad-
vanced for a variety of interpretations. The fact that these
matters are not easily resolved does not lessen the value of
paradigm cases, which can still help us locate the relevant
features for discussion.

Civil has yet another connotation, which has received relatively little attention. The lawbreaker who is civil in his
behavior will submit to arrest and punishment. Submission
is really an extension of openness and nonviolence, and for
that reason few theorists have viewed it as a distinct criterion.[16] Just as efforts to evade arrest by concealment and
violence have already been excluded from civil disobedience,
the requirement of submission at least rules out attempts to
evade arrest and punishment by flight, although it is difficult to determine just what else it excludes. Joseph Ellin
stresses the main points: "The idea of taking the penalty
probably should be understood to mean not willingness to
accept jail but rather the renunciation of all nonlegal means
(concealment, flight) of avoiding jail. What is intended is the
willingness to rely on the law alone as your protection."[17]

Perhaps most of the difficulty stems from what is called
"resisting arrest." Certainly submission does not require
complete passivity and cooperation with arresting officers for
the act to be *civil* disobedience. Some forms of noncooperation (for example, forcing the officers to carry the violaters
from the scene) might well meet the letter if not the spirit of
submission. Furthermore, nothing in this criterion excludes

16. See, for example, Bedau, "On Civil Disobedience," and John Rawls,
"The Justification of Civil Disobedience," in Bedau, *CD*, pp. 240–55.
17. "Fidelity to Law," *Soundings* 51, no. 4 (Winter 1968): 422.

the appeal to and use of existing legal procedures, although this matter will receive further attention later.[18]

The final criterion of civil disobedience is implicit in the foregoing discussion, and indeed it can be argued that the other criteria (except illegality) are its outgrowths.[19] Civil disobedience is an act of protest which, by expressing one's personal morality (e.g. dictates of conscience) and/or his conception of public morality (e.g. shared principles of justice), calls attention to a discrepancy between some law or policy and those moral standards.[20] It may be the condemnation of a failure to live up to minimal standards or the affirmation of a higher ideal.

On the basis of these criteria, my definition of civil disobedience is offered less as a formal restriction than as an attempt to highlight particular bases for the identification of acts of civil disobedience: *civil disobedience is a public, nonviolent, submissive violation of law as a form of protest.*[21] If not all lawbreaking is civil disobedience, if the what is necessary but not sufficient, the how of the action must be emphasized. I have not been content to limit the how to conscientiousness, for example. The mode in which the lawbreaking

18. But contrast the position developed by Carl Cohen, "Law, Speech, and Disobedience," in Bedau, *CD*, pp. 165–77.

19. See Francis A. Allen, "Civil Disobedience and the Legal Order," Part I, *University of Cincinnati Law Review* 36, no. 1 (Winter 1967): 9.

20. It is difficult to determine whether acts of disobedience that meet the other criteria and yet are motivated by personal interest and advantage really qualify as civil disobedience. This problem can be handled, in part, by insisting that civil disobedience have some reference to moral standards (whether private or public), although individual motives may be "neurotic or narrowly self-seeking." See Bay, "Civil Disobedience," *International Encyclopedia of the Social Sciences,* vol. 2, p. 474. I shall have more to say about this question later in this chapter.

21. Bedau tends to emphasize "frustration" more than protest. The act of civil disobedience must be designed to frustrate or thwart the law or policy, especially if it is engaged in generally. Bedau, "On Civil Disobedience," passim.

as protest or expression of conscience is conducted is crucial, and the how of civil disobedience is necessarily structured by nonviolence, openness, and submission. It should be stressed again that if this reformative definition is viewed by the reader as only stipulative, the remainder of the argument will not be affected.

Quite obviously, I am developing an ideal type which will enable me to identify acts of civil disobedience for purposes of evaluation. Many questions about the classification of any particular act will, of course, emerge. Some of these questions have already been suggested (e.g. incidental violence). I am not concerned with precisely labeling the various acts of disobedience and resistance that could be found or conceived. But there are several very clear historical examples which fit the paradigm of civil disobedience, and many of them will appear in this study. My objective is to see how a theological-ethical framework might help to evaluate those acts which, regardless of the terms employed, raise fundamental and fascinating problems about the obligation to obey the law and the justification of resistance. Such acts raise these problems precisely because of their characteristics, as one example will indicate. If in civil disobedience the agent accepts the legal penalty for his action, has he thereby satisfied the claim of the law on him? If, as some argue, the law presents him with a choice—obedience or punishment—does obedience have a prima facie claim?

CIVIL DISOBEDIENCE AND REVOLUTION

The concept of civil disobedience can be further elucidated by distinguishing it from other forms of resistance, especially rebellion and revolution. Many attempts to appraise civil disobedience from a moral standpoint have been misdirected because of their common assumption that it can be justified

only if revolution can be justified. But civil disobedience cannot be adequately assessed if it is placed *only* within the context of revolution. The two phenomena have much in common, but the differences are so important that they cannot be ignored. Perhaps the distinction can best be sharpened by viewing both civil disobedience and revolution as species of political resistance. Richard Rovere cogently argues that "civil disobedience may be a form of resistance, but not all resistance is civil disobedience. Rioting and other efforts to disrupt or usurp democratically constituted authority are forms of resistance that have nothing whatever to do with civil disobedience."[22]

Resistance always involves standing against someone or something. Whether it takes the form of bullets or ballots, it is a refusal simply to acquiesce in the actions or demands of other men. Some kind of force, which can be defined as "physical or intangible power or influence to effect change in the material or immaterial world,"[23] must be used: it may be coercion and violence or influence and persuasion. Resistance takes place in the context of conflicting ideas, values, or interests. The adjective *political* specifies the sphere within which the act of resistance occurs, and its direction. Political resistance, then, is opposition to and the use of some force against the policies, laws, or practices of a political order and the men who, in their public capacities, execute them. We must distinguish, as Leslie J. MacFarlane contends,

between ordinary acts of law breaking and acts of *political* disobedience. While there are bound to be difficult cases on the margin whatever line of distinction

22. See the confusion about resistance and civil disobedience, ranging from equation to total separation, in the collection of opinions "On Civil Disobedience, 1967," *The New York Times Magazine* (November 27, 1967). Rovere's statement appears on p. 131.

23. Paullin, *Introduction to Non-Violence*, p. 6.

is used, the vast majority of those acts of disobedience which would normally be classified as political occur when the perpetrators are motivated by the desire to secure changes in the policy, laws, government, or constitution of the state.[24]

Obviously political resistance encompasses a broad range of activity, from the dissemination of ideas in print to sabotage and regicide. Furthermore, many theologians have argued that one of the primary values of democracy is its institutionalization of resistance. Paul Ramsey suggests that in one sense "democracy means justifiable and limited resistance."[25] This institutionalized resistance (especially in the form of legal dissent and election of officials) is not always adequate. For example, in the late 1960s the cry among the opponents of the United States' involvement in Vietnam was that opposition must move from legal and institutionalized to illegal resistance.

Civil disobedience can be located on a continuum of political resistance[26] whose major extremes are nonviolent and

24. Leslie J. MacFarlane, "Justifying Political Disobedience," *Ethics* 79, no. 1 (Oct. 1968): 30. As Alan Gewirth indicates, the meaning of *political* fluctuates between moral (e.g. Aristotle) and amoral (e.g. Machiavelli) poles, just as the term *law* does. There are other meanings between these extremes. One is the rhetorical—*political* indicates the use of influence, persuasion, pressure, etc. to obtain an end. Another is the administrative—*political* indicates the existence of rules for regulating the life of some community. Thus, authority and rules, and power and influence are variously emphasized in these definitions. Gewirth, "Political Justice," in *Social Justice*, ed. Richard Brandt, (Englewood Cliffs, N.J.: Prentice-Hall, 1962.)

25. Ramsey, *Christian Ethics and the Sit-In*, p. 93. Cf. Helmut Thielicke's statement: "Resistance is legal today only in a democracy. Here legality and legitimacy do not follow separate paths. Resistance is so legal in fact that it is an accepted fact of the political routine." *Theological Ethics* (Philadelphia: Fortress Press, 1969), vol. 2, *Politics*, p. 328.

26. Rock (*Widerstand gegen die Staatsgewalt*, p. 127) views resistance as an "analogical" concept.

violent action. Often a similar distinction is drawn between active and passive resistance, but that terminology creates some difficulties. For example, passive resistance tends to imply the absence of initiative and force on the part of the resister, and also to suggest acts of omission (e.g. not paying taxes) rather than commission.[27] In order to avoid these implications, it is better to use the term *nonviolent resistance*.

Gandhi in fact rejected the term *passive resistance* as a description of his campaigns and instead employed the term *Satyagraha,* which can be understood as nonviolent resistance. His rejection had a different rationale: passive resistance appeared to be based on weakness not strength.

> Satyagraha differs from Passive Resistance as the North Pole from the South. The latter has been conceived as a weapon of the weak and does not exclude the use of physical force or violence for the purpose of gaining one's end, whereas the former has been conceived as a weapon of the strongest and excludes the use of violence in any shape or form.[28]

Actually Gandhi's point can be expressed most succinctly by the distinction between nonviolence as a way of life and nonviolence as a matter of expediency. He contends that passive resistance is employed only because a movement lacks the strength to effect its will by other, more violent means, whereas *Satyagraha* involves a fundamental commitment to a way of life which transcends the ends-means relationship. Gandhi's own analysis of nonviolent resistance led him to other distinctions which can be utilized without implying acceptance of their underpinnings in his thought.

27. See Leo Kuper, *Passive Resistance in South Africa* (New Haven: Yale University Press, 1957), p. 72. Cf. Rock, *Widerstand gegen die Staatsgewalt,* p. 127–30. In the end, Rock seems to think that the term *Gehorsamverweigerung* is more adequate.

28. Gandhi, *Non-Violent Resistance,* p. 6.

In addition to established methods of opposition within democratic political orders (e.g. voting) nonviolent resistance includes both noncooperation and civil disobedience. Noncooperation is often confused with nonresistance, but they can be distinguished. Both withdraw the main points of contact with state and society, but noncooperation remains within the arena of conflicting claims and is simply one form of resistance. Nonresistance, on the other hand, as practiced by some sectarian groups, is often an attempt to avoid implication in the arena of conflicting claims and interests and hence to eschew resistance altogether. It has no political purpose, while noncooperation presupposes such a purpose. Noncooperation, according to Gandhi, "means renunciation of the benefits of a system. . . . We, therefore, renounce the benefits of schools, courts, titles, legislatures and offices set up under the system." It also means "withdrawing all the voluntary assistance possible and refusing all its [the system's] so-called benefits,"[29] which for Gandhi had specifically political purposes. This noncooperation may involve acts of civil disobedience; but not all refusals of benefits and assistance are illegal. Presently, noncooperation by not voting or by purposely keeping one's income below taxable levels is legal, while the act most frequently labeled as noncooperation (the refusal to register for Selective Service) is illegal.

Another significant difference between civil disobedience and noncooperation rests on the degree of interaction between the dominant and subordinate groups. Generally, noncooperation is an effort to reduce interaction so much that the opposition will be forced to capitulate or at least to negotiate. Civil disobedience, on the other hand, heightens interaction between groups. It involves "the dramatic presentation of demands, compels a response by the dominant

29. Ibid., pp. 170, 238.

group, transforms the routine, relatively unconscious pattern of interaction by an infusion of emotion, moral fervour and conflict, thus providing a stimulus for reconsideration of the relations between the dominant and subordinate groups."[30] It consists of an illegal act or a series of illegal acts that require some response from the community or its officials.

Violent resistance implies not only direct harm to persons but also the unauthorized use of force. As such, it is often associated with a more extensive rejection of the existing government than civil disobedience, which has limited ends even within a revolutionary context, and it takes many not easily distinguishable forms, the most important of which is clearly revolution.

The term *revolution* was brought into the political arena from astronomy, where it was used to describe the motion of the planets, but it is by no means limited to astronomy and politics. The phrases *technological revolution, industrial revolution,* and *sexual revolution,* for example, all connote abruptness of change as well as the fact that the change strikes at the very roots of a particular system. Revolution thus indicates that the conditions under which a system has been operating are suddenly altered. Hence political revolution has been defined by C. J. Friedrich as "a sudden and violent overthrow of an established political order."[31] I wish to emphasize more clearly than Friedrich that revolution involves an alteration of the basic structure of the social or

---

30. Kuper, *Passive Resistance,* p. 74.

31. C. J. Friedrich, "An Introductory Note on Revolution," *Revolution (Nomos 8),* ed. C. J. Friedrich (New York: Atherton Press, 1967), p. 5. Paul Schrecker describes revolution as "an illegal change of the conditions of legality" ("Revolution as a Problem in the Philosophy of History," in Ibid., p. 38). See also Peter Berger, "Between System and Horde," in *Movement and Revolution,* by Peter Berger and Richard J. Neuhaus (New York: Doubleday, Anchor Book, 1970), p. 51; and Martin Rock, *Christ und Revolution,* p. 41 and passim.

political realm. The primary features of revolutionary activity, then, are (1) violence and (2) the intention of altering the social or political order in a fundamental way rather than simply replacing one set of officials with another.[32]

This typology of political resistance represents an effort to facilitate the moral assessment of civil disobedience. The most difficult question, however, remains unanswered. Is rebellion or revolutionary activity a logical implication of civil disobedience? This question could be interpreted in relation to either of the two features of revolution that I have stressed: violence or the intention to make a fundamental change in the system. Because I shall examine violence in relation to civil disobedience more fully below, this discussion will focus on the other feature of revolution. I contend that the affinities between civil disobedience and rebellion or revolutionary activity do not in fact cancel out the distinction that exists between them, which is clear in principle and must be maintained. Those who insist that the justifications for civil disobedience and rebellion are identical must argue that the act of civil disobedience is a revolutionary act.

For example, Robert Penn Warren, in justifying his refusal to sign a statement that Nicola Chiaromonte, with the collaboration of Ignazio Silone, drew up in 1960 to declare agreement with the sponsors and signatories of the "Declaration on the Right to Insubordination in the Algerian War," wrote of the resister: "If he does not have this trust in the orderly process of self-rectification for the state and society, he may very well resort to disobedience. But he should recognize that this is a *revolutionary* act. By implication he is pre-

32. From one standpoint, it is possible to view revolution as a successful rebellion, but revolution implies a fundamental change in the system while rebellion (and coup d'état) may simply suggest a shift in personnel and holders of power rather than an alteration in the structure. Although tyrannicide is often discussed in this context as one form of violent resistance, it too may not be a revolution in the sense of fundamental change.

pared to destroy the state which he disobeys." Rightly rejecting one of the statement's theses, that the essence of democracy is the right to disobedience, Warren went on to argue speciously that, because "the act of disobedience is a revolutionary act, it can be endorsed now in France only if one feels that the present government should be overthrown." Why? Because "every act of insubordination by conscience necessarily condemns a state."[33] In effect, then, no disobedience is justified unless revolution is also justified in that situation.

Stuart Brown, a philosopher, develops an argument which on first reading may appear to be very close to Warren's but contains differences which I find significant. Brown's main point is that "there is a *logical relationship between civil disobedience and civil rebellion* and that this relationship explains the suspicion and fear with which acts of civil disobedience are frequently regarded."[34] When he explains this relationship, he depends largely on an interpretation of *treason*. Civil rebellion is not easily assimilated to the general category of crimes, but it is one form the crime of treason may take. Of course, other crimes may be committed in rebellion. Because civil rebellion is "explicitly treason," it is "a crime in and of itself."

The point is one of clarification not justification. Brown contends that from the relation of treason and civil rebellion, it follows "that an act of civil disobedience may be implicitly treasonous and implicitly a crime in and of itself."[35] How qualified and tempered this statement is in contrast to Warren's view is evident. For Warren rebellion and treason are logical implications of any act of disobedience; for Brown disobedience may or may not be *implicitly* treasonous.

33. Robert Penn Warren, in "On Civil Disobedience and the Algerian War," *Yale Review* 50 (Spring 1961): 476–77, 480.
34. Brown, "Civil Disobedience," p. 678. Italics mine.
35. Ibid., p. 677.

Brown recognizes that, although the distinction between rebellion and civil disobedience is quite clear in principle, the lines may be blurred in actual cases. For example, it may be extremely difficult to determine the point at which massive civil disobedience could so disrupt the machinery of government that it would collapse. On the other hand, civil disobedience as a tactic dictated by the weakness of the rebels can merely disguise their designs until an opportune time for revolution arrives. In the meantime, nonviolent disobedience may be one way of mustering support or weakening the fiber of the community to insure a successful revolution. Certainly Brown is correct in arguing that "wherever, on grounds of mere strategy or tactics, civil disobedience is committed either as an alternative to rebellion or as part of a conspiracy to rebel, it is implicitly revolutionary and treasonous."[36] But this is a logical implication of only some, not all acts of civil disobedience. In my final chapter I shall discuss "obstructive" civil disobedience, which may well be revolutionary, at least by implication.

By emphasizing the differences between civil disobedience and revolutionary activity, I have drawn distinctions within the concept of civil disobedience that make it impossible to treat civil disobedience only within the context of revolution. Some acts of civil disobedience may be revolutionary or at least serve as means in an overall revolutionary movement, but not all acts of civil disobedience are directed at replacing the existing political system with another. There is, of course,

36. Ibid. In chapter 4 I shall further consider the question of whether in addition to the actor's intention and the act's consequences, one has also to look at the act's logic in order to determine whether it is revolutionary. I shall focus on the question of universalization, because some interpreters of civil disobedience think that tax resistance (such as Thoreau's refusal to pay his poll tax) is in its logic a revolutionary act (see Bedau, *CD*, p. 22). Certainly Thoreau's act pointed in the direction of revolution, since he chose to deny the state what he saw as its only point of contact with him.

a shared area between civil disobedience and revolution, which means that the logic of justification in the one case is not totally unrelated to the other. If we were to assume that civil disobedience is revolutionary at least by implication, the discussion would be greatly simplified: there would be only one framework of justification, and the discussion could move freely between civil disobedience and revolution without jumping a wide hiatus. But this advantage would be illusory, since it could be gained only by sacrificing careful analysis of two very complex phenomena.

THE FORMS OF CIVIL DISOBEDIENCE

In addition to questions of resistance and revolution, a gigantic web of problems clings to the concept and practice of civil disobedience. Although it is impossible fully to disentangle the problems and arrange them in neat, separate categories, careful analysis at this point will clarify some of the issues that are important for assessing civil disobedience.

One way to unravel the web is to inquire into the legitimacy of calling the following acts *civil disobedience*.

1. A Black Muslim (e.g. Muhammed Ali) refuses induction into the armed forces when his draft board rejects his claim to be a religious conscientious objector and/or a minister—an act paralleled numerous times by the Jehovah's Witnesses, who constitute the majority of imprisoned Selective Service violators.[37]

2. In protest against the war in Vietnam, Thomas Cornell of the Catholic Peace Fellowship said, "The idea is to get as many people as possible to burn their draft cards so that the government would not be able to prosecute all of them."[38]

37. See Willard Gaylin, M.D., *In the Service of Their Country: War Resisters in Prison* (New York: Viking, 1970), pp. 269–70.
38. *New Haven Register,* October 20, 1965.

3. In March 1964, seven demonstrators used their bodies, garbage, and cans to block the Manhattan approach to Triborough Bridge during rush-hour in protest of "overcrowding and unsafe conditions in East Harlem Schools."[39]

4. Twice the Supreme Court, on the grounds of lack of standing or ripeness, refused to examine the constitutionality of a Connecticut statute which made the use of contraceptives a criminal offense. The requisite standing was attained only when the executive and medical directors of the Planned Parenthood League of Connecticut were arrested as accessories in violating the statute because they gave information, instruction, and medical advice about contraceptives to married persons.[40]

5. The Freedom Rides in 1961 tested the implementation of the *Boynton* v. *Virginia* decision of the Supreme Court which prohibited segregated terminal facilities used in interstate travel.[41]

Religious-Moral and Moral-Political Bases of Disobedience

The refusal to obey a demand of the state on personal moral or religious grounds, as in case #1, is nonviolent, open, and submissive, but there is still widespread disagreement about the appropriateness of applying the term *civil disobedience* to such a case. A prominent political philosopher distinguishes between conscientious objection and civil disobedience: "A refusal to follow a legal command, because of a fundamental moral or religious objection, is 'conscientious objection.' . . . Civil disobedience is a public protest against a law or policy regarded as morally wrong for all—

39. *New York Times,* March 7, 1964, p. 1.
40. *Griswold* v. *Connecticut,* 381 U.S. 479 (1965).
41. *Boynton* v. *Virginia,* 364 U.S. 454. Cf. James Peck, *Freedom Ride* (New York: Simon and Schuster, 1961).

not just the protesters."[42] Even in religious circles there has
been a long-standing distinction between "the disobedience
required by faith" and "political resistance in general."[43]
This distinction is generally accepted, despite the fact that
churches have never found it easy to draw the line between
these kinds of disobedience. What for one group is "disobedience required by faith" (e.g. the Mennonite's or
Quaker's refusal to take the oath or to participate in military
service) is for another group "political resistance." Nevertheless, the distinction is important.

Two features are central in any discussion of acts such as
the refusal of induction on the basis of personal moral or
religious principles. First, moral principles are more private
than public, especially because they often depend on personal religious convictions. "You must obey God rather than
men" (Acts 5 : 29). Many would restrict the term *civil disobedience* to those acts which are political in the sense that
they are

> justified by moral principles which define a conception
> of civil society and the public good. . . . Being an ap-
> peal to the moral basis of public life, civil disobedience
> is a political and not primarily a religious act. It ad-
> dresses itself to the common principles of justice which
> men can require one another to follow and not to the
> aspirations of love which they cannot.[44]

42. Ernest van den Haag, "Government, Conscience, and Disobedience," *Sidney Hook and the Contemporary World: Essays on the Pragmatic Intelligence,* ed. Paul Kurtz (New York: John Day Company,
1968), pp. 113, 115.
43. Helmut Thielicke, *Politics,* pp. 344, 359. For a related distinction
between civil disobedience as "the last refuge of conscience" and as an
instrument of social protest, see Edward LeRoy Long, *War and Conscience in America* (Philadelphia: Westminster, 1968), pp. 112–20.
44. John Rawls, "The Justification of Civil Disobedience," in Bedau,
CD, pp. 246, 248.

The second feature is an implication of the first. The agent is not trying to effect general social change, but rather to "witness" to his personal values and perhaps to secure a personal exemption for himself. There is no effort to compel others either by persuasion or coercion. He primarily wants to extricate himself from evil. He confesses, "Here I stand. I cannot do otherwise. So help me God." This act is still political if that term denotes the sphere within which the activity takes place, but it is not political in the sense of an appeal to shared public moral principles that would justify a change in the law or policy. Not everyone is satisfied that the objective of change through persuasion or coercion is essential to a definition of civil disobedience. Richard Lichtman insists that

> civil disobedience may perform another, and independently valid, function. It is also the act of a man who will not permit himself to be corrupted. His defiance of society at a given point may be based on the obligation to respect his own conscience—his moral autonomy—and on a respect for truth in human relations which leads him to make this fact known to his oppressor. He may have little hope of altering the law or system of institutions he opposes, but he will not permit that law to alter him.[45]

Two fundamentally different approaches to ethics are evident in the private and public bases of disobedience. Max Weber made a similar distinction: *Gesinnungsethik,* ethic of intention or ultimate values, and *Verantwortungsethik,* ethic of responsibility.[46] While this is close to a distinction

45. Richard Lichtman's statement in *Civil Disobedience* (An Occasional Paper, The Center for the Study of Democratic Institutions, 1966), p. 17.

46. See "Politics as a Vocation," in *From Max Weber: Essays in Sociology,* ed. and trans. Hans Gerth and C. Wright Mills (New York: Oxford University Press, 1946), pp. 118 ff.

between morals and politics, it is much more a distinction between two views of the relations of ethics and politics. In the ethic of intention or ultimate values, a person is absolutely committed to a single value (e.g. pacifism) which must be actualized regardless of the broader cost. The purity of action in relation to that value is crucial. His main concern, as Weber expresses it, is that the flame of pure intention not be quenched. In the ethic of responsibility a person is concerned with a range of values. He is aware that he cannot bring all of them to fulfillment without conflict and compromise. This ethic involves a submission to political process and depends on some broader, more public vindication of its proposals. The court of appeal for a Gesinnungsethik, however, transcends the public political arena; it is interior.

Of course, these are ideal types which, in actuality, are often intermingled. Milton Mayer's account of paying only a portion of his income tax because of its contribution toward military preparations provides an instructive and typical combination of appeals. Having proclaimed, "My first responsibility is . . . to preserve my soul," he nevertheless proceeds to calculate political effectiveness—what impact will his example have?[47] Many discussions of civil disobedience are unsatisfactory because of covert shifts from one type to the other. Thus, arguments which are presented for political (or moral-political) acts are sometimes coupled with the plea that such acts be judged almost exclusively in terms of their motivation.

The critical question at this point is conceptual. Should acts of disobedience which are based only on private and

47. Milton Mayer, "The Tribute Money," in *What Can A Man Do?* ed. W. Eric Gustafson (Chicago: University of Chicago Press, 1964), pp. 77–85; also in Bedau, *CD*, pp. 127–34. Daniel Berrigan has said of his participation in the burning of draft files by the Catonsville Nine: "if my religious belief is not accepted as a substantial part of my action then the action is eviscerated of all meaning and I should be committed for insanity." *The Trial of the Catonsville Nine* (Boston: Beacon, 1970), p. 83.

personal motives with no concern about social change be considered civil disobedience? The disobedience of the early Christians would seem to be an example. Christian Bay writes, "The early Christians represented the first spectacu-lar—and highly successful—civil disobedience movement in the West."[48] Others have concluded that it is a mistake to call this Christian activity (e.g. refusing to worship the em-peror) civil disobedience since it was based on personal, private principles and was not really directed toward changing laws or policies of the political order.[49] How this question is resolved is not as important as the recognition of the distinction between private and public orientations in disobedience. I am inclined to use the term *civil disobedience* for those nonpolitical acts which exemplify the other criteria so well, but they do not constitute a major part of this study, which will focus on the moral-political bases of civil dis-obedience.

I use the phrase *moral-political bases* because, as Quentin Quade insists, "the real truth . . . is that *political* conviction (on anything of significance) is itself an *ethical* position, a judgment about human values."[50] The civil disobedience practiced by Martin Luther King, for example, was clearly moral-political. It involved a conception of public justice or the civic good based on moral principles and affirmations which did not simply concern his private, personal, or inter-personal life. Purely personal moral codes or religious-moral

48. "Civil Disobedience," in *International Encyclopedia of the Social Sciences*, 2: 475.

49. James Luther Adams says that "the disobedience of the early Chris-tians was civil disobedience only in a narrow sense." "Civil Disobedience: Its Occasions and Its Limits," *Political and Legal Obligation (Nomos 12)*, ed. J. Roland Pennock and John W. Chapman (New York: Atherton, 1970), p. 295, n. 1.

50. Quentin L. Quade, "Selective Conscientious Objection and Political Obligation," *A Conflict of Loyalties: The Case for Selective Conscientious Objection*, ed. James Finn (New York: Pegasus, 1968), p. 208.

mandates (just as self-interest) may be important motives in much civil disobedience, but this study will concentrate on those acts whose rationale includes some reference to a conception of a good or just civil society. This is primarily an enterprise in "political ethics."

Educative and Coercive Force

Cases #2 and #3 raise questions about the kind of force used in civil disobedience.[51] It may be a moral, educational force, marked by an appeal to reason, conscience, and moral sensitivity. Or it may represent an effort not merely to persuade the community that a law or policy is inconsistent with values already held but also to change fundamental attitudes—indeed, to convert members of the community. Finally, it may be coercion, defined as "the use of either physical or intangible force to *compel action contrary to the will or reasoned judgment* of the individual or group subjected to such force."[52] The primary question is: does public, nonviolent, submissive disobedience which relies heavily on coercive force constitute civil disobedience?

Case #2 is an effort to frustrate the government's purposes by making enforcement of the law too costly or too embarrassing; thus its effect is largely accomplished by coercion rather than by conversion or persuasion. Numerous other examples of coercive protest are available: troop trains have been blocked, campus buildings have been liberated, deans of colleges and universities have been locked up. Often these protests have involved both educative and coercive actions. For example, a group of nine persons calling themselves the East Coast Conspiracy to Save Lives vandalized

51. Some of this discussion of moral and coercive force has already appeared in James F. Childress, "Nonviolent Resistance: Some Conceptual and Moral Considerations," *Journal of Religious Studies* (Punjabi University, Patiala, India), 2, no. 1 (Autumn 1970): 28–44.

52. Paullin, *Introduction to Non-Violence,* p. 6.

General Electric Company files and draft board records in Philadelphia in February 1970. Their public justification referred to both educative and coercive implementation of their ends. Not only did they want to "point out" the complicity of corporations, the government, and the military in perpetuating a system of destruction, but they also wanted "to disrupt functioning of the machine of death and oppression."[53] Likewise, the more famous Catonsville Nine combined education and coercion in their protest.[54]

Because any particular protest may involve different audiences as well as different techniques, it is necessary to recognize that an act that is educative in relation to one audience may be coercive in relation to another. In the case of the destruction of General Electric Company files, the audiences included at least General Electric as the primary target, the public as bystanders through news reports, and law enforcement officials who had to respond. This act was coercive from the standpoint of General Electric, but educative from the standpoint of the general public.

Many proponents of civil disobedience recognize the place and importance of coercion in their actions. The Reverend William Sloane Coffin, Jr., a contemporary theorist and practitioner of civil disobedience, writes:

I think we must recognize that massive civil disobedience to the war would represent *not only an effort to arouse a confused and inert public,* but really a form of moral jiu-jitsu, an *effort on the part of a minority morally to coerce the majority* into a greater consciousness of the issues of the war. It would be moral coercion even if the minority practicing civil disobedience accepted the punishment of the majority, for I suspect it

53. *The Washington Post,* Feb. 21, 1970, B 2.
54. Daniel Berrigan, S.J., *The Trial of the Catonsville Nine,* p. 35.

would be embarrassing for the government to arrest thousands of citizens when the country is already so divided.[55]

But other proponents of civil disobedience refuse to acknowledge these coercive elements. Confronted with the charge that the underlying idea of his civil disobedience was "embarrassment of government," Gandhi replied, "Certainly not. A satyagrahi relies not upon embarrassment but upon self-suffering for securing relief."[56] Elsewhere he insisted upon this distinction between change by embarrassment and by conversion: "I have deliberately used the word *conversion*. For my ambition is no less than to convert the British people through non-violence, and thus to make them see the wrong they have done to India."[57] Conversion rather than coercion or even persuasion is what mattered to him.

Of course, these views would seem fatuous apart from Gandhi's conviction that the nonviolent resister's suffering can alter attitudes and actions. When attempts were made to rebut this conviction by appeals to the absence of an unambiguous historical precedent, Gandhi replied by stressing the uniqueness of his own experiment in resistance and by reiterating his fundamental principle: "The law of love will work, just as the law of gravitation will work, whether we accept it or not."[58]

P. Régamey O.P., in *Non-violence and the Christian Conscience,* followed the path that Gandhi charted. He contended that pre-Gandhian civil disobedience was violent because it both *forced* the oppressor and gave him the oppor-

---

55. Charles E. Whittaker and William Sloane Coffin, Jr., *Law, Order and Civil Disobedience* (Washington: American Enterprise Institute for Public Policy Research, 1967), pp. 39–40 (italics mine).
56. Gandhi, *Non-Violent Resistance,* p. 32.
57. Ibid., p. 227; cf. p. 285.
58. Ibid., pp. 362–63, 384.

tunity to express his violence.[59] But neither Gandhi nor
Régamey adequately distinguished two different questions.
One is the *moral* question of whether civil disobedience
ought or *ought not* to involve coercion, and the other is the
empirical matter of whether a particular act of civil disobedience actually *does* involve coercion. To answer the
moral question by denying that coercive disobedience is
ever justified does not settle the empirical issue.

Thoreau emphasized the coercive aspects of civil disobedience much more than Gandhi. No one would deny the
importance of the educative goal in Thoreau's effort to dis-
seminate his ideas, since he wrote in "Civil Disobedience":
"I am doing my part to educate my fellow-countrymen
now."[60] His reluctance to leave jail after one night (because
someone paid his poll tax) could be interpreted as a recognition of the importance of accepting punishment in order
to stimulate public consideration of slavery and the Mexican
War. But it is at least as likely that his reluctance stemmed
from the fact that his revolt had been undermined by payment to the tax collector, which reestablished the main point
of contact between Thoreau and his government. When all
these matters are considered, Thoreau's view of civil disobedience points mainly in the direction of coercion. He
construed his act as "counter friction to stop the machine"
of government.[61]

It is interesting to note that Martin Luther King's early
position was closer to Gandhi's. He summarized his position
in the Montgomery bus boycott: "Our method will be that
of persuasion, not coercion."[62] His confidence in persuasion

59. (New York: Herder and Herder, 1966), p. 212.
60. Henry David Thoreau, "Civil Disobedience," *Walden and Civil
Disobedience*, ed. Sherman Paul (Boston: Houghton Mifflin, Riverside
Edition, 1960), p. 252.
61. Ibid., p. 243.
62. *Stride Toward Freedom*, p. 48.

paralleled Gandhi's confidence in conversion because both shared the view that suffering unjust punishment is redemptive. The person who is civilly disobedient, King wrote in 1963, "breaks a law that conscience tells him is unjust, and . . . willingly accepts the penalty of imprisonment in order to *arouse the conscience of the community* over its injustice."[63] Despite this basically optimistic view of man, King stressed the importance of the crisis-situation and of "constructive, nonviolent tension"; one purpose of his action in Birmingham was "to create such a crisis and foster such a tension that a community which has constantly refused to negotiate is forced to confront the issue."[64] Later, he moved much closer to Thoreau and emphasized coercing government officials to do or to abstain from doing certain acts. In August 1967, he asserted: "Our real problem is that there is no disposition by the administration or Congress to seek fundamental remedies."[65] Civil disobedience became primarily a technique to disrupt governmental machinery or at least to prevent its smooth operation. King's projected campaign of massive civil disobedience was to be aimed at the "dislocation" of northern cities: "To dislocate the functioning of a city without destroying it can be more effective than a riot because it can be longer lasting, costly to the society but not wantonly destructive."[66]

Whether one emphasizes persuasion and even conversion or coercion depends on many factors. There are perceptions about the actual situation, for instance the people's susceptibility to attitudinal change and the government's responsiveness to the people. Assumptions about man's nature and his

63. "Letter from Birmingham Jail," in *Why We Can't Wait*, pp. 83–84. Italics mine.

64. Ibid., p. 79.

65. *New York Times*, August 16, 1967, pp. 1, 29.

66. Ibid. This statement also appears in King, *The Trumpet of Conscience* (New York: Harper and Row, 1968), p. 15.

possibilities, about the place of rationality and coercion in human communities, and about the efficacy of love in action shape these perceptions. Thus, part of the argument will necessarily take place on philosophical or theological levels, which will be explicated later in this study.

At this juncture it is imperative to make certain that such perspectives about man do not prevent us from recognizing the various kinds of force in most acts of civil disobedience. A definitional fiat to the effect that coercive acts cannot be considered civil disobedience may well confuse the discussion by obscuring the place of coercion in much civil disobedience.[67] The question of the relative weight of coercion and moral appeals will, of course, be very important in evaluating any act of civil disobedience.

Direct and Indirect Disobedience

Cases like #3, the protest against school conditions in Harlem by the violation of traffic regulations on the Triborough Bridge, are particularly interesting because they involve breaking laws that are admitted to be valid and just, and that are not being used in some covert way to buttress an unjust system. The fact is, of course, that not all laws or policies can be violated *directly* by the ordinary citizen. He can disobey a governmental order which prohibits travel to a particular foreign country, but he cannot disobey an order that another person convicted of treason be executed. In the latter case, he can engage in *indirect* resistance to focus attention on the cause he advocates.

Perhaps I can begin to clarify this distinction between direct and indirect civil disobedience with another quotation from Gandhi:

67. Cf. Mortimer J. Adler's argument in a panel discussion, the transcript of which appears in *Illinois Continuing Legal Education* 5, no. 1 (January 1967): 71–121. He tries to exclude coercive acts from civil disobedience.

> Aggressive, assertive or offensive civil disobedience is non-violent, wilful disobedience of laws of the State whose breach does not involve moral turpitude and which is undertaken as a symbol of revolt against the State. . . . Defensive civil disobedience, on the other hand, is involuntary or reluctant non-violent disobedience of such laws as are in themselves bad and obedience to which would be inconsistent with one's self-respect or human dignity.[68]

This distinction has to do with the relation between the act of civil disobedience and the evil being protested. If the evil being protested is a law which is deemed invalid or unjust (either "unjust on its face" or "unjust in its application"), the act of civil disobedience is *directly* related to the object of the protest. Examples of direct resistance are the refusal to pay taxes because the tax law is considered unjust, or to serve in the armed forces because the draft law is viewed as inequitable.

But if the specific law that is infringed is thought to be just, the act then is only *indirectly* related to the cause that is being advocated. Examples of indirect civil disobedience are Thoreau's protest against the Mexican War and slavery by refusing to pay the poll tax and recent burnings of draft cards in order to protest the war in Vietnam.[69] Usually the communication of indirect resistance depends on a symbolic connection between the act and the cause. Although such a connection is missing in case #3, it is present in the burning of draft cards, which symbolize the whole Selective Service system.

68. Gandhi, *Non-Violent Resistance*, p. 175.
69. This distinction is drawn from Bedau's "On Civil Disobedience," p. 657. He is careful to avoid confusion between direct resistance and direct action. "Direct Action is a special form of direct resistance, in which the dissenter uses his own body as the lever with which to pry loose the government's policy." Cf. also Carl Cohen's contribution to the symposium, "Civil Disobedience and the Law," *Rutgers Law Review* 21 (Fall 1966): 4–5.

Later I shall argue that, ceteris paribus, direct disobedience is more easily justified than indirect. Here, however, the question is whether indirect disobedience even constitutes an act of civil disobedience. The widespread denial that it does is another example of the tendency to move rapidly from classification to justification. Mortimer J. Adler argues that the term civil disobedience is misused when it is applied to violations of ordinances in order to call attention to dissatisfaction with some general state of affairs.[70] He, in effect, chooses to write his evaluation into the description of the act. But there seems to be no good reason to restrict the term *civil disobedience* to the breach of laws that are deemed invalid and/or immoral.

Even those interpreters of civil disobedience who are not guilty of Adler's faulty argument often simply ignore the phenomenon of indirect resistance.[71] But if this distinction between direct and indirect resistance is applied to the classical theories of civil disobedience, some interesting patterns emerge. Gandhi tended to stress direct, while Thoreau (at least in his action) stressed indirect resistance. It is hardly necessary to underline the point that this was only a matter of emphasis. King, following a pattern already suggested in our discussion of force, moved from his early preoccupation with direct resistance to a striking concentration on indirect resistance. In 1963, his famous "Letter from Birmingham Jail" affirmed a responsibility to obey just laws, along with a moral duty to repudiate unjust laws by civil disobedience.[72] Then, in his projected "dislocation" of northern cities by massive disobedience, King advocated infringing laws that were recognized as both valid and just.[73]

70. Adler, pp. 86, 89.
71. For example, John Rawls, "The Justification of Civil Disobedience" in Bedau, *CD*, pp. 240–55.
72. *Why We Can't Wait*, p. 82.
73. *New York Times*, August 16, 1967, p. 1.

Legal and Translegal Appeals

In cases #4 and 5, the disobedients appeal to positive law, and it is not entirely clear that such acts should be labeled civil disobedience. Although they are committed publicly, nonviolently, submissively, and in order to call attention to a discrepancy between a policy or law and public moral standards, they are not necessarily illegal. In fact, the defense will often argue that their clients were not engaged in civil disobedience and that their acts were illegal only in terms of an invalid or inapplicable law.

That laws may be in conflict makes it possible to speak of an act as legal and illegal at the same time. An act may be illegal according to local ordinances or state statutes but legal according to the federal Constitution. Thus, an examination of several direct action cases before the Supreme Court in the last decade reveals that officials often use trespass and breach-of-peace statutes to restrict first-amendment freedoms or to deny due process or equal protection of the laws.[74] When violations are committed under the claim of legality, what is at issue is the legitimacy of that claim.

A major proponent of the view that such acts are not civil disobedience is William L. Taylor, General Counsel for the United States Commission on Civil Rights. His thesis is that if a violation is committed under a claim of legal right, with the intention of seeking redress in the courts, it can hardly be termed civil disobedience. "Thus, almost all of the major forms of direct community action—sit-ins, freedom rides, demonstrations, picketing, and rent strikes—are properly understood as actions well within the framework of our legal system,

74. See A. E. Dick Howard, "Mr. Justice Black: The Negro Protest Movement and the Rule of Law," *Virginia Law Review* 53, no. 5 (1967): 1030–90.

rather than as civil disobedience."[75] For him civil disobedience must always have an extra- or translegal appeal.

But Taylor's view is not completely adequate. Indeed, it
can be argued that "test case" is simply "a euphemism for
civil disobedience."[76] This argument is plausible in part because "standing" is a prerequisite in our system for securing
judicial review of allegedly invalid laws. Thus, the Supreme
Court twice (in 1943 and 1961) refused to accept challenges
to the validity of a Connecticut law which prohibited the use
of contraceptives—"an uncommonly silly law" as Justice
Stewart said. The ground for this refusal was lack of standing
or ripeness, since the law had not been violated in either case.
This standard was finally met in *Griswold* v. *Connecticut*
(the case which led to the invalidation of the law), although
the appellants had not infringed the contraceptive law but
rather an aiding-and-abetting statute. This was sufficient,
since, as the court argued, "the accessory should have standing
to assert that the offense which he is charged with assisting is
not, or cannot constitutionally be, a crime."[77]

A fundamental question has to do with the perspective
from which one views the act of disobedience. Does one examine the act and the law in their total context, which would
include a decision by the highest court? Or does one focus on
the actor, his intention, and his appeals, in order to determine
whether the act is civil disobedience? Many who take the

75. William L. Taylor, "Civil Disobedience: Observations on the Strate-
gies of Protest," *Legal Aspects of the Civil Rights Movement,* ed. Donald
B. King and Charles W. Quick (Detroit: Wayne State University Press,
1965), pp. 228, 230. (This article is reprinted in Bedau, *CD,* pp. 98–105).
Cf. also Charles L. Black, Jr., "The Problem of the Compatibility of Civil
Disobedience with American Institutions of Government," *Texas Law
Review* 43, no. 4 (March 1965): 492–506.

76. Robert B. McKay, "Protest and Dissent: Action and Reaction,"
Utah Law Review 10, no. 1 (July 1966): 25.

77. 381 U.S. 479 (1965), at 481. Cf. Ibid., pp. 25–26.

first perspective refrain from describing the act as disobedience until the courts have declared the law constitutional, valid, and applicable and have determined that the act infringes the law. The act is considered retrospectively from the court's decision.[78] Civil disobedience then becomes the infringement of a *valid* law.

Others focus on the *actor's appeal* to positive law rather than the ultimate judicial decision. If the act is defended by an appeal to positive law and the judicial system rather than some translegal principle, it is not civil disobedience.[79] Not all who take the actor's perspective limit the use of the term *civil disobedience* to such acts. For some what is crucial is the *act* of disobedience even if it only violates a local ordinance and is ultimately vindicated.[80] The act is described as civil disobedience if the actor recognizes that his act is "illegal or of contested illegality" and that, at any rate, it is enforced by some public officials.[81]

I find it useful to take the actor's perspective and to focus on the act of disobedience to the demand of the state through some of its officials. This approach is especially appealing from the standpoint of moral decision-making. Morris Keeton expresses the point cogently:

> To restrict civil disobedience by definition to violations of *valid* law would have the advantage of stressing the difference between clearly legal acts and acts with no claim to legality. This claim, however, is generally in dispute

78. Cohen, "Civil Disobedience and the Law," *Rutgers Law Review* 21, no. 1 (Fall 1966): 8–9.

79. Ernst van den Haag, "Government, Conscience, and Disobedience," pp. 116–17.

80. Harrop Freeman, "Civil Disobedience and the Law," *Rutgers Law Review* 21, no. 1 (Fall 1966): 17–18.

81. Christian Bay, "Civil Disobedience: Prerequisite for Democracy in Mass Society," in Spitz, ed., *Political Theory and Social Change*, p. 166.

at the time of the decision to act, and an adequate ethical policy will use terms that provide as efficient guidance as possible over the entire range of choices to be served.[82]

I do not deny, however, that there may be a significant moral difference between breaking a law with no claim to legality (e.g. as in indirect resistance) and breaking a law with honest doubt about its validity and morality. But that is a question of justification, and up to this point I have only dealt with classification—whether the term *civil disobedience* applies to acts which appeal to the legal system and which are ultimately declared legal. At any rate, the test case is marginal to this study.

In this chapter I have tried to cast some light on the phenomenon of civil disobedience by conceptual analysis that considers definitions in the classical tradition of Thoreau, Gandhi, and King as well as the contemporary reality of protest. The distinctions I have drawn can be evaluated in terms of clarity, consistency, etc., but also in terms of their usefulness both to general reflection and to the remainder of this study, in which I try to construct a framework for the debate about the justification of civil disobedience. The tasks of describing and evaluating an act such as civil disobedience can never be fully separated, but whatever nonviolent, public, submissive, illegal acts of protests are called—whether civil disobedience or something else—they are to be distinguished from revolution and typical crimes, which raise somewhat different questions of justification.[83] Many of the problems I have exam-

---

82. Morris Keeton, "The Morality of Civil Disobedience," *Texas Law Review* 43, no. 4 (March 1965): 510–11.

83. A possible objection to my discussion is that, by emphasizing "civility" so much in the definition of civil disobedience, I have moved too easily from definition to justification—from saying that this is civil disobedience as defined (and it may or may not be justified), to saying that this is justified civil disobedience, or that civil disobedience is justified

ined here will be crucial to the discussion in chapter 4, where
I try to show how the framework developed in the other
chapters illuminates the justification of civil disobedience as
already defined.

---

disobedience. But I think this objection does not hold, since I have still
left open the central question: when is disobedience under these conditions (nonviolently, publicly, submissively, and in protest) *justified?* In a
sense, my definition sharpens one of the central moral questions (the obligation to obey the law and its limits) because it does not include certain
other features, such as violence.

II

BASES OF POLITICAL OBLIGATION:
NATURAL LAW AND THE ENDS OF THE STATE

POLITICS, ETHICS, AND THEOLOGY

The major objective of this entire study is to establish a framework within which a constructive as well as an analytic interpretation and evaluation of civil disobedience can take place. As I argued in the preface, this topic has not received careful attention in Christian social ethics for several reasons. Most importantly, the discipline's so-called situational bent denies continuity and generalization while its orientation toward action finds paramount value in the action itself rather than in critical reflection upon it. Valuable as some of these themes are in liberating Christian ethics, the liberation can become a new bondage. Without reducing situational variability to uniformity and without denying the importance of action, Christian social ethics can and must deal with right- and wrong-making characteristics that recur in numerous contexts. Indeed, to overlook these persistent factors is to surrender serious moral reflection.

Admittedly the factors that bear upon the justification of civil disobedience cannot be as neatly and systematically arranged as the term *framework* might suggest. But whatever terminology is used, there remain a set of factors which decisively affect the discussion and evaluation of civil disobedience in Christian social ethics.

The fundamental element in such a framework is a theory of political obedience, its basis and limits.[1] Such a theory could be construed as offering either motivation or justification for obedience. The two different questions it attempts to answer can be simply stated: "Why *does* a citizen obey the law?" and "Why *ought* a citizen to obey the law?" The former asks for an explanation of behavior that may draw on the psychological and sociological factors leading one to obedience, whereas the latter asks for a justification of obedience.[2] The marshaling of reasons for obedience to government is absolutely indispensable to an assessment of disobedience. Joseph Tussman rightly contends:

1. I am well aware of the difficulties of using the terms *obey* and *obedience*. (a) Not all laws can be obeyed or disobeyed. Such terms fail to indicate all the possible relationships between citizens (and public officials) and the law. While criminal law forms the model that makes sense of an emphasis on obedience, there are other laws that confer powers, create possibilities, etc. Nevertheless, because I am interested here in the " 'end product' of the legal system, where it makes its impact on the private citizen," I shall continue to use the language of obedience (H. L. A. Hart, *The Concept of Law* [Oxford: Clarendon Press, 1961], pp. 109, 113). (b) The language of obedience tends to imply "command," but the whole model of command and obedience is terribly inadequate, as Hannah Arendt demonstrates, largely because it tends to equate power with violence (*On Violence* [New York: Harcourt Brace World, 1970], chap. 2). She uses the term *support* instead of *obedience*. However, I shall use *obedience* because of traditional usage and the fact that it serves as a handy antonym of (civil) disobedience.

2. These questions may, of course, converge. The distinction between them appears in several places, e.g. H. A. Prichard, "Green's Principles of Political Obligation," in *Moral Obligation* (London: Oxford University Press, 1949), p. 82; William K. Frankena, "Obligation and Motivation in Recent Moral Philosophy," in A. I. Melden, ed., *Essays in Moral Philosophy* (Seattle, Wash.: University of Washington Press, 1958), pp. 40–81.

> There can be a right to disobey only if there is first a duty
> to obey; there can be a right to revolt only if there is also
> a duty to support. If this seems paradoxical it is less so
> than the view that there is a limit to obedience without a
> duty to obey. The limit of obedience is the fringe of the
> garment of obligation.[3]

One cannot really establish a right or a duty to disobey unless
he can also establish *in that context* the conditions under
which there would be an obligation or a duty to obey. This is
precisely what so many theologians of revolution fail to recognize.

What Dietrich Bonhoeffer said about "the ethical phenomenon" in general applies strikingly to civil disobedience; it is
a "peripheral event," an exceptional occurrence.[4] "The
'moral scrutiny' to which authority is linked is not," writes
A. P. d'Entrèves, "a matter of daily occurrence. It is resorted
to only in moments of crisis. We have not, thank God, to decide every day which laws we have to obey, and why."[5] But
when this marginal question of disobedience is raised in a
serious way, the questioner is pushed back to the bases of "political obligation." Political obligation often includes more
than obedience to rules or laws. For example, we might say
that a person has a political obligation to vote in his country's elections, although there is no law requiring him to do

3. *Obligation and the Body Politic* (New York: Oxford University Press,
1960), p. 32.
4. *Ethics*, trans. Neville Horton Smith (New York: Macmillan, 1955),
pp. 233–35.
5. "Obeying Whom?" (The Philip Maurice Deneke Lecture for 1964,
mimeographed copy), pp. 17–18. Cf. also, S. I. Benn and R. S. Peters, *The
Principles of Political Thought* (New York: Free Press, 1965), p. 354:
"Men rarely question the legitimacy of established authority when all is
going well; the problem of political obligation is urgent when the State
is sick, when someone is seriously contemplating disobedience or revolt
on principle."

so. But when I use the term *political obligation* I shall mean only the moral obligation to obey the law.

A good case can be made that political obligation, its foundation and limits, really is the core of political philosophy. Peter Laslett and W. G. Runciman contend that obligation to political authority "was and still is regarded as lying at the heart of all the problems of political philosophy." And Isaiah Berlin insists that it is "the most fundamental of all political questions."[6] Unfortunately, Christian social ethicists in recent years—especially those interested in revolution and those fearful of the language of obligations—have not given this central problem the careful attention it requires, although they have not been totally derelict in this respect. Even those who have not explicitly treated political obligation have usually operated with an implicit theory which affects their judgments about resistance.

Total neglect of the grounds of political obligation is simply impossible in the Christian context, largely because the Christian church was one of the primary forces in the emergence of divided loyalties, without which the problem of political obligation could not really be raised: "Render unto Caesar the things that are Caesar's and unto God the things that are God's" (Matthew 22:21). This passage, as many historians of political philosophy have recognized, contains an explosive political implication which, regardless of the intention of the statement, could not be ignored, especially when an independent community arose. George Sabine writes in his classic, *A History of Political Theory:* "The rise of the Christian church, as a distinct institution entitled to govern the

6. Laslett and Runciman, eds., *Philosophy, Politics and Society,* 2d ser. (Oxford: Basil Blackwell, 1962), p. ix. Berlin, "Does Political Theory Still Exist?" in ibid., p. 7, cf. pp. 12, 14. Contrast the argument by Thomas McPherson, who contends that political obligation is a question in only certain philosophical frameworks, namely those that are individualistic. *Political Obligation* (London: Routledge and Kegan Paul, 1967).

spiritual concerns of mankind in independence of the state, may not unreasonably be described as the most revolutionary event in the history of western Europe, in respect both to politics and to political philosophy."[7] Man is henceforth regarded as a citizen of two kingdoms, with distinctly separate loyalties to each.

Christian social and political thought has always centered around the relationship of these two kingdoms. Various ways of distinguishing, separating, and relating them have been conceived in response to both theological problems and practical crises. The Christian church as an independent community and institution sharpened the conflict between conscience and the state that had been expressed long before by Sophocles's Antigone and by Socrates, but it failed to resolve the intellectual and practical difficulties involved in that conflict. Although the conflict can never be resolved once and for all, Christian theologians and ethicists are still struggling to give birth to solutions that will be theoretically and practically satisfactory in relation to current as well as ideal political orders.

Moreover, the peculiarity of the political relation, and especially the presence of organized coercion in the state, are just as important for Christian reflection as the division of loyalties. Lurking behind an analysis of the peculiarity of the political relation is the question of the essence of the state; and even a cursory examination of political theory—whether religious, philosophical, or more scientific—discloses profound disagreements. Although many interpreters would accept Max Weber's contention that "it is the specific means of legitimate violence as such in the hand of human associations which determines the peculiarity of all ethical problems of politics," countless others would echo Hannah Arendt's view

7. Third ed. (New York: Holt, Rinehart and Winston, 1961), p. 180.

that "power is indeed of the essence of the state, but violence is not."[8] It is not necessary to resolve this dispute now in order to emphasize that coercive power may well be a precondition of the state, if not its essence. Furthermore, it is true that Christian thinkers have often viewed politics and the political order somewhat suspiciously because of their apparently inevitable connection with coercive power. Recognizing the prima facie conflict between participation in such an order and fulfilling the mandates of the Christian faith, especially as exemplified in the life and teachings of Jesus Christ, Christian theologians have had to establish "bridges" between that faith and political life which would avoid a denial both of the essentials of the faith and of the reality of politics.

Nevertheless, the uniqueness of the political relation, as embodied in the state, does not mean that it can be considered a special realm apart from general ethical reflection and discourse. As E. F. Carritt insisted, "The political relation is a peculiar one, but all claims and duties arise out of peculiar relations," such as the family and economic relationships.[9] An inquiry into what one ought to do in any of these relations requires us to examine that sphere in the light of general moral considerations while taking account of its specific and distinctive contours. As political philosophy is therefore essentially one branch of ethics or moral philosophy, Christian political philosophy or political ethics is one branch of Christian ethics. Richard Hauser expresses the point succinctly: "There is no special political morality but the application of Christian principles to this special state of affairs."[10]

8. Max Weber, "Politics as a Vocation," *From Max Weber: Essays in Sociology*, ed. H. H. Gerth and C. Wright Mills, p. 124; Arendt, *On Violence*, p. 51, cf. pp. 37 ff.; cf. also A. P. d'Entrèves, *The Notion of the State: An Introduction to Political Theory* (Oxford: Clarendon, 1967), passim.

9. *Morals and Politics* (Oxford: Clarendon, 1935), p. 5.

10. *Was des Kaisers Ist* (Frankfurt am Main: Josef Knecht, 1968), p. 198.

It is not surprising, then, that various disputed questions in contemporary Christian ethics cast shadows over the area of political ethics too. At least three levels can be distinguished, although they are not fully separable: analysis of context, especially the political relation; norms and principles; theological and anthropological convictions.[11] For my present purposes enough has already been indicated about the political relation and its peculiarity. As regards norms and principles, there is no agreement on how they function in moral reasoning and decision making, how many of them, if any, apply not only to interpersonal but also to the social and political spheres, and how conflicts between them can be resolved. Although in this study I shall focus on a particular moral dilemma, devoting little direct attention to other critical questions, my position on many of them will be evident at various points. After all, it can be argued, "a man's account of political obligation depends upon his account of obligation in general."[12]

On a still deeper level, any interpretation of the political sphere of action must inevitably draw on underlying assumptions about man, his nature and potentialities. Whether one holds that the state is a matrix of conflicting interests and values or the expression of shared standards—that it is a dike against sin or a portal of the kingdom—the plausibility of such assertions and others will depend on some anthropology. In the Christian context, the interpretation of man draws much of its imagery and content from one of his particular

11. This analysis is close to the "basepoints" identified and discussed by James Gustafson: theological affirmations, theories of the human self, moral principles, and interpretations of the situation. See "Context versus Principles: A Misplaced Debate in Christian Ethics," *The Harvard Theological Review* 58, no. 2 (April 1965): 171–202. Cf. also Ralph Potter, *War and Moral Discourse,* and James Sellers, *Theological Ethics* (New York: Macmillan, 1966).

12. Carritt, *Morals and Politics,* p. 5.

relations—that between himself and God. Especially significant are divine purposes for man and the way these purposes are known. The ends of the political order and its internal relationships are interpreted and evaluated in the light of these purposes. Political obligation is then seen as being dependent on these ends and/or internal relationships.

It is possible to maintain that the methods and central questions are formally identical for religious and other political ethics. Thus in all versions of political ethics, assumptions about man and the universe, moral principles and values, and interpretations of the political context shape the understanding of political obligation. Christian political thinkers hold convictions that affect their "disposition toward the world" and the ways in which they "think about their purposes and actions in the world."[13] From an analytic and critical standpoint, it is necessary to deal with the theological level, not because all else derives from it, but because it is one of the main levels on which Christian ethicists present their case. Although the complex interrelation of theological–anthropological, ethical, and empirical views cannot be reduced to deduction or entailment, a certain consistency usually obtains between these levels, and it is impossible to ignore any of them.

Some versions of "political theology" ostensibly bypass the discussion of moral principles and values, perhaps because they incorporate such principles and values in theological concepts, which then assume the normative burden. At any rate, it is impossible to hold that an answer to theological and even anthropological questions will resolve political issues, for "ethics is the concrete form of the mediation *(Vermitt-*

---

13. James Gustafson, "Theology and Ethics," *The Scope of Theology*, ed. Daniel T. Jenkins (Cleveland: World Publishing Co., 1965), pp. 119, 124.

lung) of theology and politics."[14] While resolving theological questions does not determine why we should or should not obey the law, the theological element inherent in any Christian's answers to such questions of political ethics cannot be overlooked. It sets certain limits on the range of options for constructive political ethics, and it may even provide a tentative direction and set the framework of discussion.

In testing the adequacy of certain Christian ethical positions, I shall not only apply the indispensable criteria of consistency, coherence, and comprehensiveness but also take into account the intention of many writers to provide specific guidance for Christians and others in their political actions. It should be apparent that any ethical framework, whether or not it is theologically based, must first of all give "stable and uniform results when used by persons who are certified in some non-circular way as qualified to do so."[15] Second, the results of utilizing such a framework in particular instances should not be inconsistent with our intuitive judgments about them. If a wide discrepancy between the two arises, both the framework and its applications must be reexamined. Obviously a framework of political obligation that required absolute obedience in all places at all times would be rejected because of its incompatibility with what we generally recognize as right. Finally, the framework must account for, clarify, and perhaps even redirect man's moral experience, language, institutions, and common moral traditions. For example, movements in civil rights and war resistance in the 1960s involved frequent conflicts with the state and many acts of civil

14. Trutz Rendtorff, "Politische Ethik oder 'politische Theologie'?" *Diskussion zur 'politischen Theologie,'* ed. Helmut Peukert (Mainz: Matthias-Grünewald-Verlag and Munich: Chr. Kaiser Verlag, 1969), p. 218.

15. Frederick Olafson, "General Introduction," *Society, Law and Morality*, ed. Frederick Olafson (Englewood Cliffs, N.J.: Prentice-Hall, 1961), p. 16.

disobedience. These experiences, our discourse about them, the responses of our institutions to them, the judgments based on common moral traditions—all these must be illuminated by the framework. These criteria are more encompassing than considerations of theological adequacy which, while they cannot be overlooked, are nevertheless insufficient in themselves to resolve ethical problems in the political order.

Armed with these criteria, I shall examine two major interpretations of the bases of political obligation. On the one hand, some thinkers, mainly Roman Catholic, locate the basis of this obligation in the justice which must be embodied in a law for it to qualify as a law; this is the natural law position. On the other hand, some thinkers, mainly Protestant, locate the basis in the ends of the state as defined by theological-anthropological convictions; obedience then becomes a necessary means to the attainment of those ends.

NATURAL LAW

One of the most intriguing chapters in the history of social ethics describes the checkered career of natural law. Time and again it has apparently received the knock-out punch from both theological and philosophical contenders, but it has always managed to revive before the opponent's hand could be raised in victory. Both celebration and mourning have always proved premature. This incredible resilience is due in large measure to the fact that the notion of natural law addresses itself to perennial problems of human existence in social and political structures. Perhaps it is precisely the recurrent moral criticism of law, especially in relation to resistance to the state, that propels the "eternal return of natural law."[16]

16. H. A. Rommen's phrase, *die ewige Wiederkehr des Naturrechts.* See, for example, "In Defense of Natural Law," in Hook, *L & P,* p. 105, and *The Natural Law,* trans. Thomas R. Hanley (St. Louis, Mo.: Herder, 1947).

This idea of an eternal return may, however, obscure the fact that, for a large segment of religious ethics at least, the concept of natural law has never disappeared. Since the early centuries of the Christian era it has been the dominant approach to social ethics in the Roman Catholic Church, although this historical association should not tempt one to consider natural law a Roman Catholic doctrine.[17] The traditional categories are being modified greatly under new pressures in Roman Catholic thought, and current theological developments indicate that a more open, more historical, more personalistic version of natural law may be emerging.[18] Exactly how this will affect social ethics is not yet clear. But, at least to the present time, the prevalence of the doctrine of natural law has meant that Roman Catholic reasoning about resistance is "relatively unified and closed."[19]

Particular religious and theological reasons can partly account for the enduring place of natural law in Roman Catholic thought; but even more important, as I have suggested, are the possibilities it offers for dealing with critical and persistent questions of social and political life. And the way it deals with them is strikingly evident in its treatment of obedience and disobedience. Part of the appeal of natural law has been the fact that "it appears to give a *legal basis for disobedience* to particular rules which infringe those moral principles which it incorporates by definition into its concept of law."[20] Despite its varying content, form, and justification, natural law has fulfilled a function which, according to Erik Wolf, "is clear and always the same; it serves as the foundation, boundary, and direction of positive-historical, human law; it

17. Contrast Kai Nielsen, "The Myth of Natural Law," in Hook, *L & P*, pp. 122–43.

18. See Franz Böckle, ed., *Das Naturrecht im Disput* (Düsseldorf: Patmos-Verlag, 1966), as well as the works of B. Häring and J. Fuchs.

19. Rock, *Widerstand gegen die Staatsgewalt*, p. 193.

20. Dorothy Emmet, *Justice and the Law*, The Essex Hall Lecture, 1963 (London: The Lindsey Press, 1963), p. 22. Italics mine.

is its critical guiding principle."[21] In general terms, the function can be reduced to d'Entrèves' assertion that "law is a part of ethics."[22] Distinguishing three types of theory of natural law, he insists that they have only one point in common:

> they subordinate the question of knowing what the laws have said or say at a given time and in a given place, to that of knowing whether what they say is right or wrong, *iustum vel iniustum. They thus tend to dissolve the problem of the validity of law into that of its obligatoriness. They provide us with a valuation of law which purports to be a definition.*[23]

Debate about natural law has often been confused because it involves at least three different levels of discussion—metaethical, ethical, and legal. As a metaethical theory, it purports to provide the meaning of ethical terms such as *good* and *right* and a way of justifying moral principles and values. It is therefore a form of cognitivism which holds that such principles and values are objective, and also that they can be known by natural human faculties. On this level, natural law cannot be contrasted with utilitarianism, for example, because the latter is a normative ethical position which may be defended by any metaethical theory, including natural law.[24] Thus, a utilitarian can hold that social and political institutions are

21. Erik Wolf, "Naturrecht: I. Profanes Naturrecht," *Die Religion in Geschichte und Gegenwart,* 3d ed., 4, col. 1356.

22. *Natural Law* (London: Hutchinson, 1951), p. 116.

23. A. P. d'Entrèves, "Two Questions about Law," *Existenz und Ordnung* (Festschrift für Erik Wolf zum 60. Geburtstag), ed. Thomas Würtenberger, et al. (Frankfurt am Main: Vittorio Klostermann, 1962), p. 314 (italics mine).

24. Felix Oppenheim writes, "Logically, any metaethical theory is compatible with any ethical theory." *(Moral Principles in Political Philosophy* [New York: Random House, 1968], p. 49). His view is that natural law is an application of cognitivism—either intuitionism or naturalism—in legal and political ethics (pp. 35, 49).

to be judged in terms of the "greatest good for the greatest number," although he might defend this principle by any metaethical theory such as intuitionism or naturalism.

Several objections have been raised to natural law as a metaethical theory; the main charge is that its most prominent versions commit what has been termed since G. E. Moore "the naturalistic fallacy," by moving from an ontology or metaphysics of human nature to ethical prescriptions, from "is" to "ought." This objection flows from the view that ethical and value judgments cannot be logically derived from propositions about man and the world. It is fallacious to hold that a proposition about the function of sexual organs, for example, entails the moral conclusion that artificial means of contraception ought not to be employed. Such an argument is possible only if one assumes other independent moral principles and values in whose light a factual or metaphysical statement becomes relevant.[25]

However, when the proponents of natural law contend that all laws can be viewed in ethical terms, they are not satisfied with a generalization about law and morality. Rather, they assert a logically necessary relation between law and *particular moral principles*. Any law which is inconsistent with those principles is unjust and therefore cannot engender an obligation to obedience. Natural law, on this level, comprises a set of ethical principles that vary in their content from one theory to the next, encompassing such alleged "universals" as the common good, liberty, and equality, in differing combinations. This diversity has often drawn criticism because it seems to indicate that a *universal* natural law is a fiction.

Finally, beyond the metaethical and ethical questions, natural law can be viewed as a theory about the concept of law, which it defines in moral terms. Although these three levels

25. See Nielsen, "Myth of Natural Law," in Hook, *L & P*, pp. 134–36.

can be clearly distinguished, quite often they are combined in a single theory, as in the classic synthesis of Thomistic thought. From this perspective natural law is ontological. Being and oughtness are fundamentally related in an order of reality within which there are several levels of law—eternal law, divine law, natural law, positive law. Beyond this ontological basis, Thomism also affirms that the fundamental principles of morality and law can be discerned by human reason apart from revelation. A participationist metaphysic enables one to make sense of the interconnections between the several levels of law so that if a positive law contradicts natural law it loses its status as law.

Despite such frequent interconnections, it is possible to evaluate natural law as a theory of law independently of its metaethical and ethical claims. After all, the conflation of validity and morality as a basis of one's obligation to obey the law could be defended in terms of a logically necessary relation between law and certain moral principles which are derived, for example, from a special divine decree rather than from human nature or universal values. The focus of my interest, in its most precise formulation, is the Thomistic assertion that "an unjust law is no law at all," *lex iniusta non est lex*.[26] At this point, where the debate between natural law and legal positivist theories is joined, one discerns the fundamental principles governing obedience and disobedience. I

26. Augustine, *I De Libero Arbitrio*, 5: "Non videtur esse lex quae iusta non fuerit" (Thomas Aquinas, *Summa Theologica*, 1.2, qu. 95). Jacques Maritain says that because "the positive law obliges by virtue of the Natural Law which is a participation in the Eternal Law," it must be affirmed that "an unjust law is not a law" ("Natural Law and Moral Law" in *Moral Principles of Action*, ed. Ruth Anshen, Science of Culture Series, 6 [New York: Harper, 1952], p. 76). Pope John XXIII, in "Pacem in Terris," follows St. Thomas Aquinas in holding that human law which does not correspond to right reason lacks "the true nature of law" (*The Social Teachings of the Church*, ed. Anne Fremantle [New York: New American Library, Mentor-Omega Book, 1963], p. 288).

do not suggest that all versions of natural law thus conflate validity and morality, or determine whether one should obey the law by its justice or injustice alone, or consistently defend such positions, but rather that from the standpoint of political obligation, this is one of the most important claims associated with some forms of natural law.[27]

This denial of validity to an unjust law is simply the most dramatic way of expressing the logical connection between the concept of law and certain standards of morality. The advocate of natural law is not content simply to declare a law "morally obnoxious"; he also has to "condemn it to a grammatical death through definitional execution."[28] When the phrase *unjust law* is viewed as a contradiction in terms, there can be no good reason for asserting that there is a moral obligation to obey a legal rule that does not embody justice. John Courtney Murray vigorously defends this conclusion:

> no moral issue of civil disobedience rises in the case of a legal enactment that is unjust in the proper sense. To the question "Why am I obliged to obey an unjust law?" the only answer is that I am not obliged to obey it. I cannot be bound in conscience to comply with a legislative act that does violence to my rights as a man.[29]

27. My intention is to show how this claim is present in many versions of natural law theory in the Roman Catholic Church, but also how it is qualified by other themes, including teleological and consequentialist elements. The result is that the "higher law" claim is partly modified by reference to the broader context. My contention is that even this modified position does not adequately account for political obligation, at least within certain contexts.

28. Judith Shklár, *Legalism* (Cambridge: Harvard University Press, 1964), p. 107. Felix Oppenheim writes, "Natural law theorists are especially prone to define the concept of positive law persuasively to apply only to legal rules which are just, that is, insofar as they are in agreement with the natural law itself" *(Moral Principles*, p. 45).

29. John Courtney Murray, S.J., "The Problem of Mr. Rawls's Problem," Hook, *L & P*, p. 31.

In the claim that "an unjust law is no law at all" one thus encounters a long-standing and significant perspective on political obligation and resistance.

Reflecting this long tradition of natural law, Martin Luther King echoes both St. Augustine and St. Thomas Aquinas in asserting that injustice invalidates a law:

> One may well ask: "How can you advocate breaking some laws and obeying others?" The answer lies in the fact that there are two types of laws: just and unjust. I would be the first to advocate obeying just laws. One has not only a legal but a moral responsibility to obey just laws. Conversely, one has a moral responsibility to disobey unjust laws. I would agree with St. Augustine that "an unjust law is no law at all."[30]

Because most of King's acts of civil disobedience really involved appeals to higher positive law (e.g. the federal Constitution) rather than a nonpositive moral law or the outer ranges of ideality, one might be tempted to dismiss this statement as rhetoric, but it seems to be too deeply rooted in his thinking to be so easily discounted. Although he did not develop meta-ethical and ethical theses systematically, they are also evident in his theory, especially in his reliance on philosophical personalism, stemming from Edgar S. Brightman's and L. Harold De Wolf's influence at Boston University where King took his Ph.D. degree. His discussion of the standards for determining just and unjust laws is indebted to that personalist tradition: "Any law that uplifts human personality is just. Any law that degrades human personality is unjust. All segregation statutes are unjust because segregation distorts the soul and damages the personality."[31] It is easy to agree with King that there are some laws, including those he mentioned, that are so vile they

30. "Letter from Birmingham Jail," *Why We Can't Wait*, p. 82.
31. Ibid.

should be disobeyed, but I am inquiring into the most adequate framework for interpreting and directing such moral
sensitivities in relation to law. Natural law—the theory that
there can be no legal and certainly no moral obligation when
a law is unjust—may well be inadequate in this respect.

The major alternative to natural law is some form of legal
positivism, which comes in as many varieties as natural law.
For example, positivism as a *method* focuses on a way of ap-
proaching and examining law which is widely accepted in
juridical science; as a *theory* it purports to disclose the nature
of law or legal obligation; as an *ideology* it affirms that "law
is law" *(Gesetz ist Gesetz)* and that, because of the moral value
it imputes to existing law, obedience is obligatory.[32] While
various legal positivists such as John Austin, Hans Kelsen,
and H. L. A. Hart approach these matters in quite different
ways, I shall concentrate on positivism as a theory of law, with
only an occasional reference to its ideological versions; for it
is as a theory about law that legal positivism so dramatically
and, I think, effectively assails natural law. Contending that
"the existence of law is one thing; its merit or demerit is another,"[33] legal positivists insist that legal obligation and
moral obligation may be contradictory without canceling the
former but also without necessarily making it determinative
of action.

The invectives hurled between the advocates of natural law
and the positivists most often focus on the claim that an unjust law is no law at all. The fears and even the ideological
commitments underlying the argument are most apparent in
the area of sociomoral consequences. Positivists fear that nat-

32. N. Bobbio drew these basic distinctions as interpreted by A. P.
d'Entrèves in "A Core of Good Sense: Reflections on Hart's Theory of
Natural Law" (trans. from the French), *Philosophy Today* 9 (Summer
1965): 121.

33. John Austin, *The Province of Jurisprudence Determined* (New
York: Humanities Press, 1965), p. 184.

ural law leads to anarchy, whereas proponents of natural law
fear that positivism leads to a sanctification of the existing
legal order and the individual's submission to it. Unques-
tionably some in each camp have erred in these extreme directions, but the more sophisticated theorists have not been
guilty of either. As a result the debate has often appeared
misdirected.[34]

Others attempting to present an alternative to both positions have also failed to locate and deal with the critical issues. Because I can best delineate this debate by looking at
one of the misconceptions, I shall examine Emil Brunner's
argument against the Roman Catholic position to see where
and how he misses its distinctive contours. I am not interested
in his constructive position at this point, but only in his argument against natural law. Basing his social ethics on the orders of creation, which he admits are quite similar to natural
law (indeed, historically these affinities made the Christian
appropriation of philosophical natural law possible), the
Swiss theologian stresses the dependence of these orders on
God's will and action. At first glance it might appear that
Brunner is quibbling over terms, but his opposition is more
than terminological. He rejects natural law as a competing,
higher legal system, although he admits it as a criterion of
positive law. He writes:

> If, as was fully the case in the medieval world, the "law
> of nature" implies that a law of the state must not be
> obeyed if it conflicts with the law of nature, and hence is
> unjust, the law of nature means an intolerable menace to
> the system of positive law. . . . No state law can tolerate
> a competition of this kind presented by a second legal

34. See, for example, Fuller's charges in *The Morality of Law* (New
Haven: Yale University Press, 1964), p. 123, and Hart's response, "Review
of *The Morality of Law*," *Harvard Law Review* 78 (1965): 1289–90.

system. The laws of the state actually obtaining must possess a monopoly of binding legal force; the law of nature must claim no binding legal force for itself if the legal security of the state is to remain unshaken.[35]

In effect, Brunner defends natural law to a certain extent on the metaethical and ethical levels, although he repudiates it as a theory of one's obligations in the political-legal order. His point is that "the law of nature can only *reveal* the injustice of a decree of the state; it cannot release the citizen from his duty of obeying that unjust decree."[36] Underscoring man's sinfulness, Brunner concludes that the injustice of a law cannot be a sufficient reason for denying its obligatoriness, since the state and its legal order are prerequisites for life in a fallen world. This broader theological-anthropological perspective must be considered in assessing political obedience and disobedience.

Without examining Brunner's positive alternative, I want to show that his critical analysis of the Roman Catholic perspective on obedience and disobedience simply neglects some of the fundamental aspects of the reasoning behind it. While most proponents of natural law certainly do defend some version of the conflation of validity and morality (so that an unjust law is an invalid law), for many Roman Catholic thinkers natural law is ascertained in and through positive law, customs, and traditions rather than a direct individual perception. Jacques Maritain writes: "the knowledge of the primordial aspects of natural law was first expressed in social pat-

35. Brunner, *Justice and the Social Order,* trans. Mary Hottinger (New York: Harper, 1945), p. 93. He is thinking mainly of the modern constitutional state; when he turns to "tyranny" he says that a person "who is not prepared to come to terms with the legal monstrosity of the totalitarian state has no alternative but the right to resist based solely on the law of nature" (p. 95).

36. Ibid., p. 272, n. 38, and p. 93.

terns rather than in personal judgments."[37] Furthermore, natural law may be conceived more as a qualification of the legal order than as an independent system which is directly accessible to human reason. Thus, d'Entrèves sees natural law as adding a plus sign to positive law (backed by coercive force), which could not otherwise elicit and claim voluntary obedience.[38] But even in such an approach there can be a denial that an unjust rule has the quality of law. Thus, Franz Böckle writes, "If the law itself is repealed or changed, or if it comes to an end from internal considerations (e.g. *if it becomes unjust* or impossible), then the legal obligation is entirely taken away," but he is also quite clear that there is no rival, nonhistorical legal system to which one can appeal directly.[39]

Brunner's interpretation also misses the point made again and again in classical and contemporary texts on political obligation and resistance: not every contradiction between a positive law and natural law justifies disobedience.[40] The fact that an unjust law is not binding on a citizen does not mean that he is morally permitted to or ought to disobey that law. From the premise that an unjust law is promulgated, one can only conclude that that law does not obligate him; he cannot conclude simply that he ought to disregard it without broader attention to the situation.

Because St. Thomas Aquinas's interpretation of political obligation is a classic statement of this perspective as well as

37. Jacques Maritain, *Man and the State* (Chicago: University of Chicago Press, Phoenix Books, 1956), p. 92.

38. D'Entrèves, *Notion of the State,* passim.

39. Franz Böckle, *Fundamental Concepts of Moral Theology,* trans. William Jerman (New York: Paulist Press, 1968), pp. 64–65, italics mine; Böckle, *Das Naturrecht im Disput,* pp. 133–34.

40. Karlheinz Peschke, *Naturrecht in der Kontroverse: Kritik evangelischer Theologie an der katholischen Lehre von Naturrecht und natürlicher Sittlichkeit* (Salzburg: Otto Müller, 1967), p. 162.

a significant historical influence, especially in the Roman
Catholic tradition, I shall briefly delineate his position and
show how he avoids the charges that Brunner makes. St.
Thomas contrasted just and unjust laws:

> Laws enacted by men are either just or unjust. If just,
> they draw from the eternal law, from which they derive,
> the power to oblige in conscience. . . . And if a human
> law is at variance in any particular with the natural law,
> it is no longer legal, but rather a corruption of law.[41]

In accord with Romans 13, he views all authority as ultimately derived from God: "For this reason the duty of obedience is, for the Christian, a consequence of this derivation of
authority from God, and ceases when that ceases."[42] He does
not argue, however, that obedience is a theological rather than
a moral virtue.

> Obedience is not a theological virtue, for its direct object
> is not God but the precept of any superior, whether ex-
> pressed or inferred, namely, a simple word of the superior

41. *Summa Theologica*, 1.2 qu. 96, art. 4; qu. 95, art. 2; see *Aquinas:
Selected Political Writings*, ed. A. P. d'Entrèves, trans. J. G. Dawson
(Oxford: Basil Blackwell, 1959), pp. 135, 129. There are two modes of
derivation of human law from natural law: "some derivations are made
from the natural law by way of formal conclusions: as the conclusion,
'Do no murder,' derives from the precept, 'Do harm to no man.' Other
conclusions are arrived at as determinations of particular cases. So the
natural law establishes that whoever transgresses shall be punished. But
that a man should be punished by a specific penalty is a particular determination of the natural law. Both types of derivation are to be found
in human law. But those which are arrived at in the first way are sanc-
tioned not only by human law, but by the natural law also; while those
arrived at by the second method have the validity of human law alone"
(ibid.). The former is *ius gentium*, the latter is *ius civile*.
42. *Commentary on the Sentences of Peter Lombard* as reprinted in
d'Entrèves, *Aquinas*, p. 183.

indicating his will, and which the obedient subject obeys promptly. . . . It is, however, a moral virtue, since it is a part of justice.[43]

St. Thomas can maintain this position because of his general principle that faith in Christ does not destroy the order of justice but confirms it.[44] Political obedience thus is a requirement of justice.[45]

Unjust laws may be contrary to divine laws, or they may be detrimental to human welfare. A positive law which contradicts or contravenes divine law should never be obeyed. For example, if a positive law demands idolatry, it must be disobeyed. So far, then, it appears that Brunner has rightly interpreted St. Thomas's position (although he himself would also agree, following Acts 5:29, that matters of faith cannot be dictated by the state). With regard to laws that are detrimental to the common good, however, Brunner's interpretation falls apart. St. Thomas's argument includes this evaluative element in the very definition of law, "a rational ordering of things which concern the common good; promulgated by whoever is charged with the care of the community." Distinguishing object, author, and form, he insists that a law may be unjust in terms of any of these:

> Either with respect to their object, as when a ruler enacts laws which are burdensome to his subjects and which do not make for common prosperity, but are designed better to serve his own cupidity and vainglory. Or with respect to their author; if a legislator should enact laws which exceed the powers vested in him. Or, finally with respect to

43. *Summa Theologica*, 2.2, qu. 104, art. 2; see *The Political Ideas of St. Thomas Aquinas*, ed. Dino Bigongiari (New York: Hafner, 1953), p. 162.

44. *Summa Theologica*, 2.2, qu. 104, art. 6; see d'Entrèves, *Aquinas*, p. 179.

45. Cf. Richard Hauser, *Was des Kaisers Ist*, pp. 149–83.

their form; if the burdens, even though they are concerned with the common welfare, are distributed in an
inequitable manner throughout the community. Laws
of this sort have more in common with violence than with
legality.[46]

While one is not bound to obey these unjust laws, he is also
not obligated to disobey them—contrary to Brunner's interpretation. St. Thomas continues, "Such laws do not, in consequence, oblige in conscience, except, on occasion, to avoid
scandal or disorder."[47]

This position can be summarized in different language. Although the right of disobedience (negatively, the absence of
the duty of obedience) is established by seeing whether the
decree of the ruler or the law is contrary to principles of
morality, the exercise of that right is to be avoided under
some conditions, especially when it might well lead to greater
harm for the community. These principles are at work in St.
Thomas's view of the right to resist tyranny:

the overthrowing of such government is not strictly sedi-
tion; except perhaps in the case that it is accompanied by
such disorder that the community suffers greater harm
from the consequent disturbances than it would from a
continuance of the former rule.[48]

This view has remained normative for Roman Catholic social ethics. Even the most cursory survey of recent literature is
sufficient to establish Martin Rock's thesis: the common good
(bonum commune) is "the first and last criterion for answer-

46. *Summa Theologica*, 1.2 qu. 90, art. 4; qu. 96, art. 4. See d'Entrèves,
Aquinas, pp. 113, 137.
47. *Summa Theologica*, 1.2, qu. 96, art. 4. See d'Entrèves, *Aquinas*,
p. 137.
48. *Summa Theologica*, 2.2, qu. 42, art. 2; see d'Entrèves, *Aquinas*, p.
161.

ing the question: is resistance against the power of the state permitted?"[49] This position does not appear to endanger the political-legal order or to threaten anarchy, for built-in restraints rule out deleterious acts of disobedience. Thus, the concept of natural law does not, at least in Roman Catholic circles, create the dangers that some of its opponents sense in its conflation of validity and morality. One should have expected this from its nonrevolutionary history, at least until the corollary notion of natural rights emerged. Indeed, one of the main criticisms of natural law has been its conservative endorsement of the existing order, which it often views as being in accord with the basic structure of the universe.

Apart from the alleged threat it poses to the legal order, natural law has been regarded as a necessary condition of opposition to injustice. During this century, especially in the aftermath of Nazi Germany, it has been frequently maintained that without natural law there is no possibility of criticizing and resisting unjust positive laws. For example, one defender of natural law contends that its importance is that it "affords the possibility of rebellion; it provides a court of appeal, and without it there is no court of appeal beyond the edicts of men."[50] But, while the fact that some legal posi-

49. Rock, *Widerstand gegen die Staatsgewalt*, p. 172; *Christ und Revolution*, especially chaps. 6–8; cf. Maritain, *Scholasticism and Politics* (Garden City, N. Y.: Doubleday, Image Books, 1960), p. 102. Johannes Messner writes: "The observance of orders and laws of political authority may be a moral duty, *in spite of their injustice*, on the grounds of the common good, which can impose an obligation to avoid still graver prejudice to order and peace; or it may be morally permissible on the grounds of prudence, that is, it can impose an obligation to take precautions against incurring the severe penalities attached to the refusal of obedience." (*Social Ethics: Natural Law in the Western World*, rev. ed., trans. J. J. Doherty [St. Louis, Mo.: Herder, 1965], p. 593).

50. Columba Ryan, O.P., in *Light on the Natural Law*, ed. Illtud Evans, O.P. (Baltimore: Helicon, 1965), pp. 17–18. This argument is especially common in an age which finds metaphysical reasoning unconvincing. Even Emil Brunner, who rejects natural law as a legal

tivists have held relativistic moral stances may have given credence to the idea that they cannot justify disobedience to law, not all legal positivists hold this view. Indeed, many of the utilitarians (for example, John Austin and Jeremy Bentham) assumed the legal positivist standpoint at least in part because it seemed to provide a more adequate interpretation of the human situation but also a better basis for criticizing and resisting unjust laws. Hence, instead of rejecting as irrelevant the charge of undermining an ethos which would support resistance, many legal positivists would say that this charge certainly points to one of the critical issues, but that legal positivism rather than natural law provides the most helpful stance.[51] The fact that several positivists have been sensitive to such moral issues should make it quite evident that there is no *logical* reason why a person could not say, "that is a law, but it is simply too immoral to be obeyed." And, as Hart has reminded us, "this simple presentation of the human dilemma . . . has much to be said for it."[52]

Perhaps the claim that there is no possibility of criticizing and resisting unjust laws once natural law is rejected points to a psychological rather than a logical dilemma. Certain moral principles may provide a support which impels and sustains resistance to the law, but are they absolutely necessary on the psychological level? The answer to this question

---

theory, insists upon the necessity of objective natural law (as metaethical and ethical theory) for resistance: "if there is no sacred, eternal, divine, absolute law, there is no possibility of denouncing any form of law or polity or national act as unjust" (*Justice and the Social Order*, p. 8, and passim).

51. H. L. A. Hart, "Positivism and the Separation of Law and Morals," in *Society, Law and Morality*, ed. Frederick Olafson, pp. 457 f. (reprinted from the *Harvard Law Review*, 1958).

52. Ibid., p. 458. Contrast Hans Kelsen's view in "Why Should the Law Be Obeyed?" *What is Justice?* (Los Angeles: University of California Press, 1957), pp. 257–65.

may differ according to the particular circumstances—for example, in a totalitarian state—and may also depend on whether the action is criticism of law, passive refusal to obey a demand, or violent resistance. But in any of these contexts the evidence simply fails to support the claim that any particular ethical stance is a psychological prerequisite for resistance. Resistance to the Nazi regime was so varied that it is "difficult to establish a correlation between anti-Nazi activity and a specific philosophical orientation."[53]

53. Guenter Lewy, "Resistance to Tyranny: Treason, Right or Duty?" *Western Political Quarterly* 13 (September 1960): 587; cf. Judith Shklar, *Legalism*, p. 73.
Too often empirical studies of the ethical and religious factors in resistance simply reflect the author's presuppositions about what should have been the case. An example of this is Mother Mary Alice Gallin, O.S.U., *German Resistance to Hitler: Ethical and Religious Factors* (Washington, D.C.: The Catholic University of America Press, 1969), which nevertheless makes several significant contributions to the discussion. A central thesis of her study is that "the neglect of the teaching on natural law and the lack of clarity in theological views on the right of resistance made a decision in this matter [resistance] extremely difficult" (p. 199). She sees "the key to the German dilemma" as the loss of the natural law perspective: "The 'present attitude of the essence of State and Law' was one which had lost touch with the fundamental Thomistic principle that 'Law is a dictate of right reason' " (p. 37).
It is interesting that while she seems to see the decline of doctrines of natural law as responsible in part for the fact that the resistance movement was not larger, she also assumes that those who were able to resolve the conflict of conscience in the direction of resistance reflected the natural law perspective. "The men of the Resistance Movement seldom refer directly to 'natural rights,' and the very diversity of reasons which they offer for fighting the Hitler regime creates the impression that they were not concerned with a rational explanation of any abstract 'right' or 'duty' of resistance. This can be said without in any way detracting from the *probability* that they acted in defense of fundamental human rights from a high ethical or religious motivation" (p. 39, italics mine, cf. p. 50, but ct. p. 199).
Also, while the Roman Catholic Church retained a fairly strong doctrine of natural law and the Calvinists had a fairly strong basis in tradition for a right of resistance and even revolution, these groups failed to produce more members of the resistance than the Lutheran communion, which is so often charged with having influenced the ethos of submis-

In fact, the evidence does not support even a modified claim that, although natural law is not a psychological prerequisite, it provides the most adequate psychological support for criticism and resistance.[54] The temptation to flee from situations that present conflicting claims is not uncommon—as in Sartre's famous example of the student who came to him for advice about whether he should stay with his mother or join the French resistance movement—and natural law offers some security and certainty by permitting one to redescribe one's act. If one is not really violating a law (since the order is unjust and hence invalid), one can feel a sense of legal

---

sion to the powers that be: "the particular confession to which a man belonged made little or no difference in his decision to fight against Hitler" (p. 192; cf. 199–200). Mother Mary Alice Gallin apparently defends natural law on metaethical, ethical, and legal levels with little distinction between them. The point that I would stress is that the absence of adequate doctrines of natural law cannot be taken to account for the limited resistance, since, after all, the doctrines of natural law were generally lacking in the thought of those who did resist.

On the religious and ethical motives in the opposition to Hitler, see also Ernst Wolf, "Political and Moral Motives behind the Resistance," in Hermann Graml, et al., *The German Resistance to Hitler* (Los Angeles: University of California Press, 1970), pp. 195–234; and the comprehensive, thorough analysis of the Kreisau Circle by Ger van Roon, *Neuordnung im Widerstand: Der Kreisauer Kreis innerhalb der deutschen Widerstandsbewegung* (Munich: R. Oldenbourg, 1967), especially his conclusions (pp. 470–73).

54. See the preceding note. The attempts to deal with problems raised on the ethical and metaethical levels of natural law have often had consequences in the area of obedience and resistance. For example, there have been several recent attempts to avoid particular difficulties on the ethical level by refusing to view natural law as a code and by stressing its historicity and flexibility (cf. n. 18 above). But such attempts have undermined one of the reasons frequently adduced for supporting it; for the more open, flexible, and historical the principles of natural law are, the less effective they are in supporting criticism of and resistance to law. See Louis C. Midgley, *Beyond Human Nature: The Contemporary Debate over Moral Natural Law*, The Charles E. Merrill Monograph Series in the Humanities and Social Sciences (Provo, Utah: Brigham Young University Press, 1968), especially p. 67.

justification. Yet this gain is limited if not illusory, for, as pointed out earlier, the most sensitive and carefully formulated statements about natural law deny that an unjust law is sufficient justification for disobedience in all cases. When so many other features of the moral situation, such as probable consequences, must be examined and evaluated, the doctrine of natural law cannot provide complete and final security.

Perhaps the most important problem is how to engender a "critical and independent attitude among citizens in general."[55] But certain theories of political obligation may be better than others in creating and sustaining this attitude. As Hart argues most cogently, in *The Concept of Law:*

> What surely is most needed in order to make men clear sighted in confronting the official abuse of power, is that they should preserve the sense that the certification of something as legally valid is not conclusive of the question of obedience, and that, however great the aura of majesty or authority which the official system may have, its demands must in the end be submitted to a moral scrutiny. This sense, that there is something outside the official system, by reference to which in the last resort the individual must solve his problems of obedience, is surely more likely to be kept alive among those who are accustomed to think that rules of law may be iniquitous than among those who think that nothing inquitous can anywhere have the status of law. [p. 206]

In this context, the question about natural law—quite apart from its supporters' argument that it is the strongest possible and perhaps even necessary basis of resistance and its critics' fear of anarchy—is how adequate it is as an account of and a direction for our moral experience in the political-

55. Shklar, *Legalism,* p. 72.

legal order. Most theories of natural law are "internalist" in that they locate the answer to the problem of obedience within law itself, treating law as a moral concept.[56] In the internalist view, it is meaningless to inquire into a moral obligation to fulfill our legal obligations because of what I would term a seamless fabric of obligation, whereas the positivist such as Hart stresses that obligation has legal and moral as well as other uses,[57] and that to assert a valid legal "ought" or obligation is not necessarily to assert a moral one.

"Externalist" theories, those which appeal to a nonlegal source or a moral authority outside the law, can more helpfully interpret and guide our experiences in the state. In externalist theories, a law may satisfy all the requirements of the political-legal system and thus be valid, although it so contravenes certain moral conceptions of civic justice or the common good that one has the right or even the duty to disobey it. The validity of the law is not determined by the moral justice it embodies, but rather by the rules of the particular system. As Dorothy Emmet points out in *Justice and the Law:*

> we have to distinguish between the questions (a) By what criterion do we know whether a particular rule is a rule of law?, and (b) What is the general purpose of a system of law? The Natural Law theorists conflate these questions, and since it may very well be the case that questions of justice and morality are involved in answers to (b), they assume that they must also be involved in answers to (a). [p. 9]

56. John Ladd, "Law and Morality: Internalism vs. Externalism," Hook, *L & P*, pp. 61–71.

57. See Hart, *The Concept of Law*, pp. 199, 56, 88; "Positivism and the Separation of Law and Morals," in Olafson, *Society, Law and Morality*, p. 455; "Legal and Moral Obligation," in Melden, *Essays in Moral Philosophy*. See also Richard Brandt, "The Concepts of Obligation and Duty," *Mind*, n.s. 73 (1964): 374–93.

Taking this distinction seriously, one could hold that a legal
system, in order to be a legal system, has to meet certain moral
requirements although the particular rules issued within that
system, in order to be valid, do not. Hart, adhering to legal
positivism but also to a "minimum content of natural law,"
sees this as the "core of good sense" in doctrines of natural
law.[58]

This approach offers a more cogent interpretation of our
moral experience in the political-legal order than internalist
theories do. The position that I shall develop later also distinguishes between focusing on the particular rule and on the
legal system as a whole for purposes of interpreting the basis
of the moral obligation to obey the law. I shall conjoin that
distinction with several other steps in order to establish what
natural law cannot allow, and hence to argue that there may
be a moral obligation to obey an *unjust* law (within limits).
That is, even if the rule is unjust, it may still be valid, and I
may have an obligation to obey it, depending on the particular system and the basis of my obligation within that system.
This obligation exists in addition to the prediction and evaluation of consequences which many proponents of natural
law would admit, as already indicated, in order to avoid the
conclusion that an unjust law creates an obligation to disobey or permits an automatic exercise of the right to disobey.

The distinction between a whole system and particular laws
enables one to illuminate a crucial question that most theories
of natural law cannot encompass—*indirect* disobedience. For
example, when a person recognizes that the present tax law,
despite egregious inequities, is fundamentally just as well as
valid (at least sufficiently just so as not to cancel one's obligation to obey it) but finds his protest against military spending

58. Hart, "Positivism and the Separation of Law and Morals," pp.
462–65, and *The Concept of Law*, chap. 9.

thwarted at various turns, he may select the violation of the
tax law as one way to make his stand, even though he realizes
that its effectiveness is doubtful. That particular law and
one's actions in relation to it will have to be considered in the
context of the whole system, including, of course, the effects
of disobedience on that system (as many proponents of natural
law admit), but even more importantly in terms of one's general obligation within and to that state and its legal order.
One cannot simply isolate a particular rule and consider its
justice or injustice, validity or invalidity, for the relevant
moral context is much broader.

On a deeper level, if and when natural law provides a modi-
cum of security in resistance, it does so through its claim that
the unjust rule promulgated by the state is not really a law
and that there is thus a *legal* justification for disobedience.
Undergirding this claim is a fundamental perspective on the
world that stresses coherence, order, and harmony. The contrasting perspectives that frequently support natural law and
legal positivism are evident in the famous exchange between
H. L. A. Hart and Lon Fuller. Hart argues that the doctrine
of natural law obscures the ingredients of moral decisions in
relation to law by viewing values as cohering in one system
and by ignoring the occasions which demand that we sacrifice,
or at least compromise, some of the values. He underscores the
point that many of our judgments and decisions concern the
lesser of two evils.

> Like nettles, the occasions when life forces us to choose
> between the lesser of two evils must be grasped with the
> consciousness that they are what they are. The vice of this
> use of the principle that, at certain limiting points, what
> is utterly immoral cannot be law or lawful is that it will
> serve to cloak the true nature of the problems with which
> we are faced and will encourage the romantic optimism

that all the values we cherish ultimately will fit into a
single system, that no one of them has to be sacrificed or
compromised to accommodate another.[59]

Over against this, Fuller insists that positivism finally denies
"the possibility of any bridge between the obligation to obey
the law and other moral obligations. No mediating principle
can measure their respective demands on conscience, for they
exist in wholly separate worlds."[60] On the one side, values fit
together in a system; on the other, they may well fall into
conflict in particular situations—such are the assertions of the
different theorists.

I am inclined to think that these perspectives have tremendous significance for interpreting political obedience and disobedience. In my opinion, the legal positivist stance taken by
Hart and others more fully illuminates our experience in the
political-legal order and, furthermore, more helpfully directs
our responses, by its clarity and its refusal to define law persuasively in relation to moral principles. This does not mean,
as I have shown, that a positivist theory of law ignores moral
considerations. Although some positivists have indeed ignored such questions or have even defended an ideological
position that puts a moral premium on existing law, this is
not a necessary implication of positivism as a theory of the
nature of law, specifically its denial that the justice of a particular rule determines whether it is a law. My contention is
that nothing is gained in theoretical clarity, moral guidance,
or psychological support for criticism and resistance by de-

59. Hart, "Positivism and the Separation of Law and Morals," p. 461.
Cf. *The Concept of Law*, p. 207.
60. Lon Fuller, "Positivism and Fidelity to Law: A Reply to Professor
Hart," in Olafson, *Society, Law and Morality*, p. 491. For more recent
statements of Fuller's position, see *The Morality of Law* and *Anatomy
of the Law*, A Britannica Perspective (New York: New American Library,
Mentor Book, 1969).

fending natural law as a *theory of law,* [61] although my own position on the metaethical and ethical levels may be construed as one form of natural law.

ALTERNATIVES TO NATURAL LAW

In recent Protestant thought political ethics has attempted, in the words of Ernst Wolf, "to break through to new ground beyond natural law and positivism, where the tensions between them, if not removed, might at any rate be lessened."[62] Unlike certain types of positivism, it has been concerned about the justice of law and the possibility of both criticism

61. Some proponents of versions of natural law theory would insist that the law as it is cannot be so easily determined, and that in certain contexts it can be determined only by reference to "political morality." Ronald Dworkin contends that the law includes rational criteria that possibly might be or should be used by the courts in drawing their conclusions. Obviously he is quite right that the United States Constitution "injects an extraordinary amount of our political morality into the issue of whether a law is valid" through the due process clause, the equal protection clause, etc., but he and other natural lawyers such as Lon Fuller tend to focus on the "fuzzy" areas in law, on the penumbra, whereas Hart and many of the legal positivists tend to take the clearcut laws as models.

Dworkin also argues that "in the United States, at least, almost any law which a significant number of people would be tempted to disobey on moral grounds would be doubtful—if not clearly invalid—on constitutional grounds as well." See his article "On Not Prosecuting Civil Disobedience," *The New York Review of Books* 10, no. 2. (June 6, 1968): 14; reprinted in *Trials of the Resistance* (New York: A New York Review Book, 1970). The objections that I have raised about traditional natural law theories hold, to a great extent, for Dworkin's view also, although it is certainly more helpful than most traditional statements. For some other contemporary restatements of natural law theory, see Edgar Bodenheimer, "Dicta," *Virginia Law Weekly* 22, no. 3 (1969) and J. R. Lucas, *The Principles of Politics* (Oxford: Clarendon Press, 1966), especially sections 73 and 74.

62. Quoted by Heinz-Horst Schrey, "Beyond Natural Law and Positivism: The Foundations of Law in Present-day Evangelical Theology in the German-speaking World," *Concilium: An International Review of Theology* 5, no. 3 (May 1967): 36.

and resistance. But, in contrast to some versions of natural law, Protestant ethics has focused on the relative rather than the absolute justice of law. On the question of one's obligation to obey the law, Wolf, for example, argues that an adequate interpretation cannot make obligation depend simply upon an act or decree of the state; nor can it deny validity to those rules which do not measure up to certain absolute standards. In some instances, this reinterpretation is conceived as a "search for a *tertium quid* between rational certainty and relativity in ethics and politics."[63]

I shall delineate these general alternatives to natural law first, by sketching briefly and in general terms some of their dominant themes and my major objections to them; second, by illustrating these themes in relation to selected Protestant thinkers; and third, by discussing in depth Paul Ramsey's interpretation of political obligation. More specific criticisms and my own treatment of the issues will follow.

Although many Protestant theologians appropriate some form of natural law on the metaethical or ethical levels, very few deny the title of "law" to an unjust law, and very few make obedience dependent simply on the degree of justice of each particular rule. Of course, as I have shown, few Roman Catholic thinkers interpret natural law as a higher law which is decisive for the questions of obedience and disobedience since they also insist upon an assessment of consequences in light of the common good. While on some of these points the differences between Roman Catholic and Protestant perspectives are indeed minor, nevertheless, Protestant interpretations of political obedience usually focus more on the government and its laws as a system than on its particular laws. They

63. Ernst Wolf, "Zum Protestantischen Rechtsdenken," *Peregrinatio* 2 (Munich: Chr. Kaiser Verlag, 1965); Paul Lehmann, "A Christian Alternative to Natural Law," *Die moderne Demokratie und ihr Recht* (Festschrift für Gerhard Leibholz), ed. Karl D. Bracher, et al. (Tübingen: J. C. B. Mohr/Paul Siebeck, 1966), p. 523.

evaluate particular laws not merely in relation to certain standards of justice, whether absolute or relative, but also in the context of a system of law which itself is usually evaluated in moral terms. Even more significantly, instead of dealing with obedience and disobedience primarily in relation to a rule's injustice and the consequences of disobedience, Protestants tend to concentrate on the ends and functions of the state and its laws as defined in theological-anthropological terms.

Perhaps the significance and direction of this discussion will be clear from the outset if I indicate some of the weaknesses I see in most Protestant alternatives to natural law. First, by concentrating on the ends and functions of the state and its laws, and on obedience as a means to these ends, Protestants often overlook other indispensable criteria for the moral evaluation of obedience and disobedience that cannot be forced into this framework. This weakness is an offshoot of a more fundamental one inherent in the very attempt to offer a theory of political obligation that will apply to any and every political order. The moral factors in political obligation may be distinctive in each political-legal order (or at least in each type of political-legal order). These two weaknesses point to a third: perhaps the attempt to develop a general theory of the state from the standpoint of theological-anthropolical convictions is itself misdirected. It may be that the neglect of moral factors other than the ends and functions of the state, and the failure to deal with the distinctive moral factors in each political order, stem from the effort to develop a general theory of the state rather than confronting each state in its particularity. There are other criticisms to be made of particular Protestant positions, but these are the major objections I shall try to deal with in my own constructive statement, while at the same time retaining several valuable insights of such positions.

Like theories about natural law, especially within the Roman Catholic context, these alternative positions discuss political obligation in relation to theological-anthropological perspectives, moral principles and values, and interpretations of the dominant features of the political-legal order. Because the theological and anthropological perspectives are usually correlative, I have been considering them together, but it might be instructive to separate them for this discussion.

The Thomistic interpretation of the state and political obligation is constructed on a view of man's nature, as well as the divine ordering purpose, which decisively limits the effects of sin. D'Entrèves summarizes the basis of the Thomistic theory of political obligation by means of a distinction between the state's historical origins and its rational justification.

> The idea of sin, without being rejected, is confined to narrow limits, merely to explain certain inevitable hardships of social and political experience, such as slavery, the penal character of laws, or the existence of unjust rulers. It has no part in the rational justification of the State, because political obligation is inherent in man's nature. Man is unthinkable without the State because it is only in the State and through the State that he can achieve perfection.[64]

Not sin but human particularity, which must be welded into a whole for man to reach perfection, is the rational explanation and justification of the state. Many Protestants, on the other hand, relate the necessity of political obedience very closely to the fallen condition of the world. They often understand the political order as basically representing force

64. D'Entrèves, *Aquinas,* p. xvii.

rather than authority.[65] Since such force and coercion are necessary to restrain human sinfulness, the political order is a correlate of sin. This is not to say, of course, that sin is the *reason* for the state; it may simply be the *occasion* for divine action in instituting this order. These divergent emphases may stem from two fundamental perspectives on nature: the Roman Catholic tends to think of nature from a metaphysical perspective, the Protestant often views it in historical terms.[66]

What one stresses on the anthropological level is usually correlated with one's theological affirmations. And Christian political thought sooner or later appeals to theological affirmations as well as to a doctrine of man in explicating its understanding of why one should obey the law and when one may or should disobey it. While the Roman Catholic appeals to the divine will as mediated through the natural moral law known by reason, the Protestant generally appeals to God's active will as expressed in a variety of ways. Dante Germino gives an acute summary of the major theological differences which undergird the divergencies in political thought between the rationalist approach shown in Roman Catholic and

65. See Richard Hauser, *Autorität und Macht* (Heidelberg: Lambert Schneider, 1949). But Barth indicates that Christian ethics does not hold that the "exercise of power constitutes the essence of the state, i.e. its *opus proprium,* or even a part of it. What Christian ethics must insist is that it is an *opus alienum* for the state to have to exercise power" (*Church Dogmatics,* vol. 3, pt. 4. [Edinburgh: T. & T. Clark, 1961], p. 456). This would qualify Hauser's statement about Protestant social ethics generally (including Barth): "Ihr theologisches Fundament gerade führt die protestantische Sozialethik stets wieder dahin, im Wesen des Staates und seiner Autorität den Machtcharakter vor allem zu sehen und zu betonen" (p. 13).

66. On the difference between the metaphysical and historical points of view, see the statement by Josef Fuchs, S.J.: "Coercion is a result of sin from the historical and not from the metaphysical point of view." *Natural Law,* trans. Helmut Reckter, S.J. and John A. Dowling (New York: Sheed & Ward, 1965), p. 97.

Anglican ethics, and the fideist views held by many of their opponents, including, for example, Karl Barth.

> Just as Christian rationalism in political theory presupposes a God who is the embodiment of perfect wisdom and truth and who has ordered the universe in terms of a structure which man has been given the capacity at least partially to comprehend by the use of his reason, so Christian fideism presumes a God whose primary attribute is continuous action and power, and who is perpetually engaged in directly ruling, sustaining, and even re-creating (restoring) what He has made. The voluntarist conception of God, which is the foundation of all fideist ethics, emphasizes God's active will rather than his ordering reason. Whereas the rationalist conceives of God's rule as operative in the universe through the teleological structure or design which He has fashioned, the fideist attributes to God a sovereignty unmediated by any such rational structure. The tremendous, omnipresent majesty of God cannot be diluted by any doctrine such as the Thomistic idea of a divine governance exercising itself indirectly through a "nature" possessing its own (even if God-granted) immanent laws of development.[67]

Whereas the Christian rationalist can utilize reason to ascertain the principles of right order, the fideist emphasizes faith in response to direct divine commands in all their multiplicity.

The answers to any questions about the bases and limits of political obligation will be shaped very differently, in content as well as form, by each of these theological convictions. But, because of the limited scope of his essay, Germino does not go on to indicate the way different conceptions of God's active will relate to some particular emphases *within* or even *beyond*

67. Dante L. Germino, "Two Types of Recent Christian Political Thought," *The Journal of Politics* 21 (1959): 464-65.

Christian fideism. The patterns of interpreting the divine
activity and purpose in relation to man vary greatly even
among opponents to the Thomistic theory of natural law. At
the risk of oversimplifying what is involved, three distinct but
inseparable activities of God in relation to man can be identified, and his purpose for man cannot be interpreted without
these categories: God creates; he judges, governs, and sustains;
and he redeems. There are several reasons for selecting these
theological affirmations as central for this discussion. Not
only have they been dominant for such classic interpreters of
the Christian faith as Thomas Aquinas and John Calvin, but
they have also been central in the debates about the state by
the thinkers under consideration. This is to be expected since
these affirmations capture some of the most essential general
statements about the divine-human relation and the divine
purposes for man.

In terms of Protestant ethics, the state and law can be construed as an order of creation (Paul Althaus and Werner
Elert), an order of conservation or preservation (Walter Künneth and Helmut Thielicke), an order of redemption (christological foundation as in Karl Barth and Jacques Ellul), or
an order which relates to God's creating, preserving, and redeeming will (H. H. Schrey).[68] Although I shall not discuss

68. For a discussion of this typology, see Heinz-Horst Schrey, "Beyond
Natural Law," pp. 30–36; Heinz-Horst Schrey and H. H. Walz, *The
Biblical Doctrine of Justice and Law* (London: SCM Press, 1955), particularly part 3; cf. Ernst Wolf," 'Trinitarische' oder 'Christologische'
Begründung des Rechts?" in *Recht und Institution*, ed. Hans Dombois
(Witten-Ruhr: Luther-Verlag, 1956), pp. 9–29. A cautionary word about
the general utility of this typology is in order. It is especially appropriate
for German-language theology because of its greater attention to the
theological task in Christian social ethics. American Christian social
ethics has often been so absorbed in practical, institutional problems and
their solutions that serious theological reflection has seldom been cul-
tivated. Even where it has been developed, it has often been only as an
afterthought, although there are some recent examples of increased attention to the theological locus of ethics, including the work of Paul
Lehmann.

in great detail the patterns of political obligation associated with these theological doctrines, a summary of some of the main themes that representatives of these types develop will provide the necessary background for a careful, detailed examination of Paul Ramsey's views of political obligation. Then a critique of his position will set the stage for my own interpretation.

Dealing with the state in relation to both the order of creation and the order of preservation, Emil Brunner, in *Justice and the Social Order,* recognizes both an absolute justice based on the divinely created nature of man and a relative justice referring to a reality that has fallen away from the order of creation (p. 98). He contends that the state cannot be understood fully and simply in relation to the divine will in creation ("the most comprehensive ordering of the community") but must also be viewed "as an order of preservation in the sense of coercive law and the curbing of anarchy by the use of force."

> The modification in the status of man due to evil necessitates a modification of the order of justice, not only in the sense that it becomes a coercive system of positive law, but also in the sense that the substance of this positive law cannot coincide with that of the law of nature laid down in the order of creation. That is why there *must* be a difference, if not an antithesis, between positive law and the law of nature. [p. 100]

Brunner likes to illustrate the differences between the orders of creation and preservation by referring to Jesus's saying about another sphere of relationships: while in the order of creation man and woman were to be united in an indissoluble marriage, Jesus stressed that the Mosaic recognition of divorce was an accommodation to human sin "for the hardness of your hearts" (pp. 99, 211).

As I have already pointed out, Brunner's strictures against the tradition of natural law occasionally betray a lack of discernment about its position on resistance. Despite his affinities with this tradition on some levels (e.g. his discussion of the orders of creation), another point brings him closer to some forms of positivism. He insists that the "essence of the state is not justice but power" and that its purpose is "not only, indeed not primarily, justice" (pp. 196, 208). His stress on voluntarism and sin leads to this "realistic" interpretation of the state, law, and politics. One result of these themes is his use of natural law as only a *criterion* of law rather than a higher law to which one can directly appeal. A law's divergence from the natural law does not cancel the obligation to obedience, because such divergence is expected and because the legal system as a whole is so indispensable to human life; it is an order necessary to restrain sin, even if it is unjust.

From Brunner's perspective, then, the Christian's understanding of action motivated by love must also be structured by what can be discerned in the given institutions in the light of theological-anthropological convictions. The most precise summary that he gives of his position is, "one Lord, one motive, but two kinds of command." The single motive is love, but God commands man in different ways—as creator and preserver in institutional structures and processes, and as redeemer in interpersonal relationships. Justice is appropriate in the former, love in the latter. Out of love the Christian recognizes the demands of order which are always present because of human sinfulness; thus, his *first* response is always one of conserving and preserving the given order. [69]

Some other theologians, mainly within the Lutheran tradition, have focused more exclusively on the state as a manifestation of the order of preservation. Two important repre-

69. Brunner, *The Divine Imperative*, trans. Olive Wyon (Philadelphia: Westminster Press, 1947), pp. 620, 213–14, and passim.

sentatives are Walter Künneth and Helmut Thielicke,
though their positions on resistance are somewhat different.[70]
I shall concentrate on Künneth's position. According to him,
a Christian ethics of politics can guide activity between God
and evil.[71] It provides this guidance in part by interpreting
"the principle of order" according to the biblical revelation
in order to discern the essence of the state. In a fallen world
"the order of the state represents a concrete historical realization of the divine will of preservation. . . . The reality of the
state is the political form of the divine order of preservation."[72] In the terminology of the early church, the state
represents both a punishment and a partial remedy for sin,

70. Several of their differences stem from their different methodological
approaches. Künneth tends to deduce principles from scripture and
Reformation tradition and then to apply them, while Thielicke engages
in a phenomenology of the state in the light of the biblical message.
Thielicke's greater appreciation of the contemporary context and the impossibility of a direct appeal to tradition for political ethics makes his
approach more flexible. He insists on drawing a distinction between the
intentions of the Reformers and the institutional context of their statements in political ethics. See Thielicke, *Theological Ethics*, vol. 2,
Politics, pp. 144, 374; Künneth, *Politik zwischen Dämon und Gott: Eine
christliche Ethik des Politischen* (Berlin: Lutherisches Verlagshaus, 1,
Taschenbuchauflage, 1961).

71. Künneth, *Politik*, p. 417. " 'Damonie' signifies the metaphysical
opposition to the order of preservation as God's establishment" (p. 205).
This theme of conflict is prominent in several Swedish Lutheran interpretations of Luther and constructive political ethics. Following the
major direction set by Gustaf Wingren, Gunnar Hillerdal, in *Gehorsam
gegen Gott und Menschen* (Göttingen: Vanderhoeck & Reprecht, 1954),
develops a political ethic which stands in contrast to the Barthian understanding of political life and the state. But there are several differences
between Wingren and Hillerdal, on the one hand, and Künneth, on the
other. Quite significant are the emphases by Wingren and Hillerdal on
God's ordering rather than order, on love rather than an analysis of
order, on the state as effecting justice and not merely, or mainly, order.
There is some discussion of these debates within contemporary Lutheran-
ism in Thomas G. Sanders, *Protestant Concepts of Church and State*
(Garden City, N.Y.: Doubleday, Anchor Books, 1965), chap. 1.

72. Künneth, *Politik*, pp. 89, 105.

and is thus an order of necessity *(Notverordnung).*[73] The theological idea behind such arguments is that, under the conditions of sin, the form of God's creative will is the order of preservation *(Erhaltungsordnung).*

Even an unjust, perverted state still manifests the divine will for order in Künneth's framework, which puts more emphasis on the order that persists than on the perversion. Various principles, e.g. the second table of the Decalogue, can indicate injustice in the state's structure and activity; but, like Brunner, Künneth argues that they cannot absolve from the obligation to obey the law. Even the Christian obeys the law because it is necessary for the maintenance of order which, in turn, is fundamental for the preservation of man. Künneth's tremendously high appreciation of the value of order pervades his whole discussion of resistance.[74]

A christological grounding of law has been offered by Karl Barth and modified by other theologians. In an effort to avoid the dualisms perpetuated by the two kingdoms doctrine that has been so dominant in Lutheran social ethics, Barth regards Christ as equally lord of both realms. Divine and human righteousness, the Christian community and the civil community, form concentric circles whose center is Christ and the Kingdom. Both reflect Christ although in different ways, and while the state cannot simply embody divine righteousness, it can be a parable or analogue of the Kingdom.[75]

73. Thielicke, *Politics,* p. 112; Künneth, *Politik,* pp. 93–94, 418.
74. As he recognizes; see *Die Vollmacht des Gewissens,* ed. Europäischen Publikation e.V. (Bonn: Hermann Rinn, 1956), p. 84. For a more extended discussion of Künneth's position, see my Ph.D. dissertation, *The Basis and Limits of Political Obligation* (Yale University, 1968), pp. 218–49.
75. Barth, "The Christian Community and the Civil Community," in *Community, State and Church* (Garden City, N.Y.: Doubleday, Anchor Books, 1960), pp. 168–70 and passim.

Here, as in all the other interpretations from a Christian standpoint, loyalty to God enters the discussion of loyalty to the state. The christological approach stresses, in its opposition to natural law and natural theology, that "apart from the church, nowhere is there any fundamental knowledge of the reasons which make the state legitimate and necessary." But Christ has an ontic and not merely noetic significance for the political order. That is, he is significant for the very *being* of the state, and not merely for the Christian's knowledge about it, for the state is within the christological sphere, although on a different level than the church. Barth contends that Christian conscience demands submission to authority "because in this authority we are dealing indirectly, but in reality, with the authority of Jesus Christ." While the dominant end of the state is in the order of redemption, it serves man only in a negative way, by guaranteeing the church's freedom to preach: "All that can be said from the standpoint of divine justification on the question (and the questions) of human law is summed up in this one statement: the Church *must have freedom to proclaim divine justification.*"[76]

By distinguishing between *moral-legitimist* and *positivist-providential* approaches to the state, I can clarify some divergences in the interpretation of Romans 13 and significant differences between some of these recent theories of political obligation, although these differences appear within a basic agreement that it is possible to develop a theory of the state on the basis of theological-anthropological principles. In early Christianity, the obligation of the Christian to be subject or to render obedience was viewed as an absolute, and Romans 13:1 was read in an absolutist way: "Let every person be subject to the governing authorities. For there is no

76. "Church and State," in *Community, State and Church,* pp. 140, 120, 122, 147.

authority except from God, and those that exist have been instituted by God" (R.S.V.). I call this a positivist-providential interpretation because it stresses a nonmoral view of the state, which is seen as simply posited or given by virtue of God's providential activity. As d'Entrèves summarizes this interpretation,

> The accent was laid almost exclusively on the providential character of power. The plan laid down by God must be accepted in whatever way it manifests itself. Divine sanction does not depend on the use made of power: good or bad, all power is of God. It follows that even evil power must be patiently endured.[77]

A form of disobedience, often called "passive obedience," was accepted since the Christian could not worship the emperor, although he had then to accept martyrdom or other consequences of that refusal.

But Romans 13 was open to another interpretation (which was also utilized in natural law), largely because of its statement that the holder of power is "God's servant for your good" (Romans 13:4, R.S.V.). This phrase was construed to mean that power is *legitimated* in *moral* terms (e.g. goodness and justice). Therefore, while the positivist-providential interpretation only had a basis for passive obedience, this moral-legitimist view could justify active resistance and even revolution.

It should be evident that of the positions I have sketched Walter Künneth's expresses several elements of the positivist-providential approach. Although he does not absolutely repudiate active resistance and revolution, he does insist that

77. D'Entrèves, *Notion of the State*, p. 184. For a distinction similar to the one I have drawn between moral-legitimist and positivist-providential approaches to the state, see John Howard Yoder, *The Christian Witness to the State*, Institute of Mennonite Studies, Ser. #3 (Newton, Kansas: Faith and Life Press, 1964), pp. 74 ff.

from the context of the Christian faith such action only becomes an ethical possibility *(Möglichkeit)* but does not have
an ethical justification *(Rechtfertigung)*. Karl Barth and Emil
Brunner, on the other hand, represent versions of the moral-
legitimist stance (which differ from the natural law), although they treat questions of obedience and resistance in
quite different ways because of their theological-anthropological perspectives.

An especially striking example of the way such perspectives affect the framework of reasoning about resistance is
found in the different criteria by which these two theologians
suggest that the unjust, and particularly the totalitarian,
state can be recognized. For Barth (at least in his writings
during the 1930s) the state's encroachment upon the sphere
of the church and its preaching is a sure sign of totalitarianism, necessitating a strong response from the church. For
Brunner, however, the state's infringement of the institution
of marriage as an order of creation is more significant as an
index of totalitarianism. Furthermore, Barth insists that the
"real Church must be the model and prototype of the real
State,"[78] whereas Brunner believes that the patriarchal
family is "the prototype of a just social order," and that the
patriarchal family and the just social order have "analogous"
organizations and structures.[79] Both sets of claims make
sense only because of their fundamental theological pre-

78. Barth, "Christian Community and Civil Community," *Community,
State and Church,* p. 186. Franklin Sherman gives a penetrating analysis
of christological social ethics in "The Vital Center: Toward a Chalce-
donian Social Ethic," in *The Scope of Grace,* ed. Philip J. Hefner
(Philadelphia: Fortress Press, 1964), pp. 233–56. He suggests that when a
christological ethicist tries to move from generalities to specifics, "he
develops, under the rubric of Christ as the mediator of creation, or of
cosmic Christology, a full-blown equivalent of the sort of scheme of
orders of creation or natural law developed by an ethicist of the other
type under the rubric of God-the-Father" (p. 250).

79. Brunner, *Justice and the Social Order,* pp. 189–95.

suppositions: Barth's view of the state as being within the christological sphere; and Brunner's view of the state as representing both the orders of creation and of preservation, which are sharply distinguished from redemption.

These brief comments hardly do justice to the complexity and subtlety of these types of Christian political thought. They remain suggestive rather than exhaustive. But it is clear that these Protestant discussions of the bases of political obedience tend to develop a theory of the state which stresses its purposes and functions as illuminated by theological-anthropological convictions. Their more specific differences are located within this united approach, and the Christian's obligation to obey the law is understood within this framework. Paul Ramsey's argument follows a similar pattern, although it is more instructive and useful because of its effort to relate the state and political obligation to the whole idea of God as creator, preserver, and redeemer, and because of its specific examination of civil disobedience.

CHRIST TRANSFORMING NATURAL LAW:
PAUL RAMSEY'S POLITICAL ETHICS

Among American theological ethicists no one has given more vigorous attention to the questions that form the center of this study than Paul Ramsey. As one moves to his thought after even a brief overview of the approaches to political ethics of some European Protestant thinkers, the change in atmosphere is remarkable. While most of the latters' views on political obedience emphasize the theological rather than the ethical level of discussion, for Ramsey the reverse is the case. He, too, recognizes the importance of theological affirmations for ethics, but he goes farther than most theologians in drawing out in detail their *ethical* significance. Thus, he tends to examine the theological categories of creation and redemption primarily (although not exclusively) in the ethical terms of love and justice. At the very least, he moves quickly to indicate their ethical significance.

Nowhere is this point more vivid than in Ramsey's critique of Paul Lehmann's *Ethics in a Christian Context*. The question, as Ramsey puts it, is "whether a full-bodied understanding of the Christian life can be recovered, or even articulated, simply by dwelling upon the immediate encounter of today's world with the *theological ultimates* ingredient to the Christian context, without a significant Christian *ethical analysis* and guidance fully elaborated in between." His answer is emphatically negative. Lehmann, he thinks, substitutes "Reconciliation at the moment of decision in question for the work of graceful reason and love-in-action seeking to determine and do 'justice' in actual concrete political choices."[80] Ramsey's general approach is certainly congenial to my study, although it may be susceptible to the charge that he has failed to give sufficient attention to its theological underpinning. My disagreements with his position are directed less toward method and approach than toward the results of his theological-ethical analysis of political obligation. But even in this area his analysis is, as always, thorough, rigorous, and stimulating.

Ramsey, too, is trying to find his way between or beyond natural law and positivism, although he clearly stands nearer the former than many of his European counterparts, as the several different rubrics he has used for this theological ethics indicate: "Christ transforming natural law," "love transforming justice," "faith effective through in-principled love," "faith illuminating reason," and—more recently—"mixed rule-agapism," a category inspired by William K. Fran-

80. Ramsey, *Deeds and Rules*, p. 51 (author's italics); p. 96.

kena.[81] Ramsey has affinities with the tradition of natural
law on several different levels, as will be evident in the en-
suing discussion, but he certainly does not appropriate those
elements that make it the only basis of political obligation.
Several aspects of his theological-anthropological perspective
prohibit such an appropriation. His understanding of the
Christian doctrine of man, for example, precludes a denial
of validity and obligatoriness to an unjust law. One may still
be obligated to obey a law which is unjust by moral standards
(even natural law) on the grounds of the order of the system.[82]

Ramsey's own understanding of natural law and natural
justice is greatly influenced by Jacques Maritain, whose
version of natural law is also "revisionist."[83] Thus, Ramsey
does not emphasize its ontological basis as much as its expression in historical tradition, custom, and positive law, as
well as in a community of moral reflection. Nor does he emphasize rational deduction as much as inclination (or dis-
inclination) as expressed in medias res: rather than an abstract knowledge of the human essence, there is a perception
of humanity through inclinations and disinclinations which
men experience while encountering situations and actions of
good and evil, for example, the aversion to carrying out an
atrocious deed in war.

Although Ramsey thus has much in common with some
forms of the tradition of natural law that dominates Roman

81. See the essays in Ramsey, *Nine Modern Moralists* (Englewood
Cliffs, N.J.: Prentice-Hall, 1962). These different phrases may reflect
different levels of discussion. The more theological level is expressed by
the phrase *Christ transforming natural law;* the norms of conduct are
expressed in *love transforming justice;* and the human self who formu-
lates these principles is indicated by the phrase *faith illuminating reason.*
82. *Deeds and Rules,* p. 116; *Christian Ethics and the Sit-In,* passim.
83. *Nine Modern Moralists,* pp. 217, 223.

Catholic ethics, he answers the question of political obligation in a fundamentally different way. His answer is much
closer to the Protestant alternatives to natural law and positivism, which emphasize the necessity of order in relation to
the divine will of preservation *post lapsum*. Several considerations support this interpretation: Ramsey's realism,
his view of force in the state, his concentration on the system
rather than particular laws, his view of the system as primarily serving order, and his view that one might have an
obligation to obey an unjust law.

He sees only one significant difference between Protestant
and Roman Catholic interpretations of natural law. Because
natural law has been "republished" by the Roman Catholic
Church, Ramsey contends that "the Catholic moralist after
all has no natural law of his own but *only that natural law
affirmed by the Holy Office.*"[84] At the center of this debate is
the question whether love can transform justice or whether
justice is closed to love's impulses because it has been codi-
fied or republished.

For Ramsey agape, which he understands as seeking the
good of the neighbor, is primary and distinctive in Christian
ethics.[85] Whereas many theologians stop by defining agape
as a vague notion of humanity and welfare, he thinks that a
faithful reason can discern the principles that define the
neighbor's good. But if agape is basic it is not exhaustive.
"Where Christ reigns, agape enters into a fresh determination of what it is right to do; yet Christ does not reign over a
structureless world or over men who are bereft of any sense
of natural injustice." While divine love provides the "su-

84. Ramsey, Review of *Life, Death and the Law*, *Journal of Public
Law* 11 (1962): 392, italics mine; See *Nine Modern Moralists*, p. 229.
85. Ramsey, *Basic Christian Ethics* (New York: Scribner's, 1950),
passim; see *Nine Modern Moralists*, pp. 5 f.; *Deeds and Rules*, pp. 2,
122, n. 41.

preme light" in which Christians walk, they also have some sense of justice, which for Ramsey often means notions of right and wrong generally rather than justice in a strict sense.[86] Because both elements, natural justice and love, have to be held onto as *sources* of knowledge in Christian ethics, they can neither be identified with each other nor separated. Nor is it sufficient to say, as Reinhold Niebuhr does, that they are dialectically related. Their relationship might seem to be best described as interpenetration, since justice anticipates love and love transforms justice; but even here Ramsey stresses love's transformation, revision, and elevation of justice so that they are asymmetrically related.[87]

When the Christian makes ethical judgments and decisions, he cannot fully separate these sources, pointing to norms of love and norms of justice. The moral principles and rules that he has received were formulated under the impact of both love and justice, or love-transformed justice, creating "historical deposits" which have become determinative for ethical reflection. Thus, Ramsey makes both historical and logical claims for just war principles, for example. *Historically,* principles justifying and limiting war were formulated by men trying to ascertain what love and justice would require in the use of force on behalf of the neighbor; *logically* such principles would have to be formulated now if they had not been developed and transmitted previously.[88]

---

86. *Nine Modern Moralists,* pp. 5, 1–8.

87. *Christian Ethics and the Sit-In,* pp. 126 ff. This is "mixed agapism" (see *Deeds and Rules,* p. 122).

88. *Nine Modern Moralists,* "Introduction . . . "; *War and the Christian Conscience* (Durham, N.C.: Duke University Press, 1961), pp. xix ff., 9–10, and passim. Against some charges, Ramsey insists that even rule-agapism begins with persons and then devolves rules by a process of " 'generalization' from an analysis of the requirements of love in particular actions" *(Deeds and Rules,* p. 129). But Ramsey fails to indicate who can engage in this generalization and when. Love does not begin de novo at any point in history; there is a continuity of tradition and

While grace, according to some theologians (e.g. Walter Künneth), provides the freedom to be pragmatic in resistance, in Ramsey's view it provides substantive moral norms. Its main function is illumination, for it aids man's perception of norms and their meaning. "We should affirm . . . that right and wrong action, justice or injustice, have not yet been adequately defined so long as love has not also entered to reshape, enlarge, sensitize and sovereignly direct our *apprehensions* (based on nature alone) of the *meaning* of right and wrong action or of the just and the unjust."[89]

According to Ramsey, grace (love) puts certain restrictions on conduct, including means to ends. Prudence (or the principle of proportion) comes into play only after there has been a clear differentiation between permitted and prohibited action; and the difference between these two cannot be established merely by reflecting on consequences of actions. Ramsey insists that "[h]ow we do what we do is as important as our goals."[90] Although this emphasis is crucial in his treatment of the use of force in acts of resistance, I would suggest that his understanding of political obligation follows the pattern that is dominant in many Protestant alternatives to natural law. Observance of the law is viewed primarily as a means or condition of preserving and maintaining order. The fundamental consideration, then, is not whether an individual owes others obedience to the laws of the state because he has promised to obey, or consented to obey, or benefited from the obedience of others. Rather,

a deposit of moral wisdom. When love is clothed for action, it always *logically* leads to certain principles which *historically* have been associated with love. Thus, no person can readily begin with persons and their claims independently of the interpretation and evaluation of these claims in the light of *rule*-agapism. This is a necessary qualification of his statement about a process of generalization.

89. *Nine Modern Moralists*, p. 5. Italics mine.
90. *War and the Christian Conscience*, p. 6.

at this point, love-transformed justice focuses on the ends and functions of the state and the effects of obedience and disobedience instead of the political relation.

To develop Ramsey's answer to the question "Why ought we to obey the law?" it is necessary to turn to his "theological ethical justification of legality and order." Among love's principles are order and observance of law. "Order is a provision of pure rule-agapism that has general validity; and, within this, obedience to law is certainly a summary rule."[91] How does love come to *these* principles? Answering this question will require an examination of (1) the importance of order among the neighbor's needs that love attempts to meet and (2) the importance of observance of law for the maintenance of order.

For Ramsey there are two concepts of *general* rules: the first includes those that derive from the discernment of the "meaning of essential humanity" by faith-illuminated reason; the second includes those rules of practices which afford the "best possible social existence" as this is ascertained, again, by faith-illuminated reason. But if order is a rule of general validity in Christian ethics, under which concept does it fall? Or does it, like promise-keeping, fall under both? It would seem that order falls among those principles which "at one and the same time express generally what love requires in particular acts and what love requires as a practice." Order is both a requirement of essential humanity and social practice; "there will be an inner pressure within acts that seek to be concretely loving also toward order (and not only order so far as it is just) as among the fundamental needs of men. . . . An act that goes wide of this rule because it is 'seen' to be the most love-fulfilling thing to do can only seem so."[92]

91. *Christian Ethics and the Sit-In*, p. 76; *Deeds and Rules*, p. 116; cf. *Christian Ethics and the Sit-In*, p. 77.

92. *Deeds and Rules*, pp. 143, and passim; 143; 116.

Order is not the only value or norm which determines the
morality of political conduct. Along with order, and in dialectical relation to it, is the concept of justice. At this point
justice clearly means less than the total concepts of right and
wrong; it refers to the structuring of institutions and of
relationships within institutions. Ramsey is close to Brunner
in his assertion that injustice is never the sole justification
for resistance, for one can say that order is "for the sake of
justice since the only real political justice is an ordered
justice; yet justice is no less for the sake of order."[93] But
Ramsey wants to affirm more than this about order since
he insists that there is a certain "primacy of order to justice."
This primacy of order to justice sometimes seems to mean
that if the purpose of one's institutions and activity is order,
justice will be a product of it because, in a way similar to
one of Lon Fuller's arguments, goodness and justice have
more coherence than evil and injustice. At other times, this
order seems to be more simply a presupposition of justice,
a prerequisite for the establishment of justice. But clearly
Ramsey always affirms that the "present unjust order" is better than disorder.[94]

On the theological level, Ramsey's alternative to both
Brunner and Barth is,"to connect *every* ethical consideration
with the *whole* idea of God." "If God be God, then every
ethical, legal, and marital consideration must be connected
with the *whole* idea of God."[95] He does not suggest that

93. "The Uses of Power," *The Perkins School of Theology Journal* 18
(Fall 1964): 18. Reprinted in Ramsey, *The Just War* (New York: Scribner's,
1968). Cf. *Christian Ethics and the Sit-In*, pp. 48–49.

94. *Christian Ethics and the Sit-In*, p. 119. For his emphasis on both
justice and order, see *Who Speaks for the Church?* (New York: Abingdon,
1967), p. 156.

95. *Nine Modern Moralists*, p. 208 (author's italics). His point is that
this way of proceeding was suggested by Brunner, who failed to develop
it fully (see p. 207). Ramsey, "Marriage Law and Biblical Covenant,"
Religion and the Public Order 1963, ed. Donald Giannella (Chicago:
University of Chicago Press, 1964), pp. 75 f.

every ethical or legal idea will be explicated by the whole doctrine of God in the same way or with the same emphasis on God as creator, ruler and preserver, and redeemer.

A chief problem . . . remains for Christian ethical analysis. This is the question how, in moral decision and action, the Christian's response to God the Creator, his response to God the Ruler and Preserver of this fallen world, and his response to God the Redeemer *stand in indivisible relation to each other; and where the stress falls in cases of concrete decision.*[96]

The stress in questions of obedience and resistance falls on God as ruler and preserver, for naked human relations cannot actualize "fellow humanity" apart from "garments of skin" (Genesis 3:21), which symbolize God's restraining grace in such institutions as the state and the legal order. Such institutional arrangements are expressions of God's governance and preservation of a fallen world. Ramsey indicates the affinities of his position along these lines with the Lutheran interpretation of the state, which appears in Künneth's and Thielicke's thought, among others, as an "order of necessity." For Ramsey, then, in contrast to Barth, the Fall and God's governance of man *post lapsum* and pre-resurrection are "decisively important for Christian political theory."[97] He offers a "realistic interpretation of the state and its law as God's governance of a fallen world."[98]

Because order is a—perhaps *the*—primary end of the state, a fundamental consideration in the act of disobedience is the effect it will have on this order. Although nothing in my argument denies the presence in Ramsey's political ethics

96. *Christian Ethics and the Sit-In*, pp. 126–27. Italics mine.
97. "The Uses of Power," *The Just War*, pp. 7, 5–6, n. 2.
98. *Christian Ethics and the Sit-In*, p. 47. For Ramsey's dialectical understanding of man in political existence, see *The Just War*, especially p. 92.

of several other principles—e.g. the prohibition of the direct use of force against an innocent party—which would enter the overall evaluation of acts of disobedience, nonetheless political obedience is based primarily on the preservation of order. The fact that the end is order rather than happiness does not make the approach less teleological.

Yet because this view of political obligation is not unambiguously teleological, perhaps many of its themes could be restated in terms of my positive argument about fair play in the next chapter although Ramsey's position, in contrast to mine, derives its force primarily from a view of man as sinner. Order could be viewed as a synonym of justice: "a disposition or arrangement of equal and unequal things in such a way as to allocate each to its own place."[99] Furthermore, it is necessary to ask whether order cannot be viewed as a present requirement rather than as an end and consequence. Certainly it is possible to view the state in its activity as order and ordering rather than simply having the effect of establishing and maintaining order. However, from the standpoint of disobedience, matters look somewhat different.

If we try to understand the act of disobedience as itself disordering rather than having disruptive consequences, several difficulties emerge. The main one is that it becomes a tautology to say that disobeying the law is a disordering act. Surely Ramsey does not mean this, since observance of law is only a summary rule of love while order is a rule of general validity. Perhaps this point can be expressed by the dual connotation of *order:* a command and a structured state of affairs. Disobedience itself is disordering only in the former sense; it is a violation of a command or demand. It may be, but is not necessarily, a disruption of a structured state of

99. St. Augustine' statement; see d'Entrèves, *The Notion of the State*, p. 159.

affairs, except in the restricted sense that a person has re-fused some particular demands of his role in the structure and patterned relations.

Although Ramsey's position may be most adequately in-terpreted as employing the term *order* in both senses, this is not entirely clear. But if he uses *order* primarily in the con-sequentialist sense, it is difficult to avoid an interesting prob-lem. To base the obligation to obey the laws on the con-sequences of obedience in contrast to those of disobedience, as evaluated in the light of order, is to fail to supply a founda-tion for *universal* obedience, *secret* as well as public. For if I know that everyone else will continue to obey the law, that my secret act of disobedience will have no effect on anyone's attitudes toward obedience, and that it thus will in no way undermine the practice of authority and obedience, there is no obligation on me to obey.[100] I am assuming, of course, that no moral principles or rules such as the pro-hibition against murder are violated.

An example of the sort of case I have in mind is ignoring a stop sign on a deserted road late at night when it is clear that no other vehicles are in the area. If my point holds that, under such conditions within a teleological framework even of the rule-utilitarian sort, there would be no obligation to obey the law, then this interpretation stands in some tension with our general intuitive judgments about obedience and

100. This argument is influenced by David Lyons, *Forms and Limits of Utilitarianism* (Oxford: Clarendon Press, 1965). Another in-teresting possibility in interpreting Ramsey's position on political ob-ligation is his relatively recent appropriation of some of John Rawls's work. See Ramsey, "Two Concepts of General Rules in Christian Ethics," *Ethics* 76, no. 3 (April 1966): 192–207. A revised version is printed in *Deeds and Rules,* pp. 123–44. I have discussed this matter more fully in my dissertation, *The Basis and Limits of Political Obligation,* pp. 295–99. For some of Ramsey's views on political obligation, especially a re-statement of the divided loyalties, in the context of an analysis of selective conscientious objection, see *The Just War,* chap. 5.

disobedience, as I shall contend in the next chapter. Of course, few theories of political obligation are fully and consistently teleological, especially when their defenders recognize different moral principles, as Ramsey does. Furthermore, his writings after *Christian Ethics and the Sit-In* show that he would supplement his discussion of order by the generalization argument ("What would happen if everyone did that?"), which may well overcome many of my objections and which will receive further attention in chapter 4.[101]

I shall conclude this section on Ramsey by looking at the way one of his opponents in the so-called context-principle debate views political obligation. Joseph Fletcher's notion of love is notoriously difficult to specify, but certainly it is consequentialist and even unabashedly utilitarian when it enters the social and political spheres. "The Christian love ethic, searching seriously for a social policy, forms a coalition with the utilitarian principle of the 'greatest good of the greatest number.' "[102] This is love's method and procedure.

For Fletcher as for Ramsey the claim of order is important. Although order is required because of the human good it serves, it is never an absolute, because at every point one evaluates the whole situation—the degree of injustice, the value of order, etc.—all under the consequentialist, utilitarian umbrella. The question for Fletcher is what makes for a better state of affairs?

> We have a moral obligation to obey civil law, for order's sake; and we have a moral obligation to be situational (even disobeying the law) for love's sake. . . . Neither the state nor its laws is boss for the situationalist; when there is a conflict, he decides for the higher law of love.

101. See *Deeds and Rules,* chap. 6.
102. *Moral Responsibility: Situation Ethics at Work* (Philadelphia: Westminster, 1967), p. 19.

He has to weigh immediate and remote consequences
as well as local and broader interests, but if the scales
go against law, so does he.[103]

The differences between Ramsey and Fletcher are great,
although both agree about the centrality of love in Christian
ethics. For Ramsey love is in-principled; for Fletcher it is
supra-principled.[104] Whereas Fletcher is teleological and
utilitarian, Ramsey strongly asserts that "the reduction of
Christian ethics to teleology is nearly the same thing as
abandoning it."[105] Nevertheless, one should not overlook a
basic similarity between their two approaches to political obligation; observance of law is justified as a means of preserving
order for love's sake. This similarity persists, although Ramsey views order as a rule of general validity and Fletcher
views it (and all other requirements) as a summary rule.
Thus, partly because of his theological-anthropological perspective, Ramsey is less willing to speak about love requiring
a violation of order than Fletcher is. Furthermore, Fletcher
recognizes no intrinsic restrictions on the means of resistance,
whereas Ramsey sees some conduct as being always contrary
to love, e.g. the direct use of force against innocent persons.

Obviously, Ramsey is not a consequentialist or utilitarian
in the same way or to the same extent that Fletcher is. But
my argument does not profess to deal with Ramsey's whole
ethical theory—only the basis of political obedience. An
ethicist, just as the proverbial man on the street, may have
a variety of principles, some teleological, some deontological.
My contention is that Ramsey's interpretation of political
obedience is fundamentally teleological, as indeed every ade-

103. *Situation Ethics: The New Morality* (Philadelphia: Westminster,
1966), p. 101.
104. See Fletcher's "Reflection and Reply," *The Situation Ethics
Debate,* ed. Harvey Cox (Philadelphia: Westminster, 1968), p. 260.
105. *Deeds and Rules,* p. 109.

quate theory must be to some extent. But he has perhaps put too much emphasis on the demand of order because of his theological-ethical approach, although his emphasis on this end of the state does not mean that he denies other ends. Certainly his framework for reasoning about resistance is structured largely by this concentration on order, for the questions that he asks are to a great extent determined by this value, as is certainly the case in his *Christian Ethics and the Sit-In*. Nothing in my argument so far should be taken as indicating that order plays no role in my analysis of political obligation and the justification of disobedience. Rather, because it has been so emphasized to the exclusion of some other important features of the political relation, and because it has often been viewed as providing the answer to political obligation generally (or in tension with justice), I think it is advisable to see what else can be said about political obligation and then show how order sets certain clear limits on the act of disobedience.

THEOLOGY AND THE ENDS OF THE STATE

The criticisms that I have directed against many Protestant alternatives to natural law as a basis of political obligation can suggest some other possible directions. Martin Rock, a Roman Catholic who has written one of the most comprehensive studies of resistance from a theological standpoint, contends that the diversity of Protestant positions on such questions represents particular dogmatic presuppositions.[106] I have explored the relation between certain interpretations of political obligation and theological affirmations in this chapter because these theologians appeal to theological propositions that interact with their interpretations of moral principles and values and their analyses of the state.

106. *Widerstand gegen die Staatsgewalt*, pp. 192, 60, 62, 65.

These three elements—theological-anthropological perspectives, moral principles and values, and analysis of the state—are combined to constitute a theory of political obligation in most political ethics from a Christian standpoint.

Beyond the analytic statement that a discussion of the theological-anthropological level cannot be avoided in delineating these positions, my normative view is that theological affirmations should provide an interpretative framework for moral experience, not the premises from which moral conclusions are derived. Moral experience as reflected in common discourse and language, institutions and practices, as well as philosophical analysis, can be set within the theological context of God's relation to man, which shapes reflection without directing it toward a specific goal.[107] Although no attempt should be made to relate all ethical questions and answers to theological propositions, such propositions, and the basic affirmations they signify, should illuminate political obligation both directly and indirectly through their impact on views of moral values and principles and interpretations of the state.

With Ramsey, I stress that the *whole* idea of God is indispensable for Christian social ethics. God's creating, ordering (sustaining and restraining), and redeeming purposes and actions cannot be separated, although they as well as our re-

107. For example, the view of man as a sinner would seem to rule out some anarchistic approaches, although I shall argue later that the realist interpretation of man does not exhaust the rationale of the state and political activity. My view of the way one handles moral experience in relation to theological affirmations stands in sharp contrast to the procedure employed by Jacques Ellul, who writes: "Were we to take the experience of law as the point of departure for our analysis, we could be sure of reaching no result whatsoever. . . . Rather, in order to perceive the elements of law, we must begin with what God reveals to us in his creation and in his covenant." *The Theological Foundation of Law*, trans. Marguerite Wieser (Garden City, N.Y.: Doubleday, 1960), p. 75.

sponses can be distinguished. Human institutions, including
the state, can be illuminated by these theological ideas; for
God through such institutions creates new possibilities for
man, sustains human existence, restrains recalcitrant individuals and groups, and provides improved qualities of life.
None of these themes can be ignored in a Christian's reflection about the state, its ends and relations, and his responsibility to it.[108]

Many recent Protestant interpretations of political obligation can be criticized on the grounds that they construe the
ends of the state too narrowly in relation to certain theological themes such as the preservation of order, and that they
thus fail to bring the entire scope and range of divine purposes to bear on this set of problems. For example, an important objection to Künneth is that, although the divine will to
preserve man through order is essential to a Christian interpretation of political life, it is not the only or even the primary
element in such an interpretation. By so emphasizing that the
state which maintains order by force and coercion is a correlate of sin and God's restraining will, Künneth implies that
it has no purpose or function apart from man's sin. My position is closer to the Roman Catholic tradition, which understands the state in relation to human particularity and the
diversity of human interests, projects, and needs even apart
from human perversity that requires restraint. I would stress
that the state has a function for the "puzzled man," who is
sincerely trying to determine what he ought to do in relation
to other men, as well as for the "bad man" who wants to avoid
such considerations and responsibilities.[109]

Just as an emphasis on preservation tends to lead to a stress

108. My use and development of these themes are indebted to the work
of James Gustafson and, indirectly, H. Richard Niebuhr. See Gustafson,
"A Theology of Christian Community?" in *Man in Community*, ed.
Egbert de Vries (New York: Association Press, 1966), pp. 175–93.

109. Hart, *The Concept of Law*, pp. 38 ff.

on the necessity for certain actions and structures in relation to sin, so an emphasis on creation or redemption often leads to a neglect of the place of sin and evil and the need to restrain them by force and coercion. While some Roman Catholic thought, operating from the standpoint of creation, moves in this direction,[110] Karl Barth's thought (especially in its later development) had little room for these themes from the standpoint of redemption.[111] At any rate, a view of political obligation developed within a theory of the state as defined by theological-anthropological convictions must take account of all three aspects of human experience—which are expressed theologically as creation, preservation and judgment, and redemption—if the state and political activities are to be adequately interpreted and directed.

Although this theological perspective does not directly provide norms for the justification and limitation of political obedience, it excludes certain approaches to them. More positively, a *pluralist* approach is most consistent with an adequate, balanced interpretation of God's creative, ruling, and redeeming will.[112] Thus, no single principle or value receives

110. See Pope John XXIII's encyclical "Pacem in Terris": "the whole reason for the existence of civil authorities is the realization of the common good" (*The Social Teachings of the Church*, ed. Anne Fremantle, p. 289). Paul Ramsey criticizes this view in "Pacem in Terris," *Religion in Life* 33 (Winter 1963–64): 116–35 (reprinted in *The Just War*, pp. 70–90).

111. See n. 65 in this chapter. Two of the recent attempts in American Protestant ethics to deal with social and political life mainly from the standpoint of redemption while not ignoring other motifs can be seen in Charles West, *Ethics, Violence and Revolution*, Special Ser. #208 (New York: Council on Religion and International Affairs, 1969), especially pp. 37 ff, and Douglas Sturm, "A Critique of American Protestant Social and Political Thought," *The Journal of Politics* 26, no. 4 (Nov. 1964): 896–913.

112. My pluralist perspective is influenced by W. D. Ross, *The Right and the Good* (Oxford: Clarendon Press, 1930) and *Foundations of Ethics* (Oxford: Clarendon Press, 1939); see also H. J. McCloskey, *Meta-Ethics and Normative Ethics* (The Hague: Martinus Nijhoff, 1969).

exclusive attention. For example, excessive concentration on the principle of order is avoided—although its importance for a full understanding of the state is not denied—because God's relation to man through institutions cannot be reduced to mere preservation. Justice must be considered, along with other principles, because of God's creative and redemptive purposes. This pluralism connotes not only a multiplicity of ethical principles but also (a) that their application in particular cases may lead to incompatible and even contradictory judgments, and (b) that, with only a few exceptions, their weights and priorities are not clearly discernible. The simplicity of dealing with political obligation in the light of a single or dominant principle is forsaken in order to deal concretely with each political order on its own terms. Whatever else it means, this pluralism at least denies that the utilitarian approach exhausts the range of moral reasoning, particularly in the political sphere, although this case has yet to be established.

Beyond the concentration on limited theological notions (such as preservation) and limited moral principles and values (such as order that combines evaluative and descriptive elements), there are other significant weaknesses in most Protestant explanations of political obligation as one critical element in a framework for dealing with resistance. Most of these converge on the third major level of discussion, the analysis of the state, although it cannot be divorced from theological-anthropological and moral concerns. Such theories of political obligation stress the ends and functions served by the system of political authority and then construe observance of law mainly as a means to or a condition of the fulfillment of those ends and functions, regardless of their particular content.[113] While the most general value usually is

113. Douglas Sturm (in "A Critique of American Protestant Social and Political Thought") contends that American Protestant social and po-

humanity or human welfare, most theologians specify and delineate it in terms of their theological-anthropological convictions, as, for example, in the claim that human welfare between the Fall and the Resurrection requires that the state and its laws be considered an order of preservation, with all that this implies for obedience.

A significant philosophical parallel to this approach to political obligation is rule-utilitarianism, at least in some of its forms. One form of rule-utilitarianism holds that greater good is attained by securing obedience to de facto rules and laws. Thus, because the state with its structure of authority and obedience is necessary to create a greater good in the world, one can speak of a moral obligation to obey its laws. As A. C. Ewing argues, one of the effects of disobeying the law is the subversion of the general rules on which people base their expectations. Although he admits that much moral experience seems to require a pluralist framework, he finally is "not sure that it cannot be ultimately explained on utilitarian grounds *provided we recognise other goods besides pleasure and take adequate account of the desirable effects of having some general rules on which people can rely.*"[114] Viewing the

---

litical thought (it is interesting that he does not consider either Paul Ramsey or Paul Lehmann) is primarily *pragmatic* (Reinhold Niebuhr) and secondarily *situational* (Joseph Sittler and H. Richard Niebuhr), in contrast to his other two types, *finalistic* or teleological and *formalistic*. The finalistic or teleological approach focuses on the social and political order "from the perspective of its final cause, its purposes, and ends" (p. 903). At the opposite pole is the pragmatic approach, which is "oriented toward the interpretation of the means necessary to preserve associations from destruction" (p. 904). While I recognize the contributions of this typology, I would suggest that it might be better to understand both the pragmatic and finalistic approaches as basically teleological, although their views of the ends—e.g. whether ultimate or proximate, lofty or mundane, positive or negative—are, of course, quite different.

114. *The Individual, the State and World Government* (New York: Macmillan, 1947), p. 216 (italics mine).

ends of the state under the general rubrics of human welfare and needs as well as more specific headings such as security, liberty, and justice, J. Roland Pennock advances another form of this argument: "The ends of the state—of all political organization—require law for their realization. To them, law is the essential means. An obligation to obey and support the state entails an obligation to obey its law, at least in general."[115] From this perspective, to answer the question whether one should obey or disobey requires looking at the effects of the proposed action on the ends of the state or the state's fulfillment of its ends.

Of course, one possible objection to my attempt to indicate the basic affinity between many Protestant approaches to political obligation and some forms of rule-utilitarianism is that I am ignoring what happens when a particular form of argument is placed within a theological context; but my response is that the theological context may not modify the reasoning even when it changes its terms and adds new dimensions.[116] Thus, despite Paul Ramsey's insistence on the uniqueness of the notion of order in Christian social ethics, the content of the dominant end or function may not alter the mode of reasoning.[117]

However, one possible result of certain theological contexts is that the state is placed in a broad cosmic perspective that reduces the sense of human enterprise and project as well as the sense of the state as a cooperative endeavor. Certain theological perspectives can contribute to *alienation* by removing institutions from the ongoing activity of human creation and

115. "The Obligation to Obey the Law and the Ends of the State," Hook, *L & P*, p. 79.

116. Contrast what happens when theologians use the concept of responsibility in a theological framework; see Albert R. Jonsen, *Responsibility in Modern Religious Ethics* (Cleveland: Corpus Publications, 1968).

117. *Deeds and Rules*, p. 115.

maintenance in their attempt to attribute too much to the continuing divine activity. From such perspectives human agents are separated from their projects and products, including the state, as is evident in some versions of what I have called the positivist-providential view of the state. But whether this happens or not depends in part on whether one stresses God's institution and continued governance of the state in relation to his purposes or simply reflects on the state in the light of those divine purposes, known either by revelation or natural reason, to determine whether the state is fulfilling its mandate. The latter approach is most congenial to this study, although it should be stressed that we are raising, without developing, one of the persistent and fundamental problems in religious ethics: the relation between a transcendent God and human activity of all kinds.

Another possible objection to my emphasis on the parallel between many Protestant views of political obligation and some forms of rule-utilitarianism is that I am overlooking the strongly deontological character of much Protestant ethics; but this objection, I think, ignores some of the possible relations between deontological and teleological positions. First, while a thinker may be a pluralist with a primary emphasis on deontological criteria, he may rely almost exclusively on teleological forms of argument in discussing political obedience, although his deontological criteria will certainly affect his views of resistance, for example, in such matters as the use and direction of force. Second, deontological and teleological interpretations are often combined in the same theory of political obligation. Thus, on the ultimate level the values and principles by which the ends and functions of the state are assessed may be established deontologically (e.g. God wills them), but political obedience may be based on the state's fulfillment of its ends and functions—a more teleological argument, although it is derived rather than ultimate.

The critical question is, which level of discussion is more important for the framework within which the discussion of obedience and disobedience is conducted? Alan Gewirth indicates one such combination of deontological and teleological elements in a theory of political obligation:

> In the Middle Ages . . . a different kind of *deontological* justification of government was widely current. This is that "the powers that be are ordained of God" (Romans 13:1). Here . . . a *utilitarian* basis was attached: the reason why God ordained that there be governments is that these were needed as punishments and remedies of original sin.[118]

While this combination specifically concerns the justification of the state, it also structures the argument about political obligation. If these points hold, one may well have a "derived utilitarian" view of the moral reasons for obedience, although the perspective is more generally pluralist.

Whatever the conclusions about the relation between such theories and rule-utilitarianism, Protestant reasoning about resistance generally occurs within a framework which bases political obligation on the necessity of the state to realize certain ends or fulfill certain functions for man. While such an approach is both helpful and necessary, to focus exclusively on the ends and functions of the state and one's action as affecting those ends and functions, is to ignore much that is important to establishing and limiting political obligation within certain contexts. Of course, from such a standpoint one can justify the state over against no-state or anarchy, but this does little to advance the discussion of political obligation. Furthermore, one can establish that particular forms of

---

118. Alan Gewirth, Introduction, *Political Philosophy*, ed. Alan Gewirth (New York: Macmillan, 1965), p. 21. Italics mine.

the state are better than others because they fulfill more values (e.g. justice, liberty, security, welfare) with less cost. Since basic human needs are better met by some states than others, Christians and other men have a duty to work for and support such states. These are important considerations in political ethics, whether theological or philosophical, but the pressing question remains: what obligation does a person have to obey the *given* state, especially when its form is a constitutional democracy? It may well be that neither the view of obedience as a condition of a state's fulfillment of its functions nor the view of a duty to support states that fulfill certain ends can adequately account for political obligation in certain contexts—one's moral obligation to obey these laws of *this particular* state.

Most Protestant analyses of the political-legal sphere—at least as far as the question of political obligation is concerned —are inadequate because of their concentration on the ends and functions of the state, although nothing in my argument denies that these considerations are very important. Such analyses generally overlook the critical distinction between *the reasons for government in general* and *the reasons for my obedience to the laws of this particular state*. While these reasons may be identical or at least overlap in most instances, they may be quite different in a particular context, for an obligation to obey the law may be independent of the state's purposes and functions although it presupposes them. Interpreting the state in terms of God's purposes as creator, preserver, and redeemer (or the correlative doctrines of man) may provide reasons for government in general, but it may not indicate why I ought to obey the laws of this particular government. My point, which will be developed in detail in the next chapter, is that political obligation in a constitutional democracy can best be understood mainly as based on the duty of fair play, although it in many respects presupposes certain ends and functions of the state. For example, there would be no practice of refraining from crossing the lawn if it had no point (that is, if it served no purpose, fulfilled no function, or achieved no end). We may well agree that its ends and functions are worthy, although we may also stress that refraining from crossing the lawn is based more on a sense of fair play than on its possible effect on the practice or the ends and functions of the practice.

This distinction between the reasons for the state and the reasons for my obedience to the laws of this particular state is often overlooked because of another, more basic, flaw in many theories of political obligation. Their central question, "Why ought I to obey the law?" is meaningless as a general question. No single criterion or set of criteria will cover all possible political and legal orders in the same way, and if this question is viewed as a search for general criteria applicable to every situation, it is misleading if not pointless. It is rather like the question "Why ought I to read books?" which cannot be answered without specifying particular sorts of books, e.g. spiritual, educational, pornographic.[119] Too many theological-ethical frameworks for assessing resistance are unhelpful because they attempt to develop the basis of political obligation so as to cover *any and every* political order instead of recognizing that different principles may be relevant to different orders. It is impossible to delineate the necessary and sufficient conditions of political obligation for all contexts.

By starting, then, with a particular context, such as a relatively just constitutional democracy, an examination of the question "Why ought I to obey the law?" can be quite instructive, especially if other guidelines are observed. First, in examining a relatively just constitutional democracy, it is necessary not only to inquire about its ends and functions but also to look at internal relations, seeking any peculiar features which seem to weigh heavily in the determination of an obli-

119. H. A. Prichard, "Green's Principles," pp. 85 f.

gation to obey the law. Second, inquiry into the general principles of obligation, their hierarchy and interconnections, if any, is indeed both possible and valuable. Benn and Peters express the point very well in *The Principles of Social and Political Thought:* "While no formula could provide necessary and sufficient conditions for obedience in every situation, the maxims offered may still act as guides for reflection."[120]

In conclusion, there are several different ways of examining political obligation and resistance with varying degrees of concreteness. One might start from moral principles, their content, form, and justification and then move to their application and effects in actual social practices. Thus, one could start with the antinomy between the individual conscience and the law, examine it for a coherent, consistent picture, and finally see whether emphasis on one side or the other would lead to consequences which would be undesirable in the light of such principles as preservation of social order or fairness. A second approach is to examine actual social practices and see whether certain principles (e.g. equality and liberty) are upheld. If so, then one asks what is permitted or prohibited within these practices and constructs a pragmatic code on this basis. Certainly positive features of this second approach are its immediacy and concreteness, although both general approaches may well come to the same conclusions.

---

120. P. 81; cf. chap. 14. Their formulation and the position that I am developing stand in sharp contrast to T. D. Weldon's argument that one can only say to a person who objects that he does not see why he should obey an order to surrender his pigs even if it is the law: "Well, this is Great Britain, isn't it?" To try to push the question one step further and say "Why should I obey the laws of England?" is to ask a pointless question of the same sort as "Why should I obey the laws of cricket?" (*The Vocabulary of Politics* [Harmondsworth, Eng.: Penguin, 1953], pp. 57–62). A similar but more open position is developed by Margaret Macdonald in "The Language of Political Theory," in *Logic and Language* (1st ser.), ed. Antony Flew (New York: Doubleday, Anchor Books, 1965), pp. 174–94.

These summaries are built on the methods of Ernest van den Haag and Sidney Hook, respectively.[121] I would emphasize, however, that the methodological point can be strained, for just as in the context-principle debate (which it closely parallels), the procedure is usually more dialectical. In the one case, a thinker examines *principles* without ignoring actual practices; in the other, he examines *practices* without ignoring various principles.

This study, utilizing aspects of both approaches, calls into question the adequacy of most Protestant interpretations of political obligation because they fail to examine definite contexts, because they focus on the ends of the state apart from particular relations within it, and because they usually raise a question that cannot be answered. I shall try to offer a more specific answer to a more specific question which both recognizes the distinctive features of a constitutional democracy and, furthermore, moves beyond a consideration of the ends and functions of the state to relations between men as citizens within that order. This procedure is justified on the grounds that a purely teleological interpretation of political obligation does not afford an adequate account of our experiences in a democratic polity, although it does account for some of them and may even be more important for other types of political order. In part, then, I am suggesting that one of the first tasks of political ethics might be to reduce the importance of theories of the state regardless of their content and basis, and rather to start with the concrete phenomenon of a particular state and inquire into the moral principles that structure one's obligation to obey the laws within that context.

121. See Sidney Hook, "Social Protest and Civil Disobedience," in *Moral Problems in Contemporary Society: Essays in Humanistic Ethics*, ed. Paul Kurtz (Englewood Cliffs, N.J.: Prentice-Hall, 1969), pp. 161–72, and Ernest van den Haag, "Government, Conscience, and Disobedience," in Kurtz, *Sidney Hook and the Contemporary World*, pp. 105–20.

III

BASES OF POLITICAL OBLIGATION: RELATIONS BETWEEN CITIZENS

CHRISTIAN AND NEIGHBOR IN THE POLITICAL ORDER

One of the most unfortunate aspects of the debate about dissent and civil disobedience between former Supreme Court Justice Abe Fortas and Howard Zinn is that only two limited and inadequate alternatives receive a hearing. If only two positions on the matter existed, it would be necessary to side with Zinn, but there are other alternatives. On the one hand, Fortas tends to abstract the rule of law from its sociopolitical context, particularly the ends that it supports. Concentrating on the rule of law, he asserts: "Each of us owes a duty of obedience to law. This is a moral as well as a legal imperative."[1] Because he does not proceed to develop the moral basis of obedience to law, one must assume that he means the rule of law intrinsically obligates, at least within the democratic context. On the other hand, Zinn contends: "To urge the right of citizens to disobey unjust laws, and the duty of citizens to disobey dangerous laws, is of the very essence of democracy, which assumes that government and its laws are not sacred,

1. Abe Fortas, *Concerning Dissent and Civil Disobedience* (New York: New American Library, Signet Book, 1968), p. 11.

but are instruments, serving certain ends: life, liberty, happiness. The instruments are dispensable. The ends are not."[2]

Fortas needs to inquire more deeply into the ends and functions of a particular rule of law; Zinn needs to recognize the importance of instruments of order for man's perilous conditions. But these objections do not get to the heart of the matter, for neither approach adequately deals with the moral basis of obedience within a constitutional democracy. While Fortas simply asserts this basis without exploring it, Zinn simply reduces it to the moral ends of law and government. I too would emphasize such ends, but the cooperative enterprise of democratic government may create some moral obligation to obedience which cannot be reduced to its ends. In developing the way such an obligation is created, I shall first establish a positive theological-ethical rationale for moving in this direction (to complement the negative argument of the preceding chapter) and then sketch the main outlines of this basis of political obligation. Because there are several affinities, as well as several significant differences, between my endeavor and Ernst Wolf's recent attempts to redirect Christian political ethics, I shall briefly analyze his position.

According to Wolf, Christian political ethics has been preoccupied with a theology of the state, but because an inquiry into the source and essence of the state is not properly theological, the theologian should let sociologists and jurists describe the state in its concrete givenness and should instead focus on how the Christian out of love ought to relate to it. He denies that the theologian, on theological grounds, can inquire into the essence of the state, propound a doctrine of the state, and then derive "particular ethical directions." In addition to this theological argument, Wolf contends that

2. Zinn, *Disobedience and Democracy*, p. 120.

such a doctrine or theology of the state obscures its concrete reality.[3]

Furthermore, he insists that in Romans 13:1–7, Paul used the customary technical-political terminology of his day instead of offering a theological interpretation of the state's essence and meaning. Viewing the state in its givenness and "naked facticity," Paul's purpose was to direct Christian conduct within that context.[4] His exhortation does not point to absolute, uncritical "obedience" to the powers that be, since in the setting of Romans, agape rather than obedience is dominant; any interpretation which ignores that obedience is subordinate to and controlled by agape is misleading.[5]

I shall not attempt to assess Wolf's *exegetical* argument (although, according to Ernst Käsemann, it represents a significant turning-point in discussions about Romans 13:1–7),[6] for my interest is rather in its conceptual adequacy and fruitfulness. This approach to Christian political ethics hinges on a distinction between a theory of the state and a theory of the *relation* between the individual (Christian) and the state. Although the theologian, according to Wolf, should not develop a theory of the state, its essence, meaning and source, he can and should interpret this relation. Such a view is not totally new in theological reflection, and one can find elements

3. Wolf, "Die Königsherrschaft Christi," pp. 41, 42, 36. His main opposition is to a theological metaphysics of the state, which he finds in most Protestant interpretations (p. 26).

4. Ibid., pp. 39 ff.; also, Wolf, "Politischer Gottesdienst," especially pp. 54–60.

5. Other interpreters have also stressed that the verb ὑποτάσσεσθαι (in Romans 13: 1, 5), which is usually assumed to mean "to obey," really has a broader meaning. See C. E. B. Cranfield, *A Commentary on Romans 12–13*, Scottish Journal of Theology Occasional Papers No. 12 (Edinburgh: Oliver and Boyd, 1965), pp. 69–72.

6. Ernst Käsemann, "Römer 13: 1–7 in unserer Generation," *Zeitschrift für Theologie und Kirche* 56 (1959): 374; cf. pp. 371, 343.

of it in Martin Luther's political ethics, for, as J. W. Allen indicates, "Luther's 'theory' is really simply a theory of the individual in relation to constituted authority. He had no theory of the State at all. The duty of the subject is not really a duty owed to the magistrate: it is a duty to God."[7]

Thus, Wolf rejects attempts to find a *christological* foundation for the state and law as well as attempts to base them on orders of creation or preservation. Usually he is represented as a Barthian who retains the Lutheran "two-kingdoms" stance only within the "brackets of christology," but clearly he extends Barth's position in such a way that the extension seems to be equivalent to a modification.[8] Their differences can be expressed succinctly: "E. Wolf's further development of Barth's view implies at the same time a correction of it, in that what he supplies is precisely *not a christological ground for the state, but a christological ground for the attitude of the Christian toward the civil powers.*"[9] Therefore the Chris-

---

7. J. W. Allen, *A History of Political Thought in the Sixteenth Century* (New York: Barnes and Noble, 1960), p. 23. There are good reasons for relating some of Wolf's emphases to Luther's position. In addition to Wolf's explicit dependence at points, the general thrust of his ethics as a whole would seem much closer to Luther's "On the Liberty of the Christian Man" than to more recent Lutheran ethics as developed by Elert and Künneth, among others. A few of the similar themes will be sketched below; their centrality rather than the analysis of order and law characterizes both Wolf and Luther in contrast to Künneth, although one would not deny that there are seeds of the conservative Lutheran position in Luther. From the Mennonite tradition, John Howard Yoder develops some similar points; he contends that "the witness to the state has never been *based on* a theory about what the state is and should be in itself, nor has it been rendered *for the sake* of the state 'in itself' " (*The Christian Witness to the State,* p. 77).

8. "Königsherrschaft Christi und lutherische Zwei-Reiche-Lehre," *Peregrinatio II* (Munich: Chr. Kaiser Verlag, 1965), p. 229.

9. Hans-Werner Bartsch, "A New Theological Approach to Christian Social Ethics," John Bennett, *Christian Social Ethics,* p. 63, n. 16 (italics mine). Bartsch's own position has several affinities with Wolf's. On Wolf's corrective to Barth's position, see Wolfhart Pannenberg, "Zur

tian's attitude, relation, and political ethics are christologi-
cally based, although the state is not.

Instead of implying that all powers have been effectively
and actually subordinated to Christ, the affirmation of the
Lordship of Christ indicates that the Christian is freed " 'to
accept' the state in its 'worldliness' as a task of human activity
in obedience to the command of God."[10] A risk of focusing on
political obedience and disobedience, as I have, is that the
Christian's responsibility will be too narrowly construed as
one of obedience or disobedience, when these alternatives exhaust neither his responsibility nor the possibilities of most
situations. Wolf certainly avoids this pitfall, for "acceptance"
(Annahme) cannot be identified with a passive acquiescence
in the given structures; it is, rather, an act of sharing responsibility with the state for human welfare. Thus, for Wolf, the
category of "coresponsibility" (Mitverantwortlichkeit) re-
places that of obedience or subordination, which has so domi-
nated many other political ethics, at least until recently when
revolution and social change became central.[11]

From Wolf's perspective the theologian attempts to clarify
the foundations for responsible judgments and decisions as

Theologie des Rechts," Zeitschrift für Evangelische Ethik 7 (1963): 11.
Cf. Bruno Schüller S.J., Die Herrschaft Christi und das weltliche Recht:
Die christologische Rechtsbegründung in der neueren protestantischen
Theologie, Analecta Gregoriana (Rome: Verlagsbuchhandlung der Päpst-
lichen Gregorianischen Universität, 1963) 128: 257.

10. Wolf, "Die Königsherrschaft Christi," pp. 23-24. Wolf also comments on article 5 of the Barmen declaration: "This is no longer a theo-
logical-metaphysical discussion of the state, but of its task; and stress is
laid on its humanness" ("Political and Moral Motives Behind the Resistance," Hermann Graml, et al., The German Resistance to Hitler, p.
214). For a good discussion of the issues at stake in the debate about a
christological interpretation of the powers, see Clinton D. Morrison, The
Powers That Be, Studies in Biblical Theology, no. 29 (London: SCM
Press, 1960).

11. "Politischer Gottesdienst," p. 62.

they are made in the political sphere in response to Christ. He delineates "personal-ethical responsibility" rather than a doctrine of the state, which should be replaced by an evangelical doctrine of "political virtues" (not only obedience) to be exercised in the act of "acceptance." This open context of responsibility requires a formation of the self and its activity in accordance with love of one's neighbor. Love is thus the ethical foundation for the Christian's relation to the state, but the state itself is no object of love. It must be understood, as Hans-Werner Bartsch writes, "in terms of, and in the light of, our neighbor. We must see the relation of the Christian to the superior powers only as a special form of the relation of the Christian to his neighbor."[12]

I find this perspective quite illuminating, but because it has some serious weaknesses, I wish to use it only as a point of departure. A few critical comments will indicate these weaknesses and suggest alternative directions. Wolf is largely right in what he affirms and wrong in what he denies. His argument for concentrating on the relation of the individual to the state is most instructive; it rightly locates the moral problem, which appears not merely in some duty to an order of preservation but mainly in duties and obligations to one's neighbors as they are presented in and through the state, law, and political processes as well as other institutional contexts.

Nevertheless, unless fundamental institutional questions are wrongly ignored, the Christian ethicist also has to consider elements of a *theory* of the state, for example, by delineating the way divine purposes for man cast light upon human institutions, as I indicated in the last chapter. Wolf does not exclude this task as completely as some of his statements suggest; for he admits, although only on a secondary level, that the ends of institutions must be examined in the light of gen-

12. See Hans-Werner Bartsch ("New Theological Approach," p. 67), who is following Wolf.

eral theological convictions.[13] This task is clearly secondary because it does not constitute a presupposition of an interpretation of the Christian's conduct toward the state—in contrast to what I have argued. Furthermore, it involves not the state's structure of power and order but rather its ends and aims, particularly in relation to humanity and the *salus publica*.

At first glance such an approach might appear to be sufficient, but by failing to delineate the principles and anthropological bases for interpreting the neighbor's good, Wolf does not clarify and illuminate the elements of moral-political decisions. Perhaps his command-obedience model requires that he leave this question open, and other theological and religious factors (e.g. the fear of self-righteousness), as well as a fear of ideology, lead him to circumscribe carefully the sphere and function of principles. But whatever its rationale, his approach is seriously debilitated by a refusal to indicate what is involved in the humanity *(Menschsein)* or human welfare *(Wohl)* which the Christian is supposed to seek and which forms the criterion for a denial of obedience to the state.[14]

There is a more serious difficulty: although Wolf draws a very instructive distinction between the ends of the state and

13. See "Die Königsherrschaft Christi," p. 41. Bartsch's interpretation appears to be more anti-institutional than Wolf's. Although he is in basic agreement with much of Wolf's interpretation of Romans 13: 1–7, Käsemann thinks that the phrase *instituted by God* expresses more than the bare facticity of the state ("Römer 13: 1–7," p. 373). For another statement of Käsemann's own position, see "Principles of the Interpretation of Romans 13," *New Testament Questions of Today,* trans. W. J. Montague (Philadelphia: Fortress Press, 1969), pp. 196–216.

14. Paul Ramsey writes, "One's individual existence is significantly affected when he gets married, or makes a promise, or when a needy neighbor claims him. One is bound to other persons in a *specifiable* way. One is established in a particular moral office—that of husband, or promiser, or neighbor—within the general Christian moral office of doing in each action anything that on the whole will make this a more loving universe" *(Deeds and Rules,* p. 164).

the Christian's relation to the state, he does not sufficiently develop the ramifications of that distinction. He rightly suggests that Christian political ethics deals with the "naked facticity" of the state, but at least as an extension of his interpretation, I would contend that Christian political ethics must deal with the particularities and peculiarities of the political order that Christian citizens confront. To eschew this task by claiming that it is not properly theological is to forget that Christian political ethics is *not merely* a theological enterprise. The "fellow man" may also be a "fellow citizen" in a constitutional democracy, and this role relation may determine the content of the claim that he makes upon the Christian.

I shall assume that the Christian is to orient himself toward the fulfillment of his neighbor's needs, which should thus be a constant motivation, intention, and direction of his action. Fletcher's cool calculation of good consequences is insufficient, for there are particular claims (e.g. promise-keeping) which have some weight independent of consequences.[15] By my promise I create a bond with a neighbor as well as engender certain expectations. Fulfilling that promise is a prima facie obligation, although it may well be in conflict with other obligations and moral principles. In political obligation I am mainly concerned to establish that obedience to the law in a democratic order is a moral obligation that can be most adequately accounted for not in terms of consequences but of certain political relations, particularly as a specification of the duty of fair play.

Too much Christian social ethics has bemoaned the in-

15. For an excellent critique of tendencies in contemporary Christian ethics to make love the sole norm and to equate love with beneficience, see Arthur J. Dyck, "Referent-Models of Loving: A Philosophical and Theological Analysis of Love in Ethical Theory and Moral Practice," *Harvard Theological Review* 61 (1968): 525–45.

creasing infrequency of direct, I-thou relations between the agent and his neighbor. Sometimes this regret has been more implicit than explicit, more felt than expressed. At any rate, it is impossible to construe the moral situation along the lines of the parable of the Good Samaritan, as some theologians do.[16] A quick glance at the complications relating to so-called Good Samaritan actions, laws, and policies in twentieth-century society all too clearly demonstrates that.[17] Instead of longing for those interpersonal, direct relations, it is urgent that we analyze precisely what is involved in *indirect* relations between Christians and their neighbors, for such relations are no less real and important than the direct, unmediated ones. The claims upon one another stem not only from abstract humanity or interpersonal encounter but also from a specification of that humanity in and through "rules, roles, and relations," which constitute the institutional matrix of obligation.[18] Thus, the role of "fellow citizen" in a democratic political order may well be a significant factor in moral judgments and decisions, since one's neighbor is also one's fellow citizen.

Love is important not merely as a quality of relationships (such as brotherhood) or as a norm but also as an orientation of the self toward the needs of one's neighbor. A central quality of love is imaginative sensitivity, which enables one to recognize his obligations to other persons. A distinction must be drawn between *recognition* of obligation and *constitution* of obligation;[19] for it may well be that an obligation is consti-

16. See Thomas Oden, *Radical Obedience: The Ethics of Rudolf Bultmann* (Philadelphia: Westminster, 1964), p. 123.

17. See James M. Ratcliffe, ed., *The Good Samaritan and the Law* (New York: Doubleday, Anchor Books, 1966).

18. As Dorothy Emmet suggests in *Rules, Roles and Relations* (New York: St. Martin's, 1966).

19. For this distinction, see George Schrader, "Autonomy, Heteronomy, and Moral Imperatives," *Journal of Philosophy* 60 (1963): 65–77.

tuted by such a principle as fairness, although it is recognized
most clearly in and through love. In a certain sense, then, justice and fairness in society depend on love, which involves
imaginatively putting oneself in another's place—an act which
presupposes recognition of the other as a particular person
both within and beyond his roles.[20]

The Christian's love, and also his perception or recognition
of obligation, are structured by some distinctive factors, particularly his ultimate loyalty and framework of interpretation. The framework in part derives from the loyalty because
the One to whom the Christian is loyal has particular purposes for man that help him interpret what is going on. This
framework and ultimate loyalty—and hence the divided
loyalty of the Christian—do not necessarily make the obligations of Christian citizens different from those of other
citizens: some obligations are established by general moral
principles, such as justice and fairness, that are shared by
Christians and non-Christians alike. Thus, both reason and
faith, nature and grace, are involved in a relation that can
best be described as reason illumined by faith.[21]

This argument about the relation of the Christian and his
neighbor in the political order is the bridgework to a theory
of political obligation. The general point is that "we think

20. See Wolfhart Pannenberg, *What is Man?* trans. Duane A. Priebe
(Philadelphia: Fortress, 1970), chap. 8, esp. p. 98. William K. Frankena
makes a different but related point about the derivation of obligations:
"all our prima facie duties *presuppose* the principle of benevolence, but
they do not all *follow from* it alone, although some of them do, including the principle of utility or beneficence. The principle of benevolence [as the prior prima facie obligation to do good and prevent harm]
is a necessary condition of all our prima facie duties, but a sufficient condition of only some of them." *Ethics* (Englewood Cliffs, N.J.: Prentice-
Hall, 1963), p. 38.

21. Cf. the discussion of Ramsey in chapter 3 and also Wolf, "Die
Königsherrschaft Christi," pp. 56, 58, and "Kirche, Staat, Gesellschaft,"
Peregrinatio II, p. 283.

it is our duty to obey or to support any authority or society when and only when we think that by so doing we can affect other men as we ought."[22] More specifically, affecting other men has to do not only with love, benevolence, beneficence, and utility but also with the claims that emerge out of the relationships between citizens in a democratic political order. Not just the ends of the enterprise, but the *activity* itself forms the matrix of political obligation, especially because the democratic state is a *cooperative task,* although it, like all states, involves subordination.

POLITICAL OBLIGATION IN A CONSTITUTIONAL DEMOCRACY: THE DUTY OF FAIR PLAY

Following the argument that I have developed, I shall examine the moral factors at work in a particular context and ask "Why ought we to obey the law in a constitutional democracy?" Often a prima facie obligation to obey the law under this system is affirmed with no indication of its basis,[23] although several principles may be relevant moral reasons for obedience. Recognizing an obligation to obey the laws of Athens because of several converging duties, Socrates, in the *Crito,* represented the laws as saying "we maintain that anyone who disobeys is guilty of doing wrong on three separate counts: first because we are his parents, and secondly because we are his guardians, and thirdly because, after promising obedience, he is neither obeying us nor persuading us to change our decision if we are at fault in any way."[24]

While I shall return later to other moral reasons for obedi-

22. Carritt, *Morals and Politics,* p. 198.
23. See Fortas, *Concerning Dissent,* and Mulford Q. Sibley, *The Obligation to Disobey: Conscience and the Law,* Special Studies no. 209 (New York: Council on Religion and International Affairs, 1970).
24. *Plato: The Collected Dialogues,* ed. Edith Hamilton and Huntington Cairns, Bollingen Series, vol. 71. (New York: Pantheon, 1961), p. 37.

ence (and disobedience), in this section I want to discuss one
of the bases of political obligation that has seldom been identified. Although theologians generally overlook it for the reasons I have already suggested, at least one element in political
obligation in a constitutional democracy is the duty of *fair
play*. I shall attempt to show the significance of such a perspective for understanding the grounds and limits of an obligation to obey the law; for my view of the task of ethics (including political ethics) is that it can deepen our awareness of the
various components as well as the totality of moral situations
by pressing certain perspectives to their conclusions. As Margaret Macdonald stresses, the value of the political theorists
"is not in the general information they give about the basis of
political obligation but in their skill in emphasizing at a critical moment a criterion which is tending to be overlooked or
denied."[25]

Because, as Sidney Hook rightly observes, originality in discussing political obligation "is almost always a sign of er-
ror",[26] it is necessary to indicate how my interpretation relates to some other theories. Basically, it is a modified contract
theory which draws on game analogies; its modifications are
attempts to overcome weaknesses of traditional contract theories as well as to account for contemporary experiences in constitutional democracies. In contrast to some forms of natural
law, contract theories generally do not assign the obligation
to obey the law to the justice or morality of the particular
law; nor do they, in contrast to some teleological theories,
concentrate on the effects of obedience and disobedience on
the state and its ends. Rather, they examine the form of the
act of obedience, which may be described as fidelity, gratitude,

25. "The Language of Political Theory," in Flew, *Logic and Language*, 1st ser., p. 194.
26. Hook, *The Paradoxes of Freedom* (Berkeley: University of California Press, 1964), p. 106.

fair play, and so forth. Thus, from this perspective, one has a moral obligation to obey the law because the act of obedience is a certain kind of act within the context of certain relations and transactions.

Usually the moral principle supporting this obligation is fidelity, or fulfilling one's contracts and promises.[27] But such an application of the duty of fidelity encounters a critical question: when and to whom did one consent or promise? An easy answer can be given in the case of aliens who become naturalized citizens, for they take an explicit oath which qualifies as consent to the status of membership in a particular state. However, because of the absence of acts of explicit consent in the lives of most citizens, contract theorists often resort to the concept of "tacit consent,"[28] which according to John Locke is rendered by living under a government's protection. He suggests that

> every man that hath any possession or enjoyment of any part of the dominions of any government doth thereby give his tacit consent, and is as far forth obliged to obedience to the laws of that government during such enjoyment as any one under it; whether this his possession be of land to him and his heirs for ever, or a lodging only for a week; or whether it be barely travelling freely on the highway; and in effect it reaches as far as the very being of anyone within the territories of that government.[29]

A serious difficulty mars this argument, for, as J. P. Plamenatz

27. J. P. Plamenatz, *Consent, Freedom and Political Obligation*, 2d ed. (London: Oxford University Press, 1968), p. 162.

28. For some of the main problems that contract theory encounters, see Alan Gewirth, "Political Justice," in Brandt, *Social Justice*. Important contemporary reinterpretations of contract theory include Joseph Tussman, *Obligation and the Body Politic*, and Michael Walzer, *Obligations: Essays on Disobedience, War, and Citizenship* (Cambridge, Mass.: Harvard University Press, 1970).

29. Locke, *Second Treatise on Government*, sec. 119.

insists, "If consent can be *implied* by some of the things that
he [Locke] maintains *imply* it, then there never existed any
government but rules with the unanimous and continuous
consent of all its subjects."[30] Furthermore, if there is no possibility of emigration, tacit consent offers little help in explaining political obligation.

Others have tried to circumvent these difficulties by con-
ceding that no deliberate performative act directed toward
incurring an obligation is presupposed, although they recognize an obligation based on gratitude, which is established
through the reception of benefits.[31] Such an obligation, then,
"would not arise out of consent, but would be no more
than a special case of the general obligation to help persons
who benefit us."[32] Voluntary acts are involved in both the
consent-promising and benefits models of political obligation,
although the former stresses one's own previous acts, as does
the duty of reparation, while the latter may stress the voluntary acts of others in creating the benefits as well as one's
voluntary acceptance of them. Regardless of the direction of
the voluntary act in the benefits model, it can afford only a
weak obligation to obey the laws, especially because one can
think of stronger debts of gratitude (e.g. to parents) that we
seldom place higher than the obligation to obey the laws.[33]
Perhaps, then, the obligation to obey the law is not primarily
based on gratitude, although this may be one motive in obedience.

Despite their weaknesses these social contract theories have
highlighted some important features of the foundations of

30. *Consent,* pp. 7–8.
31. Cf., for example, Howard Warrender, *The Political Philosophy of
Hobbes* (Oxford: Clarendon Press, 1957), pp. 233–36, 51–52.
32. Plamenatz, *Consent,* p. 24.
33. A. C. Ewing, *The Individual, the State and World Government,*
pp. 218 ff., 18; Carritt, *Ethical and Political Thinking,* p. 149.

political obligation, at least within certain contexts. H. L. A. Hart summarizes some of their strengths and weaknesses:

> The social-contract theorists rightly fastened on the fact that the obligation to obey the law is not merely a special case of benevolence (direct or indirect), but something which arises between members of a particular political society out of their mutual relationship. Their mistake was to identify *this* right-creating situation of mutual restrictions with the paradigm case of promising; there are of course important similarities, and these are just the points which all special rights have in common, viz., that they arise out of special relationships between human beings and not out of the character of the action to be done or its effects.[34]

The genuine contributions of contract theory can be retained in a modified version, which is more plausible than the model of fidelity to promises or contracts and which provides a stronger obligation than gratitude. For, as John Rawls contends, "[t]here is a gap in the stock of moral concepts used by philosophers into which the concept of the duty of fair play fits quite naturally." Despite its clear affinities with these other concepts, the "duty of fair play stands beside other prima facie duties such as fidelity and gratitude as a basic moral notion; yet it is not to be confused with them."[35] This reinterpretation of social contract theory is deeply indebted to the work not only of John Rawls, but also of H. L. A. Hart and David Lyons, among others. While these thinkers do not agree at every point, I am more interested in developing a coherent theory than in elucidating the peculiarities of each viewpoint.

34. "Are There Any Natural Rights?" *Philosophical Review* 64 (1955): 186.

35. "Justice as Fairness," *Justice and Social Policy,* ed. Frederick Olafson (Englewood Cliffs, N.J.: Prentice-Hall, 1961), pp. 95–96, n. 15.

First it is necessary to indicate the place and significance of fairness and fair play in our moral notions, especially because some critics, such as Erich Fromm, deny that these *are* fundamental moral notions and insist instead that they are clearly secondary, parasitic, incompatible with love, and dependent upon a capitalist society. According to Fromm, "the development of fairness ethics is the particular ethical contribution of capitalist society," whose whole existence is determined by exchange on the market. Fairness eliminates the use of force and fraud in such an exchange. Fromm contends that the principle of fairness in dealings (not to be confused with the Golden Rule) is a nonproductive orientation of the self and that it is incompatible with the principle of love expressed in the Jewish-Christian tradition.[36]

My argument against such a contention is that, while love will indeed sometimes demand actions which go beyond fairness, it will rarely, if ever, require actions that are unfair or institutional structures that are unfair, primarily because fairness is tied up with the recognition of persons. As Rawls puts it, "acknowledging the duty of fair play is a necessary part of the criterion for recognizing another as a person with similar interests and feelings as oneself."[37] Furthermore, to be oriented toward another person in love—which I have contended is a fundamental disposition of the Christian as well as a more general human virtue—means to recognize him as a person and to acknowledge various prima facie duties such as fairness and fair play which may not themselves be deduced from love. Fairness is justice expressed specifically in competitive and cooperative practices; and while fairness and

36. Erich Fromm, *The Art of Loving* (New York: Harper and Row, Harper Colophon Book, 1962), pp. 129–33; cf. Fromm, *Beyond the Chains of Illusion* (New York: Simon and Schuster, 1962), p. 86; *Man for Himself* (New York: Fawcett, 1967), p. 119.

37. "Justice as Fairness," in Olafson, *Justice and Social Policy*, p. 96.

love are interrelated, they are not identical, so that it is impossible to view love as the sole norm. Lyons also ties the concept of fairness directly into the notion of *social* behavior: "One who acts unfairly is to that extent not a responsible human being, not a responsible member of society, not a social creature."[38]

Fairness sets limits on the ways we attempt to achieve ends in social and political activities. Furthermore, its significance is somewhat independent of the moral content or substance of the particular rule or rules of the practice. Because it restricts the way we pursue our ends rather than determining the ends themselves, it is a *secondary* rather than a *primary* virtue, in Alasdair MacIntyre's terms.[39] Secondary virtues, which are concerned with how we do what we do, are nevertheless as fundamental to the moral life as the primary ones that establish our projects. At this point I only want to indicate, contrary to Fromm and others, that fairness and fair play are important moral considerations, especially in social and political life. Indeed, I would contend that to overlook them, or even to stress their incompatibility with love, is to exclude the possibility of evaluating (other than condemning) and directing institutional life in terms of its basic structure and the relations and conduct within it. Fairness and fair play are indispensable in social and political morality and ethics.

Even if fair play is a fundamental moral notion, closely connected with what it means to recognize another person as a person, its actual significance may well vary in different cultures and in different times and places. Many factors ac-

38. Lyons, *Utilitarianism,* p. 177.
39. Alasdair MacIntyre, *Secularization and Moral Change* (London: Oxford University Press, 1967), p. 24. I do not claim, as Rawls does, that the secondary virtue of fairness is absolute with respect to utility. See Rawls, "Legal Obligation and the Duty of Fair Play," in Hook, *L & P,* pp. 13, 17–18.

count for this variation, but it is interesting to note ways in which the virtue of fair play is inculcated in the United States. While Robert Bellah's renowned essay "Civil Religion in America" deals with trenscendent symbols, it does not give sufficient attention to public moral standards and values, although some of these are implicit in it and although he sees "the central tradition of the American civil religion not as a form of national self-worship but as the subordination of the nation to ethical principles that transcend it and in terms of which it should be judged."[40] Nevertheless, it is possible to view fairness and fair play as among the central ethical principles in American civil religion, and to see them as transmitted to the young through the public schools, and also to a great extent through competitive sports and games.[41] Further sociological and social psychological analyses of fair play and its transmission would be most useful, particularly in determining the conditions under which it is valued or denigrated.

It might be useful to draw a general sketch of this fair play theory of political obligation before I examine some of its features more closely. It has an externalist rather than an internalist theory of law, and it presupposes that certain positive ends or purposes are attained by the state, e.g. justice, security, and so forth. Among the other interesting fea-

40. Robert Bellah, *Beyond Belief: Essays on Religion in a Post-Traditional World* (New York: Harper and Row, 1970), p. 168.

41. Phillip E. Hammond, "Commentary on 'Civil Religion in America,'" in *The Religious Situation 1968,* ed. Donald R. Cutler (Boston: Beacon, 1968), pp. 381–88. Hammond's analysis, which Bellah finds "attractive," is an attempt to locate the structures in and through which the culture that Bellah describes as "civil religion" lives. His point is that, in a situation in which everybody can claim to know "God's will on earth," decisions are made in conformity with that will only through "competition of ideas within the rules of the game. Ideologically, sovereignty belongs to God, but operationally His will is known through majority vote, fair play, or some such enabling rules" (pp. 383–84).

tures of this theory is its answer to another question: to whom is political obedience owed? It is not owed to all men, to humanity in general, or to the state as an institution, but rather to one's fellow citizens, who thus have a right to or are entitled to claim it. The obligation is incurred by the acceptance of the benefits of an ordered body politic (recognized as relatively just), which would not have been possible without the general obedience and cooperation of one's fellow citizens. Although the acceptance of benefits may appear to make this obligation dependent on the debt of gratitude, the emphasis is significantly different. When it comes my turn to obey the laws, I have an obligation to do so (although it can be outweighed by other moral reasons and obligations), not because I thereby show proper gratitude for the benefits received, but because I thereby act fairly in relation to those whose obedience made the structure and benefits possible. Disobedience is a refusal to restrict my freedom as others have restricted theirs. This is roughly analogous to refusing to take the field so that the other team can have their turn at bat; the duty of fair play is violated in both cases.

As a denial that individuals are just so many indiscriminate targets on which good (e.g. happiness) can be dropped, this theory of political obligation stresses the *relations* between individuals within institutional contexts. The obligation to obey the law emerges out of a special relationship between citizens, which also has analogies in other relationships such as voluntary associations. In contrast to teleological and consequentialist theories, both traditional contract theory and this modified version of it are retrospective in that they focus on past acts rather than future states of affairs. These past acts are also voluntary although not necessarily deliberate. While teleological and consequentialist theories concentrate on the *effects* of the activity of ruling and obeying or the *effects* of the act of obedience or disobedience, for my theory the activity and its special relationships themselves are crucial, although the effects too have an important place. The point is that the act of obedience in a constitutional democracy is in itself an act of justice as well as an act with certain consequences, such as the contribution to the maintenance of the state which is essential for justice, utility, and other values.

Having sketched an overview of this theory, I shall analyze some of its features in more detail. It is interesting to compare the duty of fair play with the apparently similar duty of "playing the game," which E. F. Carritt considers only to deny that it is really a duty. The duty of playing the game, as he interprets it, is the obligation to do what would have good results or fulfill some claim *if* others cooperated; or, in its negative form, it is the obligation to refrain from doing what would have bad results or would negate legitimate claims if everyone did it.[42] An example of this alleged duty in its negative form can be put this way: "You should not make the short cut across the grass even alone and after dark, for if everybody did so the lawn would be spoilt." After examining cases in which a similar line of reasoning would lead to ludicrous results, Carritt concludes that there is no duty to play the game because he does not see "how an actual obligation can depend upon any unfulfilled condition (whose fulfillment may be very improbable), but only on a condition which my action itself will fulfill."[43]

A fundamental defect in this analysis is its concentration on future, unfulfilled conditions under which duty would take effect. The perspective seems to be that of a person deciding whether to set up or to take part in a game when he cannot be certain that others will occupy their assigned posi-

42. Carritt, *Ethical and Political Thinking*, p. 109. The generalization argument will be discussed more fully in chapter 4.
43. Ibid., p. 110.

tions. But another perspective is gained if one pictures another player entering a game already in process and trying to determine the legitimate demands that can be placed upon him. This second perspective suggests some important features of "playing the game" that Carritt missed.

The case of crossing the lawn is a good one for examination. If the general practice is to avoid crossing the lawn except in emergencies, the fact that my behavior will not be observed and thus cannot be a bad example to others is not the only consideration. The question "But what if everyone did that?" will not be especially penetrating in this context unless it brings to attention the fact that one is making an unjustified exception in the context of the practice. But this really brings us to the question of fair play. For in a generally useful practice, such as not crossing the lawn, where others have submitted to the rules for common benefits that we too have enjoyed, the refusal to follow the rule even unobserved subjects us to the charge of failing to play the game and thus of acting unfairly.

This, of course, is not to suggest that a de facto rule cannot be justifiably broken when it comes one's turn to obey, but it does suggest the relevance of evaluative considerations other than the act's consequences. Thus by concentrating on future, unfulfilled conditions in playing the game, Carritt failed to take account of relevant past actions of others in adhering to the rules and my own acceptance of benefits from the common enterprise.[44] As John Rawls contends, "It is sufficient that one has knowingly participated in and accepted the benefits of a practice acknowledged to be fair."[45]

44. Much of the analysis of the last paragraph is influenced by David Lyons. See especially his distinction: "In general, it is necessary to distinguish between our reasons for criticizing certain modes of behaviour, on the one hand, and the consequences of that behaviour, on the other" (Utilitarianism, p. 172).

45. "Justice as Fairness," in Olafson, Justice and Social Policy, p. 94.

These factors engender an obligation based on the duty of fair play.

One way to clarify further what is involved in the duty of fair play is to ask what it means to act unfairly or to be guilty of unfair play. I can explicate this set of notions best by beginning with the context of a practice that has been defined as "any form of activity specified by a system of rules which defines offices, roles, moves, penalties, defenses, and so on, and which gives the activity its structure."[46] Then a distinction must be drawn between applying the rule of a practice to acts, and applying the principle of fairness to them. For example, a local government has a statute requiring a permit for parades, and a group protesting housing conditions commits civil disobedience by violating that law. Of course, the first judgment is that a law has been violated, but to determine whether the act of violation was unfair requires further, broader considerations. David Lyons has given a penetrating summary of the relation of the rules of a practice to standards of fairness:

> the rules of the useful, co-operative practices themselves are not concerned with fairness. The rules of *de facto* practices require that we perform, or refrain from, acts of this or that kind, under these or those circumstances. Considerations of fairness, gratitude, and fidelity are, in contrast, critical considerations, not subordinate to or determined by any *de facto* rules (not even the rules of conventional morality). Thus, when we apply such notions as fairness, gratitude, and fidelity in morals, we are not performing moves in a game. We are rather con-

46. "Two Concepts of Rules," *Philosophical Review* 64 (Jan. 1955): 3, n. 1. Also, "Justice as Fairness," in Olafson, *Justice and Social Policy*, p. 80, n. 2. See the last reference for examples: "games and rituals, trials and parliaments, markets and systems of property." *Institution* would often serve as a synonym.

cerned and occupied with the basic critical and self-critical operations of morality itself—of morality, as opposed to conventions and codes.[47]

An action is judged as fair or unfair less in relation to the de facto rules and the conduct they require than in relation to the conduct and expectations of other participants, for it is in relation to them that I am either bearing a fair share of the load by obeying the rules when my turn comes, or being unfair by refusing to submit. If someone focuses on my act of violating a particular rule, he can only say that I have done what was prohibited by that rule. If he broadens the context, he can speak of the effects of my action on the joint enterprise. But one can and should add, as a factor in analysis and evaluation, that I have benefited from the obedience of *other members* (citizens) who restricted their freedom partly in expectation that I and others would obey in our turn. At this point the criterion of fairness as applied to an individual's acts is clearly very important. In any association or organization a "free rider," who accepts the benefits of that institutional arrangement without shouldering his share of the burdens and responsibilities, is guilty of unfair play.

I have emphasized violating the rules of a practice because of my interest in the question of civil disobedience, but one may also act unfairly by "taking advantage of loop-holes or ambiguities in rules, availing oneself of unexpected or special circumstances which make it impossible to enforce them, insisting that the rules be enforced to one's advantage when they should be suspended, and more generally, acting contrary to the intention of a practice."[48] Beyond this recognition of the range of judgments of unfairness, other points

47. Lyons, *Utilitarianism,* pp. 196–97.
48. Rawls, "Justice as Fairness," in Olafson, *Justice and Social Policy,* p. 95.

need to be stressed. First, a verdict of unfair play can be justified without showing that the practice or other persons were harmed by the act. Thus, it is not necessary to demonstrate that the act set a bad example, or undermined the practice, or diminished the share of benefits that other participants receive.

A second point is raised by David Lyons, who contends that the act of unfair play includes the description of seeking one's own advantage and of exploiting the efforts and contributions of others.[49] This raises several interesting questions about civil disobedience. For example, what if the disobedient does not pursue his own interest but what he understands as the public good? And what if he is making a significant contribution to the practice in other ways? Under these circumstances is his act unfair? These and other questions will occupy my attention in the next chapter when I try to determine some of the conditions for justifying civil disobedience.

Third, if the practice empowers officials to enforce demands, a disobedient will often be punished, not because he acted unfairly but because he violated certain rules. Because this essential distinction is often overlooked in discussions of civil disobedience, the fairness principle is frequently construed as requiring that a legal penalty be exacted for acts of civil disobedience. Ronald Dworkin, in a brilliant article, "On Not Prosecuting Civil Disobedience," which focuses on issues raised by the trial of Dr. Benjamin Spock, William Sloane Coffin, Jr., and others, summarizes the moral argument that many seem to make for enforcement of the law:

> [they] seem to rely on a fundamental moral argument that it would be unfair, not merely impractical, to let

49. See Lyons, *Utilitarianism*, pp. 175–77.

the dissenter go unpunished. They think it would be unfair . . . because society could not function if everyone disobeyed laws he disapproved of or found disadvantageous. If the government tolerates those few who will not "play the game," it allows them to secure the benefits of everyone else's deference to law, without shouldering the burdens.[50]

But as far as I can see, the argument that I have defended implies nothing about enforcing the law and demanding penalties.

Political obligation in a relatively just constitutional democracy emerges at least in part from what Hart calls the "mutuality of restrictions,"[51] within which an argument for an obligation to adhere to the rules based on fairness makes sense. The ends of the enterprise cannot be attained apart from general (although not necessarily universal) submission to its rules and thus mutual restriction of freedom. As I have contended, disobedience—or the refusal to abide by the rules and to restrict one's freedom of action as one's fellow citizens have—is unfair regardless of its effect or lack of effect on the attainment of the ends of the enterprise. Although there is thus a moral obligation to obey the law, it is not absolute, and it does not require that the government prosecute, convict, and punish the disobedient, however noble and conscientious his motives. Some mistakenly think the fairness

50. Ronald Dworkin, "Civil Disobedience: The Case Against Prosecution," *The New York Review of Books* 10, no. 11 (June 6, 1968): 14, reprinted in *Trials of the Resistance,* p. 52. Another very important and related issue is "jury nullification." See Joseph Sax, "Conscience and Anarchy: The Prosecution of War Resisters," *Yale Review* 57, no. 4 (June 1968): 481–94, reprinted in Sax, "Dicta," *Virginia Law Weekly,* vol. 22, nos. 4, 5 (1969). Cf. also William Kunstler, "Dissent and the Jury," in *Delivered into Resistance* (New Haven: Advocate Press, 1969), pp. 50–59.

51. Hart, "Are There Any Natural Rights?" *Philosophical Review* 64 (1955): 185 f.

argument implies that exacting a penalty, whether a fine or imprisonment, is justified—and indeed mandatory—because it will restore the balance of restrictions and freedom by forcibly restricting the disobedient's freedom after his refusal to restrict it voluntarily through obedience.

But while the act of disobedience may be unfair in relation to other participants in the practice, it is not necessarily unfair for officials simply to refrain from prosecuting the disobedient, especially the civil disobedient. Too many other factors, including some that Dworkin discusses, are (or should be) operative; for example, in the decision to prosecute or not to prosecute draft dissenters like Spock such factors as the threat to public order, the necessity of deterrence, the motives of the actors, and the loss to society when several of its most loyal citizens are punished, were relevant. It is considerations like these rather than the moral arguments from fair play that are critical, since punishment cannot restore the "mutuality of restrictions." Regardless of the direction in which they point in a given case, these factors are more important than the moral obligation to obey the law for the debate about prosecution, especially because penalties are affixed to rules, not in order to ensure an equal and fair distribution of restrictions, but rather to accomplish quite different aims.

An obligation is one reason for obedience. Arising out of a special and limited relationship, political obligation is owed to specific persons (not as men, but as citizens) rather than to the government which, however, is authorized to enforce obedience in the interest of society as a whole. The cardinal consideration, then, is not enforcement or punishment, but the *moral* claim that can be made by other members of the body politic, who may choose to relinquish that claim or to excuse its violations because of the worthy motives of the actors. Throughout I have assumed the perspective of the actor in civil disobedience rather than that of society or the state through its prosecutors and courts, but even from the latter perspective, nothing in the fairness argument requires prosecution and punishment of civil disobedience.

The actor in civil disobedience in a democracy may have an obligation to obey the law that cannot be reduced to the general requirement of benevolence or love of neighbor because it stems from the relations between men as *citizens* in a democratic polity. Viewed less as a legal than a moral-political category, *citizenship,* as Michael Walzer indicates, is defined by the two substantive values of protection and responsibility; for the citizen both receives protection of life, liberty, and so forth from the state and participates in the process of "ruling and being ruled." Protection and responsibility are not simply vertical but also horizontal, since in a democracy we have more than a series of discrete connections between single individuals and the state.[52] The metaphor of horizontal relations stresses that citizens are bound to each other both in protection and in the exercise of responsibility in the cooperative enterprise of democratic polity.

I can illustrate why this role relation of citizenship is so critical to my argument by examining one aspect of Thoreau's thought. I have already suggested the importance of looking at indirect relations in institutional contexts to understand political obligation. Thoreau, however, reduced the importance of the institutional matrix by contending that "the government is best which governs not at all" and that "any man more right than his neighbors constitutes a majority of one already." Beyond these well-known and oft-quoted sentences lies another and perhaps more significant index of his anti-institutional theme. While he partly defended his action of not paying his poll tax by stressing that

52. Walzer, *Obligations,* p. 225 as well as all of chap. 10. Cf. p. 207.

he did pay his "highway tax," Thoreau's reasons for paying the latter had nothing to do with obligations mediated through the institutional order, but rather, as he put it, "because I am as desirous of being a good neighbor as I am of being a bad subject."[53] In contrast to my position, such an argument recognizes only a "private" obligation (stemming from neighborliness, friendship, and the like) far removed from politics, although the environment within which this obligation is incurred may be shaped by the state, which may also provide the occasion and means for its fulfillment.[54] Thoreau thus does recognize obligations to others in society, but ignores obligations to others in *political* relations or in *political society*.

Without in any way ignoring the importance of the distinction between state and society, I want to stress for purposes of this analysis the significance of the role relation of citizenship within the democratic state. In calling our attention to the differences within citizenship in modern democracies, Walzer distinguishes between the oppressed citizen, the alienated citizen, and the pluralist citizen in terms of their relation to the substantive values of protection and responsibility. While the *oppressed* citizen receives less protection of life, liberty, property, and welfare and also can rarely exercise political responsibility effectively, the *alienated* citizen receives protection but chooses to boycott the state by refraining from participation in the political process.[55] Several minority groups in the ghetto and elsewhere are examples of oppressed citizens deprived of full protection and effective participation. An example of the alienated citi-

53. Thoreau, "Civil Disobedience," in *Walden and Civil Disobedience,* pp. 235, 244, 252.
54. This sentence is drawn from Walzer *(Obligations,* p. 89) who uses it in a different context.
55. Ibid., esp. pp. 226–27.

zen is the suburbanite who receives full protection but who, for a variety of reasons, including perhaps his preoccupation with the private sphere of family life and so forth, avoids the political process.

It is interesting to consider Thoreau in relation to these categories. Although he claimed to eschew the protection of the government ("For my own part, I should not like to think that I ever rely on the Protection of the State") he nevertheless conceded that, despite his declared war on the state, "I will still make what use and get what advantage of her as I can." He was clearly alienated from and engaged in a boycott of the state. Not only did he refuse to avail himself of existing machinery for political change, but he also declared: "I am not responsible for the successful working of the machinery of society."[56]

Walzer's third category, the *pluralist* citizen, expresses both descriptive and normative elements; that is, it describes what is normally at work in much contemporary citizenship and the best arrangements under present conditions. The pluralist citizen receives protection and shares in government in and through his membership in a variety of groups.[57] An analysis of political obligation in terms of fair play, of course, is most instructive and cogent in relation to the pluralist citizen, for the oppressed citizen is often deprived of the benefits and opportunities that are prerequisites for such an obligation, while the alienated citizen often refuses to acknowledge that the regime is basically just.

These distinctions in kinds of citizenship raise another significant question in a striking way: what are the necessary and sufficient conditions for the emergence of political obligation based on fair play? My discussion will not be exhaustive, but it will attempt to delineate the most important

56. Thoreau, "Civil Disobedience," pp. 247, 252; 249, cf. pp. 243–44.
57. Walzer, *Obligations*, p. 227.

of these conditions, some of which have already been adumbrated. My central contention is that political obligation emerging out of the relationships between citizens presupposes the general utility and justice of the fundamental structure of the body politic. In a way similar to some of the theological ethical arguments examined in the last chapter, some insist that the duty to support just, useful systems of government is sufficient to account for our obligation to obey the law in practically all contexts. Thus John Macmurray contends that

> political obligation is a derivative and indirect moral
> obligation. . . . The moral obligation to act justly then
> carries with it a derivative obligation to maintain the
> means to justice, and this is a system of effective law.
> We have, therefore, a moral obligation to maintain the
> law as the necessary means to justice. Here, if anywhere,
> to will the end is to will the means to it.[58]

Certainly all men have a duty to work to establish and strengthen just and useful institutions, but such a general duty, which is directed to all men by virtue of their humanity, may well be augmented by a distinctive and special obligation based on special relationships between citizens within a constitutional democracy.[59]

While a just and efficient political structure is the *object* of some of our general duties, it is also a *condition* of political obligation based on the duty of fair play. Without

---

58. *Persons in Relation* (London: Faber and Faber, 1961), p. 196.

59. In his second essay on civil disobedience, "The Justification of Civil Disobedience," (in Bedau, *CD*), Rawls is much clearer that there is a moral or natural duty to support just and efficient institutions than he was in "Legal Obligation and the Duty of Fair Play," in Hook, *L & P*. Had this point been stronger in the earlier essay, some of the criticisms directed against it would perhaps have been forestalled. See the other essays in the volume edited by Hook which criticize Rawls's position.

suggesting that such a structure exists only in a constitutional democracy, I am inquiring into the meaning of political obligation within this particular context. Whether this analysis extends to other contexts is subject to further study.[60] Neither perfect justice nor maximal utility of the fundamental structure is a condition, for such requirements would force us to roam in never-never land. Any political system is imperfect, although some are better than others.

If utility is a prerequisite for the emergence of political obligation based on fair play, why not just appeal directly to it without reference to fairness? The problem with such an argument, and its theological variants, is that although it provides strong support for the necessity of a state and laws, it offers only weak support for any particular state and one's obligation to obey it. If the utilitarian argument remains strictly utilitarian, it would require the state to be maximally efficient and useful, while the argument from fairness requires only *some* usefulness.[61] But certainly there is an obligation of fair play only in situations in which the "total benefits distributed" outweigh the "total burdens required." If this condition is not met, the practice has no point.[62]

A similar argument holds for the condition that the practice must be just. While the requirement of utility only establishes that the institution as a whole must produce a

60. See Milton R. Konvitz, "Civil Disobedience and the Duty of Fair Play," Hook, *L & P*, pp. 20 f.

61. Lyons, *Utilitarianism*.

62. In his treatment of the relationship which he calls "mutuality of restrictions," Hart does not explicitly limit the derivation of an obligation to useful enterprises. See "Are There Any Natural Rights?" *Philosophical Review* 64 (1955): 185–86. David Lyons, on the other hand, explicitly imposes a condition of usefulness or utility for the development of an obligation of fair play. He refers to the matrix for the emergence of this obligation as "useful, co-operative, *de facto* practices" (*Utilitarianism*, pp. 190 f., 164 ff.). Lyons also lists several other prerequisites for an argument from fairness.

greater balance of good over evil, the requirements of justice
and fairness control the distribution of benefits and opportunities of participation and thus ensure that all those within
the practice both benefit from it and are free to participate
in its direction. It is important to stress again that I am now
concerned with the *basic structure* (e.g. constitution) of the
practice and not all its particular laws, since the question of
whether the duty of fair play holds in relation to unjust laws
in a fundamentally just system will be considered later. Just
as there is no requirement of maximal utility from the state,
so there is no requirement of perfect justice, especially because my theological-anthropological perspective emphasizes
that perfect justice is impossible under the human condition,
although it does not narrowly circumscribe the limits of relative justice, which thus remains open to new and indeterminate possibilities.[63] While perfect justice is impossible, the
structure can, nevertheless, embody such a high degree of
justice that it can be termed fundamentally just.

What standards of justice must be met for a structure to
qualify as "just"?[64] Because I hold equal liberty as the central principle, the constitution and basic structure of the
democracy should affirm and develop *equally everyone's
liberty* to the extent permitted by the demands of order,
since obviously absolute liberty is anarchy. This equal liberty
must be viewed in both positive and negative ways.[65] In its

63. See Reinhold Niebuhr's various writings on this subject, including
The Nature and Destiny of Man, vol. 2 (New York: Scribner's, 1949), esp.
chap. 9.

64. Rawls writes, "I have drawn on the contractarian tradition not for
a general theory of political obligation but to clarify the concept of justice." "Justice as Fairness," in Olafson, *Justice and Social Policy*, p. 106,
n. 23. Furthermore, he works from well-defined principles of justice which
men in the original hypothetical position could accept for their institutions.

65. Isaiah Berlin uses this distinction but in a different way; see his
"Two Concepts of Liberty," *Four Essays on Liberty* (New York: Oxford
University Press, Galaxy Books, 1969), pp. 118–72.

negative sense, it is the commitment to create, extend, and maintain freedom from government's, society's, and other individuals' encroachment upon one's private sphere, upon family, conscience, self-determination, and so forth; because political life does not fulfill all human needs, it is essential that such a private sphere be protected. In its positive sense, equal liberty means equal opportunity to participate in the activities of the public sphere, the activities of ruling and being ruled.

Instead of trying to present a comprehensive analysis of the condition of justice, I shall try to illustrate how it works. It is impossible to make the case that an obligation to obey the law on the grounds of fair play rests on a person who has been systematically excluded from the benefits of the state or who has been denied both negative and positive liberty. An obvious example of such an oppressed citizen is the Negro in many southern states who, at least in the past, has been denied most of the elementary benefits of a democratic political order, e.g. equal protection of the laws, security of person and property, and the opportunity to participate in the election of his government. An argument that he should obey state laws cannot appeal to fair play, for his exclusion from the system is so flagrant that any discussion of the distribution of restrictions of freedom, which is central to fair play, would be irrelevant. Of course, the absence of a political obligation on such grounds does not mean that a citizen, even an oppressed one, is morally free to disregard, resist, and overturn the authority, since other moral reasons (e.g. the prevention of unnecessary suffering) may dictate obedience. Furthermore, certain laws (such as prohibitions of cruelty) remain obligatory because they embody other moral principles.

Nevertheless, in the case I described, the argument for obedience cannot take place on the grounds of justice, fairness, and fair play, which are central to democratic life. On those grounds alone, indeed, the systematically oppressed citizen is free to disobey. A more interesting question, however, is whether a citizen who has *not* been so excluded has a moral obligation, based on fair play, to obey an *unjust law* in a fundamentally just system. I shall turn to that question after I move beyond such external conditions as the structure of the state to consider internal conditions in obligations based on fair play.

Practically all contract theory, as I have suggested, stresses that voluntary actions engender political obligation. Without considering all the ramifications of this topic, I shall state briefly some of its significant issues. From the perspective of contract theory, political obligation stems from an individual's past actions and is thus constructed or artificial rather than natural. A natural obligation emerges from natural relationships such as that between children and parents.[66] Contract theory in its different forms continues to strike responsive chords largely because of its effort to view the citizen as voluntarily incurring an obligation to obey the laws of the state. Such voluntarism hardly exhausts the claims of most theorists, since they also want to view the past act(s) as deliberate and, furthermore, as directed toward incurring an obligation. Thus they frequently have recourse to the performative acts of promising to obey or consenting to be governed in explicating the basis of political obligation, as I have indicated. The alternative theory, based on gratitude, eliminates the deliberate act, although it retains the voluntary act of receiving benefits from the state as well as the voluntary acts of others in submission.

66. Cf. Robert Paul Wolff, "An Analysis of the Concept of Political Loyalty," *Political Man and Social Man,* ed. Robert Paul Wolff (New York: Random House, 1966), pp. 218–40, for a helpful typology which includes these categories.

Voluntary associations (including the church) have long functioned as models for various contractual and democratic theories.[67] In such associations it does make sense to use the categories of promising to obey the rules or authorizing the organization to make decisions that will bind the agent, although in the state one must recognize the absence of explicit commitments, deliberate choice, and deliberate incurring of obligation except in rare instances. How are previous voluntary actions interpreted in the theory of fair play? Certainly acceptance of benefits such as protection is a necessary condition for the operation of the claims of fair play; often participation in the political process is involved too. Also, as I have suggested, one takes cognizance of the previous voluntary actions of others in maintaining this ongoing structure since general, although not universal, submission is necessary for its survival.

There is, however, yet another factor which is overlooked in interpretations that focus only on "acquiescence and willing enjoyment." This is recognition, acknowledgment, and acceptance of the basic structure of the political order as just and fair.[68] Obviously many alienated citizens in contemporary democracies, particularly in the United States, have called into question the justice and utility of a structure which allows, even if it does not demand, policies such as the Vietnam war and conditions such as racism. The argument from fair play is certainly not applicable to the "revolutionary" who denies that the structure is fundamentally just.

67. Cf. A. S. P. Woodhouse, ed., Introduction, *Puritanism and Liberty,* 2d ed. (Chicago: University of Chicago Press, 1951), and A. D. Lindsay, *The Modern Democratic State* (New York: Oxford University Press, Galaxy Books, 1962), chap. 5.

68. Lyons, *Utilitarianism,* p. 191. Cf. Rawls's statement: "These conditions will obtain if a practice is correctly acknowledged to be fair, for in this case all who participate in it will benefit from it" ("Justice as Fairness," in Olafson, *Justice and Social Policy,* p. 94).

He declares his intention both to break with and to break the system. Insofar as rational discourse is possible, it has to proceed on the level of the justice of the system, not the fair play of obedience. The argument for an obligation based on fair play presupposes not only the justice of the system but also its recognition and acknowledgment. However, for most pluralist citizens, acceptance of the justice of the basic system can be assumed in the absence of explicit and circumstantial evidence to the contrary. The strongest positive evidence comes, not from the acceptance of benefits but from participation in the system, e.g. free elections.[69]

The contract metaphor has often been associated with a view of the state as a structure designed and constructed by predominantly rational men, while its critics have often been fond of conservative and more organic metaphors. Voluntary associations with their features of the *Gesellschaft,* and the state interpreted in their light, have often been viewed almost exclusively as the effects of rational decisions and human design. Nothing in my argument implies this. While I have assumed an ongoing enterprise of political order that has not only been created but also sustained by human activity, I have never supposed that such activity is strictly and simply rational—too many other factors are present and indeed indispensable, including elements of community or relations of *Gemeinschaft.*[70] Even though the state is the result of human activity, it is not necessarily an artifact of design.

Likewise, another criticism that has been leveled against

69. Another important question is action on behalf of another group that is systematically excluded from benefits and protection; cf. Walzer's interesting discussion, *Obligations,* chap. 3, esp. pp. 68–70.

70. Cf. Davis and Good, eds., *Reinhold Niebuhr on Politics,* pp. 99–104, 244 ff. For the typology of *Gemeinschaft* and *Gesellschaft,* see Ferdinand Tönnies, *Community and Society,* trans. and ed. Charles Loomis (New York: Harper and Row, Torchbook, 1963).

traditional social contract theory does not affect my interpretation. Many critics have charged that contract theory in its various forms is individualistic because it focuses on the rational, autonomous individual who will freely create obligations, although he appears to be previously unbound.[71] Without doubt these themes are congruent with if not required by most contract theories, but my interpretation of political obligation as based in part on fair play within a relatively just constitutional democracy does not deny that a citizen has other obligations (many of which are natural rather than voluntarily incurred), nor that some of these other obligations and duties (such as preventing suffering) must also be considered in an analysis of obedience and disobedience. Certainly, even within the context that I have described, other moral reasons for obedience are significant; but my contention is that political obligation within such a context can be illuminated by the model of fair play.

UNJUST LAWS AND POLICIES IN A
RELATIVELY JUST SYSTEM

Instead of examining civil disobedience only or even primarily in a revolutionary situation such as Nazi Germany, I have concentrated on a relatively just system, a constitutional democracy, in light of the constant question "How are we to understand our obligation to obey the law in such a context?" If my analysis is accurate, it is also possible—in contrast to the claims of theories of natural law—that there

71. Cf. Thomas McPherson, *Political Obligation*, especially chap. 5. For other arguments against models of political obligation such as I have defended, see John Ladd, "Legal and Moral Obligation," in *Political and Legal Obligation (Nomos 12)*, pp. 3–35, followed by critical responses. One of Ladd's central criticisms is that the concept of political obligation stresses too much the legal order as a whole instead of individual laws, and that it is thus morally objectionable. I have given my reasons for defending the opposing view.

can be an obligation to obey an *unjust* law within the democratic context. Explication of this thesis requires a brief examination of democracy, its meaning, justification, and descriptive adequacy.

At least three different approaches can be used in discussing civil disobedience and political obligation in democracies. First, one can reject the democratic ideal *in toto* and consequently deny that any democracy can claim a man's allegiance. Second, one can agree with justifications offered for democracy and yet contend that the ideal is never actually achieved and therefore no particular "democracy" engenders an obligation to obedience. Finally, one may argue that a particular law is so inconsistent with the democratic regime of which it is a part that it is not obligatory.[72]

In theological circles there have been several efforts to justify democracy that go beyond the justification of the state and government in general. Although theologians representing such divergent perspectives as Walter Rauschenbusch, Karl Barth, and Reinhold Niebuhr have joined in these efforts, Niebuhr's thought has perhaps been the most important. His pattern of argument includes the formal elements sketched in chapter 2: theological-anthropological convictions and moral principles and values. Thus, he sees democracy's justification as most securely lodged, not in the liberal creed but in the theological interpretation of man as a sinner who nevertheless has indeterminate possibilities for good.[73] Furthermore, democracy of all possible governmental forms best fulfills the demands of liberty and equality

72. These three levels are developed in David Spitz, "Democracy and the Problem of Civil Disobedience," *The American Political Science Review* 48, no. 2 (June 1954), 386–403.

73. See his discussion in *The Children of Light and the Children of Darkness* (New York: Scribner's, 1944) and the relevant sections in *Reinhold Niebuhr On Politics*. Cf. also Daniel P. Moynihan, "Nirvana Now," *The American Scholar* 36, no. 4 (Autumn, 1967).

(the regulative principles of justice) and order. Niebuhr's view is best expressed in his epigram, "Man's capacity for justice makes democracy possible; but man's inclination to injustice makes democracy necessary."[74] He and most theologians—in spite of occasional ecstatic evaluations such as in the Social Gospel—have given tempered judgments of democracy, as echoed in the "pessimistic faith" he and Paul Sigmund affirm by drawing on Winston Churchill: "we believe that democracy is the worst form of government on earth except for all others ever tried."[75]

This Christian realist justification of democracy as presented by Niebuhr and many others has been very influential partly because it can be so easily expressed in nontheological language; it is also quite cogent, largely because it can take account of man's potentialities and limitations, agreements and conflicts, shared values and competing interests. Properly stated, its view of man is dialectical, and its realism—especially as combined with a pluralist interpretation of the way democracy can and should work—leads to an emphasis on establishing rules and procedures within which a variety of self-interested groups and individuals can present their claims. Competing claims are tolerated without respect to their content in this open marketplace, and their supporters can expect to receive a measure of justice by compromise. Such realist themes as tolerance, compromise, and justice

74. *Reinhold Niebuhr on Politics,* p. 186.
75. Paul Sigmund and Reinhold Niebuhr, *The Democratic Experience* (New York: Praeger, 1969), p. vi. Dante Germino writes: "The defense of democracy should rest on the quite tenable, empirical proposition that such institutions and procedures [e.g. periodic elections, representative institutions, the rule of law] . . . are the most adequate structural means for promoting and preserving conditions conducive to the open society that have thus far been devised for industrialized societies with a high rate of literacy and social mobility" (*Beyond Ideology: The Revival of Political Theory* [New York: Harper and Row, 1967], p. 232).

could be instructively examined, but enough has been suggested for my purposes.

Despite my basic agreement with much of this realist-pluralist interpretation and justification of democracy, I must admit to having a few serious reservations, the primary one being that realism in combination with pluralism tends to correspond to, and even nourish, an ethos that vindicates the expression of private interests rather than the pursuit of the public or common good.[76] While I do not deny the importance of that expression in struggling for one's due in the expectation of compromise leading to justice, such an interpretation cannot adequately represent and support the common good. Not all the problems faced by modern societies are those of distributive injustice; critical problems such as public order, the natural environment, and foreign policy require a different interpretation and direction. It is possible, then, to recognize and support the institutional achievements of liberal democracy (such as toleration and majority rule) while wondering whether the system has allowed expression to some of the highest reaches of the human spirit.[77]

Another level of argument is more urgent from my standpoint, since one can never simply equate democratic theory and democratic practice without a careful examination of what is taking place. It is possible to agree that democracy is justified, whether from the standpoint of Christian realism or some other position, and yet to deny that any existing order which unfurls the banner of democracy really embodies or even approximates that ideal. Thus, the question of the descriptive accuracy—in contrast to the normative

76. See Joseph Tussman, *Obligation and the Body Politic;* Robert Paul Wolff, *The Poverty of Liberalism* (Boston: Beacon, 1968), chap. 4, "Tolerance"; as well as themes in the Roman Catholic natural law tradition.
77. Dante Germino, *Beyond Ideology: The   Revival of Political Theory,* p. 227.

adequacy—of democratic theory is absolutely fundamental, and it converges with the question of the relevance of the fair play model to current democratic life in industrial societies.

Some important factors to consider are the accountability and responsiveness of the government to the will of the people and the capacity of the electorate to make discerning judgments. According to many critics, both factors must be judged negatively because democracy has been derailed. The structure of modern industrial society, as Herbert Marcuse sees it, "rigs the rules of the game"[78] so that it abrogates any obligation to play the democratic game by its rules. While democracy should be "an open play of forces," it is presently clogged and even closed because of the way its rules and procedures are rigged. Although some critics assert that a conspiracy exists, others attribute the difficulty to "background limitations" that predetermine the responses of citizens by establishing a certain frame of mind and values. Under such conditions, abstract and indiscriminate tolerance necessarily becomes repressive and discriminate tolerance in favor of the status quo. Despite formal impartiality, radical alternatives simply cannot get a hearing because tolerance of all ideas does not work in a democracy which has a "totalitarian organization."

Thus, Marcuse calls for discriminate tolerance, which would deny that all views have an equal right to be expressed and heard (e.g. opposition to the extension of social security) and which would tolerate the left rather than the right, for "there are movements that should not be tolerated if an improvement and pacification of human life is to be at-

78. Herbert Marcuse, "Repressive Tolerance," in Robert Paul Wolff, et al., *A Critique of Pure Tolerance* (Boston: Beacon, 1965), p. 92; Marcuse, *One-Dimensional Man* (Boston: Beacon, paperbound, 1966), pp. 256–57.

tained."[79] In the present context, he maintains, it is necessary to have negative, critical thinking expressed by the radical students and intellectuals who have little patience with the tolerance and compromises of the democratic game. Seymour M. Lipset sees

an international revolutionary movement of students and youth that expresses in almost unadulterated form the ethic of absolute ends. These youths are almost completely uninhibited and uncontrolled, since they have no relations to the parties and organizations that have some sort of interest in adhering to the rules of the game and accept the need for compromise. Their politics is often expressive rather than instrumental. The New Left groups also have no clear concept of any road to power, of a way of effecting major social change. They are ready and willing to use tactics that violate the normal democratic game.[80]

Marcuse's view is obviously more subtle than most theories of conspiracy; but its description of what takes place in pluralistic democracy oversimplifies the facts, mainly because of his predisposition (and that of radicals generally) to conclude that unjust and evil laws and policies, and continued support for them by the people, indicate that "someone somewhere"—or at least general conditions—so confine and limit the people that they cannot make a truly free judgment. This predisposition is grounded in the radical's inveterate confidence in the goodness of man, which leads him to construe what is happening in peculiar ways. Thus, one self-described young radical writes.

79. Herbert Marcuse, *Five Lectures* (Boston: Beacon, 1970), p. 99.
80. Seymour M. Lipset, "The Possible Effects of Student Activism on International Politics," *Students in Revolt,* ed. Seymour M. Lipset and Philip G. Altbach (Boston: Houghton Mifflin, 1969), p. 512.

The Silent Majority do not bother me, for they are good. They are disturbed and angered by someone dropping a two-ounce bomb in Alexander's, but if there were freedom of the press in this country and they were fairly informed, I believe they would realize the proportion between a two-ounce bomb going off in Alexander's and the two tons of U.S. bombs that have been dropped every minute for the last four years in Vietnam. If allowed, they would be proportionately outraged.[81]

But it is difficult, if not impossible, to make the case that sufficient information and opposing value judgments about Vietnam have been unavailable to the American people. Indeed, it may be necessary to renounce absolute faith in the goodness of the people and their capacity to choose rightly rather than to try to make all incidents conform to it. More fundamental questions in this connection, however, are: whether one is willing to sacrifice the institutional machinery of democracy, including toleration, in order to achieve the ends that Marcuse and others propose; and whether one would be willing to accept the alternative structures that he presents only in outline form, for those structures are projected on the basis of a view of man that is far removed from the realism of Reinhold Niebuhr.[82]

While I am convinced that we need to nourish an ethos of democratic participation that will take us beyond pluralism to a certain extent, especially by emphasizing the common good, I do not think that such parts of the institutional

81. Gregory H. C. Knox, "Notes of a Young Radical," *Saturday Review* (August 15, 1970): 49.

82. In addition to Marcuse's discussion of toleration, see *An Essay on Liberation* (Boston: Beacon, 1969), pp. 79–91. Again, I do not deny the legitimacy of certain complaints about pluralism—indeed I accept some of them. For a fuller discussion of the issues involved in contemporary debates about pluralism, see William E. Connolly, ed., *The Bias of Pluralism* (New York: Atherton, 1969).

machinery of democracy as toleration and majority rule must be dismantled. Many contemporary critics are too willing to sacrifice democracy's rules and procedures in order to achieve their ends, since they contend that certain results are more important than preserving the game itself. But many of them seem to be laboring under a fundamental misconception about democracy, which views the failure to achieve certain ends in the political process as conclusive evidence that the system is not functioning properly. In fact, however, democracy refers primarily to just *procedures* rather than just results, which explains why unjust laws can be passed and evil policies enacted in a basically just system. Although the Constitution establishes certain boundaries (such as freedom of speech) that cannot be ignored in achieving political ends and affords some broad directions, democracy is defined more by method than content, procedure than substance, how than what. If someone contends that our most important goals and aims could be achieved more efficiently within another governmental framework, he should not try to make his case on democratic grounds, for there is a distinction between democracy and good government, although the democrat holds that the latter can best be realized through the former.[83]

The fact that a constitutional democracy does not guarantee that any particular ends will be achieved helps to explain how there can be a moral obligation to obey unjust laws. The issue now is neither a rejection of the ideal of democracy nor a denial that the existing political order is basically democratic, but rather that a particular law or policy jars with democracy and its underlying patterns of justice. Basic to my argument is the realization that a just constitution and a set of procedures do not ensure that an

83. Henry B. Mayo, *An Introduction to Democratic Theory* (New York: Oxford University Press, 1960), chaps. 1 and 2.

individual's own interpretation of justice will prevail in the public forum, or that he will be in the majority. In such a context, civil disobedience and obedience can be viewed "as part of the broader problem of the political role of minority groups in a nation dedicated, in general, to the principle of majority rule."[84] Because other citizens have submitted to this system, which would not have survived without general submission, and because I have accepted the benefits of their restricted liberty, it would be unfair for me to violate the laws and policies which (at least indirectly in a representative democracy) are the results of majority decision according to the procedures of this relatively just system. Rawls contends that submission to a democratic constitution involves acceptance of the principle of majority rule:

> In agreeing to a democratic constitution (as an instance of imperfect procedural justice) one accepts at the same time the principle of majority rule. Assuming that the constitution is just and that we have accepted and plan to continue to accept its benefits, we then have both an obligation and a natural duty (and in any case the duty) to comply with what the majority enacts even though it may be unjust. In this way we become bound to follow unjust laws, not always, of course, but provided that the injustice does not exceed certain limits. We recognize that we must run the risk of suffering from the defects of one another's sense of justice; this burden we are prepared to carry as long as it is more or less evenly distributed or does not weigh too heavily.[85]

One's obligation to obey unjust laws stems from the fact that,

84. Francis Allen, "Civil Disobedience and the Legal Order," part 2, *University of Cincinnati Law Review* 36 (Spring 1967): 188.
85. Rawls, "The Justification of Civil Disobedience," in Bedau, *CD,* p. 245.

in doing so, one shares the burdens, risks, and restrictions of cooperation in a project of fallible men whose sense of justice is not sharply honed and is frequently dulled by their propensity toward injustice.

One interpreter has criticized the use of the fair play model on the grounds that it is "pertinent only under certain highly idealized conditions."[86] Without discussing all the ramifications of this point, I would suggest that rather than being idealized and thus unreal, the conditions for using the fair play model to illuminate political obligation in contemporary democracies are minimal and are generally present unless the democratic machinery is so clogged that a *revolution* is indicated. I do not, of course, suggest that disobedience is never justified unless revolution is warranted; I am only trying to establish the basis of this obligation to obey the law in a democracy without, at this point, trying to determine its limits or when it can be overridden.

Some arguments that the model of fair play is to a great extent irrelevant stem from the assumption that each particular law has to distribute burdens and restrictions equally or fairly before obedience to it is obligatory. Thus, Joseph Ellin denies that the fair play model is "a reasonably close model of law," "since it would seem that a large body of law, and notably criminal law, prohibits conduct to which only a small minority are tempted and so cannot be understood as mutual forbearance for mutual gain."[87] Among his examples are laws which set age requirements for drinking liquor and those which impose restrictions on resident aliens. But such an interpretation overlooks the way the fair play argument deals with the system as a whole rather than each particular law. A tax law that imposes an unfair burden on certain economic classes might still create an obligation

86. Ellin, "Fidelity to Law," pp. 430–31, n. 6.
87. Ibid., pp. 417–18.

based on fair play because of its existence within a relatively just system and because of all the other factors that I have stressed in relation to fair play. The same point would hold for unfair draft selection, for in contrast to some arguments from natural law which are concerned primarily, if not exclusively, with the justice of a particular law in dealing with obedience and disobedience, this argument from fair play considers the relatively just system as a whole and the internal relations between citizens within it. What is at issue is the sharing of the burdens of the cooperative enterprise as a whole, although certainly particular laws may be so grossly inequitable, unfair, and unjust that one's obligation to them in nullified.

While many political philosophers recognize that a democracy imposes on its citizens a greater duty of obedience than other political orders, their explanations of this stronger obligation vary greatly. It is possible to argue, as Sidney Hook does, that the obligation to obey unjust laws in a democratic state is a *political* rather than a *directly moral* obligation since it is part of the commitment that one makes as a democrat, although it is, of course, not absolutely binding. He compares it to accepting an umpire's decision.[88] For him, consistency with one's democratic "onlook" may rule out much disobedience to law.

Other theorists stress that a democracy's amenability to internal changes through argument and legal political action increases the obligation to obey its laws. This emphasis appears in Paul Ramsey's interpretation of democracy as institutionalized resistance:

in democratic societies, the moral right to resist and not co-operate with injustice takes form in the various legal

88. Sidney Hook, "Law, Justice, and Obedience," in Hook, *L & P*, p. 57; cf. chap. 3 of Hook's *The Paradoxes of Freedom*.

ways in which citizens may engage in changing the law.
In this sense, democracy means justifiable and limited
resistance. . . . The operation in any legal system of procedures for transforming the law and thus to resist and
not ultimately accept or co-operate with evil or injustice
emphasizes all the more the duty every citizen has to
observe and obey the law.[89]

Because both views—the one stressing political commitment
and the other stressing institutionalization of resistance—
focus on important features of the citizen's relation to the
democratic state, it is possible to appreciate their force without admitting that they fully account for this increased obligation. For a fuller account the model of fair play is useful.

Still other points need to be made about unjust laws in a
relatively just democracy. First, at least by implication, I
have suggested that decisions about obedience and disobedience in an unjust system depend on considerations other
than fair play and, of course, involve the possibility of revolution. Even within a relatively just system, the existence of
unjust laws and policies seems to call into question the
quality of the system as a whole, for at some point the in-
justices in laws and policies can become so bad, and perhaps
so numerous, that they indicate an unjust system. When a
person seriously asks what he ought to do (obey, civilly disobey, revolt, etc.) in a crisis of state, he will often consider
whether a putatively unjust policy such as the military involvement of the United States in Vietnam indicates that the
system is corrupt, whether countless abortive efforts to alter
it further suggest that the system is not capable of redemption, and whether, therefore, any obligation to obey the system's laws is abrogated. Although it is impossible to indi-

89. Ramsey, *Christian Ethics and the Sit-In*, p. 93; cf. Carritt, *Morals
and Politics*, p. 215.

cate precisely the point at which unjust laws, considered both qualitatively and quantitatively, symbolize and signify that the system is unjust, that does not mean such a point does not exist. From the standpoint of individuals and groups, systematic exclusion from the benefits and responsibilities of the political order cancels any obligation based on fair play, as shown in my earlier example about Negroes in a southern state, although other moral and prudential reasons may preclude revolution and even demand obedience.

Second, although the obligation based on fair play stems from relationships and transactions rather than the content of particular laws, nothing in my argument implies that this content is an absolutely open matter or that all forms of conduct can become obligatory because of fair play. Because political obligation depends less on the nature of the conduct required by the law than on the relationships between citizens, it exhibits what Hart calls "independence of content," although this independence is not absolute.[90] While I shall discuss in the next chapter conditions under which one may justifiably break the law, I now want to examine the possibility that certain acts cannot become obligatory even within the context I have sketched. An example from the area of promises will suffice.

Since the obligation derives from the promise itself rather than *what* is promised, there is independence of content. I think we would deny, however, that by making a promise someone can take on an obligation to kill an innocent person; thus no one has an obligation to the Mafia to kill an innocent person simply because he has promised to do so to save his own life or in exchange for a favor. In such a case,

90. Hart, "Legal and Moral Obligation," in Melden, *Essays in Moral Philosophy,* p. 100. Of course, I have in view primarily laws which do not depend for their moral weight on other principles such as the moral prohibition of killing.

no obligation is involved because the promise is voided or invalidated. As Hart suggests, "Morals like law may have principles of 'public policy' and render 'void' a promise that involved from the start doing something patently immoral."[91] The question of the limits on the independence of content was raised in a critical way in the discussion of the significance of loyalty oaths to Hitler during the Nazi era.[92]

In principle, it is clear that there is no absolute independence of content in political obligation, but in practice it is very difficult to specify the kinds of laws and acts that are excluded. Thus Rawls insists that we have an obligation to obey unjust laws "within limits," but he fails to delineate these limits.[93] For beyond such obvious limits as killing an innocent person and some of the restrictions of the Constitution, specification is practically impossible, although the question becomes critical in morally serious inquiries as to whether one should obey or disobey. This question, of course, often converges with the previous question about whether and when an unjust law signifies an unjust system and hence allows the cancellation of obligation, at least as based on fair play.

A third major question concerns the stringency of political obligation based on fair play. To this point I have concentrated on the conditions and lineaments of such an obligation rather than its stringency and weight. If the conditions that I have described engender an obligation, such an obligation is not absolute, for it does not bind one to obey the law under all circumstances. One can describe the duty of fair play and any obligations based on it as prima facie. It may

91. Ibid., p. 102.
92. Gallin, *German Resistance to Hitler*, pp. 139 ff.
93. Rawls, "The Justification of Civil Disobedience," in Bedau, *CD*, p. 245.

well be in a given situation that the claim from other citizens that we obey the law on grounds of fair play seems legitimate but also that it conflicts with the claim that we engage in effective, even if civilly disobedient, action to alter a particular governmental policy that appears to be unjust. Both of these are prima facie rather than actual obligations because they indicate features of an act that catch our attention and make it appear to be right or wrong. Fulfilling promises is prima facie obligatory although it may not be *actually* obligatory because of its other features (e.g. violation of a debt of gratitude). W. D. Ross, one of the foremost defenders of this mode of reasoning, thinks that he can show that the so-called conflict of duties is nonexistent, for "while an act may well be *prima facie* obligatory in respect of one characteristic and *prima facie* forbidden in virtue of another, it becomes obligatory or forbidden only in virtue of the totality of its ethically relevant characteristics."[94]

Beyond the fact that it is not an absolute obligation, a prima facie obligation to obey the law, based on fair play, may be interpreted in at least two different ways.[95] One could say that the actual fact of disobedience is always relevant—that when the conditions of fair play are given, there is an obligation to obey the law, although it can be outweighed and overridden by other prima facie obligations. On the other hand, one could say that *considering* the fact of disobedience is always relevant. The first, stronger claim is the one I want to make. Thus, an act of disobedience that takes place in a nexus of claims including the conditions which establish obligations based on fair play, *tends* to be wrong. Under such conditions, the fact that the act infringes

94. Ross, *Foundations of Ethics,* p. 86.
95. Richard Wasserstrom, "The Obligation to Obey the Law," *U.C.L.A. Law Review* 10, no. 4 (May 1963): 783–84.

a law counts against it. Departure from a prima facie obligation requires justification.

An alternative to viewing political obligation based on fair play as prima facie has been proposed by H. L. A. Hart, who suggests that the distinction between prima facie and actual obligations obscures what is at stake in moral decisions. As he sees it, what is at stake can best be expressed in the language of the "lesser of two moral evils," of sacrificing an obligation for the sake of a greater good, for there is no contradiction in saying, "I *ought not* to do it though I *have an obligation to him* to do it."[96] Stating the issues in terms of a sacrifice rather than a net or actual obligation may remind us of the difficult moral decisions that have to be made in obedience and disobedience. Nevertheless, I shall continue to use the language of prima facie and actual obligations in order to stress that some obligations may override others. Thus one can speak of an actual obligation *despite* two or more prima facie obligations, though it may well be that when we reach the end of our moral tether we can only say "here are two moral obligations, one of which has to be sacrificed."

My contention, then, is that the duty of fair play is essential to interpreting political obligation in a relatively just constitutional democracy, although it alone is *not sufficient* for decisions about obedience since other prima facie obligations may conflict with it. Just what my argument that the act of political obedience itself is an *act of justice or fairness (fair play)* actually means, can best be indicated through an examination of civil disobedience and its justification.

96. Hart, "Are There Any Natural Rights?" *Philosophical Review* 64 (1955): 186.

IV

THE JUSTIFICATION OF CIVIL DISOBEDIENCE

CIVIL DISOBEDIENCE AND MORAL JUSTIFICATION

For a variety of reasons many contemporary theologians are very suspicious of any attempt to talk about the justification of resistance.[1] Several, including Walter Künneth and Helmut Thielicke, have so great a fear of legalism in the sense of self-righteousness that they deny the place of ethical justification. To try to justify an act is to try to make oneself righteous, but righteousness is a gift from God. Thus, Künneth, as I have indicated, takes this religious problem and draws a distinction between the ethical *possibility (Möglichkeit)* and the ethical *justification (Rechtfertigung)* of re-

---

1. In this chapter I am concentrating on ethical justification rather than ethical decision-making. Yet this distinction is not a separation, for these two processes are intimately interconnected. Justification has the ring of ex post facto reasoning, but it may also be prospective, as in the case of a person trying to determine which course of action is the right one to take in protesting a certain law. He examines the morally relevant features of the act and tries to assess their significance separately and collectively. I do not suggest that decision-making involves only this rational, justificatory process (see James M. Gustafson, "Moral Discernment in the Christian Life," in *Norm and Context in Christian Ethics,* ed. Gene H. Outka and Paul Ramsey [New York: Scribner's, 1968], pp. 17–36). But the arguments, reasons, and guides that are used in justification are also used in deliberation, which is preparation for decision-making.

sistance. Man in the political sphere must be directed, not toward a moral justification but toward grace alone, as the forgiveness of sin, which provides the possibility of resistance.[2] For Karl Barth, on the other hand, the possibility of resistance comes through a "pure heart and clean hands and untroubled conscience," which result from an awareness of the divine command in the situation.[3] While he does not deny that ethical reasoning about the constant direction of the divine command has a place, he eventually finds this constancy to be secondary to the uniqueness of the command in each situation. Neither Barth nor Künneth believes that action can be ethically justified. For Barth such justification is replaced by an inner certainty of God's command; for Künneth it is replaced by an assurance of religious justification.

Not only fear of legalism and an effort to preserve God's sovereign freedom prompt theologians to view ethical justification as both dangerous and ultimately impossible. Much of the contemporary discussion about context and principles revolves around the question of whether there can be any moral code that will adequately cover practical situations. It also voices the widespread suspicion that justification is almost synonymous with rationalization and that man's greatest peril is a false sense of security.

2. *Das Widerstandsrecht als theologisch-ethisches Problem* (Munich: Claudius-Verlag, 1954), p. 17; "Die heutige Position-theologisch," in *Widerstandsrecht und Grenzen der Staatsgewalt,* ed. Bernhard Pfister and Gerhard Hildmann (Berlin: Duncker und Humblot, 1956), pp. 100, 121. Jacques Ellul also writes: "I even say that it is not so much violence itself as justification of violence that is unacceptable to Christian faith." (*Violence,* trans. Cecelia Gaul Kings, [New York: Seabury, 1969], p. 140). Sometimes Künneth speaks of a duty of resistance, although he still denies that resistance can be justified (Pfister and Hildmann, *Widerstandsrecht,* pp. 99–100). But, as Martin Rock suggests, it is difficult to understand how there can be a duty of resistance and yet no justified resistance. (Rock, *Widerstand gegen die Staatsgewalt,* p. 41; see p. 204, n. 81).

3. Barth, *Church Dogmatics,* vol. 3, pt. 4, p. 450.

The task of justification can be clarified by distinguishing between three terms: justify, excuse, and explain. To explain an act is to locate and present its cause, which perhaps will be discussed in terms of the agent's motives: for example, he committed the crime because he needed money. To say that an act is excused is to say that it is wrong, but that because of some special circumstances the agent is not responsible and hence not guilty: for example, the plea of insanity may be accepted as an excuse in a murder case. If, however, a plea of necessary self-defense is made, it is a justifying rather than an excusing reason; for the claim is that while the act would normally have been bad or unlawful, this circumstance has rendered it good, or at least permissible. "When a merely excusing circumstance is present, then, the act remains objectively immoral, but the agent is not guilty, because not responsible; whereas when a justifying circumstance is present, the agent is perfectly responsible, but his act is rendered objectively lawful."[4]

Justification is demanded only when there is some reason to think that an act is bad or wrong. Usually there is a conflict between a particular act and a rule, or more generally a conflict of duties. Justification consists not only of giving reasons for the act in question but also of showing that they outweigh the reasons against it. Civil disobedience must be justified, if my argument in the last chapter is correct, because there is a prima facie obligation to obey the law, at least within certain contexts. Any act that involves infringement of the law thus requires justification.

To whom is this justification directed? Who demands it? It is a part of what it means to be a social being. A person offers reasons for his actions, including civil disobedience, when they are subject to some dispute on moral grounds.

4. Eric D'Arcy, *Human Acts: An Essay in their Moral Evaluation* (Oxford: Clarendon, 1963), p. 81.

He builds his case before several different groups: government officials, fellow-citizens, collaborators in disobedience, and ultimately his own conscience. Perhaps this task of justification is more imperative for civil disobedience in a democracy than for many other acts that also apparently violate obligations because, at least in some of its forms, it is an act of communication which appeals to the community to view certain moral-political questions in a new light and to respond accordingly. Civil disobedience is thus intimately connected with justification. For example, one tries to show how significant one's cause is for the body politic, but this is only one of several levels that may be involved in justification. Richard McCormick indicates that "morally justifiable" means

> that a person (or persons) has submitted to the processes of justification demanded of any socially responsible person. It does not mean, because of its complexity and prudential character, certainly that the protest is objectively justifiable.[5]

One must, of course, distinguish between the rational justification offered by the philosopher or theologian and everyday justification.[6] The former deals with the question of civil disobedience in general terms (e.g. what *case* can be made for civil disobedience?), whereas the latter focuses on the immediate problem of obeying or disobeying this law. But such a distinction must not obscure the ways in which the framework of justification developed by the ethicist, whether theological or philosophical, can illuminate everyday justification.

5. Richard McCormick, "Notes on Moral Theology," *Theological Studies* 30, no. 4 (December 1969): 671.

6. Robert S. Summers, "Legal Philosophy Today—An Introduction," *Essays in Legal Philosophy*, ed. Robert S. Summers (Berkeley: University of California Press, 1968), pp. 5–6.

It is impossible for the ethicist or anyone else to construct a "principle, a code, a theory" that will determine the necessary and sufficient conditions of justified civil disobedience. As Ernest van den Haag rightly insists, "We cannot state a principle of sufficient specificity and generality to permit us to deduce from it when to follow law and when not to obey it."[7] The alternative is not to eschew this task of ethics by simply allowing a situational grasp of the right action, whether it be from intuition or a divine command; for it *is* possible to delineate some principles and procedures for the justification of civil disobedience. These cannot be employed mechanically, and furthermore there will be disagreement at practically every point about the values and norms and their relevance to a particular situation. Nevertheless, these principles and procedures highlight certain questions that cannot be avoided in any responsible assessment of civil disobedience in a constitutional democracy whose basic structure is generally just and to whose citizens one has an obligation based on the duty of fair play. If these questions have the aura of common sense, it is because they are simply specifications, for civil disobedience, of the criteria that are appropriate for any act.

The justification of civil disobedience involves several steps.[8] The first is to justify the cause, which usually consists of showing that a law or policy is unjust or that certain conditions in the society need to be rectified. Second, one must determine whether disobedience is justified by inquiring whether the obligation to obey the law is overridden or canceled. Third, even if disobedience is justified, one must try

7. Ernest van den Haag, "Government, Conscience, and Disobedience," pp. 110–11.
8. My present formulation of these four steps is indebted to the excellent study by Leslie J. MacFarlane, "Justifying Political Disobedience," *Ethics* 79, no. 1 (Oct. 1968): 24–55. Cf. also, Rock, *Christ und Revolution*, pp. 128 ff.

to determine the forms it may take or means it may employ, e.g. whether disobedience should be coercive or persuasive and whether any particular forms of action are ruled out (e.g. the direct provocation of police attack). Finally, one must justify the probable consequences—not merely the direct but also the indirect and obliquely intentional consequences. Although the critical questions of order and success enter here, it is important to note that they appear only after several other points have been established. This arrangement is especially significant, as too many theologians make order the primary consideration.

The artificiality of separating these steps should be evident. Certainly steps two and three must be considered together, since some forms of resistance, such as those involving submission to arrest and punishment, may affect the charge that an obligation is being infringed. However, these steps are arranged serially so that the justification of each step depends on the justification of the previous one.[9] They indicate only formal procedures and questions which must be applied concretely to particular acts of disobedience in particular sorts of state. Thus, my discussion of canceling or overriding the obligation to obey the law will depend on my interpretation of fair play as at least one basis of that obligation within a relatively just democratic state. The limits and possibilities of such an endeavor should be clear: "while general ethical reasoning cannot by itself *prove*, it may *help* us to see that an action is wrong."[10] Acts are more or less justified according to the various features they present, but there is rarely an absolute yes or no, particularly in matters as complex as civil disobedience.

9. Cf. MacFarlane, "Justifying Political Disobedience," *Ethics* 79, no. 1 (Oct. 1968): 53.
10. A. C. Ewing, *The Individual, the State and World Government*, p. 4. Author's italics.

In light of this four-step pattern, I shall examine civil disobedience in relation to the charge of unfairness, its forms and means (e.g. direct and indirect, coercive and educative), and its consequences (e.g. the debates about political effectiveness and disorder). Before I develop these arguments, however, two points should be made. First, in concentrating on civil disobedience, I do not assume that other illegal acts which fall outside its boundaries (such as illegal abortions) cannot be justified. My concentration on civil disobedience is simply an effort both to narrow the range of illegal acts for my discussion and, at the same time, to deal with an important phenomenon in contemporary democratic life which raises distinctive problems of justification, especially in relation to theories of political obligation. Furthermore, as I indicated in chapter 1, I am most interested in civil disobedience as a political act which attempts to effect change by communication and persuasion or other forms of force rather than as a witness to one's personal values or as a test case. The other points I made about the ambit of civil disobedience in chapter 1 also hold for this discussion.

Second, I shall comment only briefly on the first major step —the justification of the cause—which is, of course, fundamental to any justification of civil disobedience. In the course of this discussion, I give little direct attention to the determination of unjust or immoral laws and policies, or to the causes for which one might violate admittedly valid and just laws, in order to focus attention on another question: once the actor thinks that some laws or policies or states of affairs violate moral-political standards, what *other* factors are required for justification of civil disobedience? Such a question is important because it is easy to move from an enthusiastic endorsement of goals to an uncritical endorsement of means, as was evident in the civil rights movement in the early 1960s, and it is likely that the current acceptability of civil disobedience as a means of political action is partially due to its earlier association with such goals as civil rights.

But civil disobedience for even the most worthy causes and objectives raises moral and not merely tactical questions. In defending, for example, the attempted voyage of the *Golden Rule* into the United States' nuclear testing area in the Pacific, the first task is to demonstrate the legitimacy of the cause (opposition to nuclear weapons in general and nuclear testing in particular), although the legitimacy of the cause alone does not permit one to conclude that civil disobedience is justified.[11] While the same argument applies to other causes, the first task in justifying civil disobedience is to show how a particular law (e.g. the draft law), a particular policy (e.g. U.S. involvement in Vietnam), or a state of affairs (e.g. racism) demands rectification. Obviously such an argument will draw on general moral-political standards in order to show that the objective is both worthy and imperative. It will also involve many assumptions about social and political affairs; for instance, in the case of the voyage of the *Golden Rule*, assumptions were made about the place of nuclear

---

11. As Howard Zinn seems to imply (*Disobedience and Democracy*, passim). My position stresses the necessity of justifying disobedience when there is a conflict between one's moral principles and the obligation to obey the law. An opposing position is defended by Michael Walzer, who states that "men have a prima facie obligation to honor the engagements they have explicitly made, to defend the groups and uphold the ideals to which they have committed themselves, even against the state, so long as their disobedience of laws or legally authorized commands does not threaten the very existence of the larger society or endanger the lives of its citizens. It is obedience to the state, when one has a duty to disobey, that must be justified." ("The Obligation to Disobey," *Ethics* 77 [April 1967]: 170–71). This essay is reprinted in Walzer's *Obligations: Essays on Disobedience, War, and Citizenship*, where he somewhat qualifies this claim: "*Sometimes* it is obedience to the state, when one has a duty to disobey, that must be justified" (p. 17, italics mine).

weapons in a world of conflict and especially about the whole question of deterrence.[12]

Although I do not develop its ramifications, I do emphasize the justification of the cause, since some proponents and opponents of civil disobedience think that if it is justified for any one objective, then it is justified for all. Such an assertion includes several confused claims. One is an empirical claim that when civil disobedience becomes accepted as a major technique of political action, it is utilized for unworthy as well as worthy ends. I shall discuss this claim later. Another claim, made on logical grounds, is that anyone who justifies civil disobedience on behalf of one cause has to justify it for all. Such a claim simply does not hold. There is a clear difference between justifying civil disobedience on behalf of civil rights and justifying it on behalf of oppressing a minority group, and to justify the former is not to justify the latter. I shall return to this point when I discuss the generalization argument.

CIVIL DISOBEDIENCE AND THE PRINCIPLE OF FAIRNESS

A most significant question is how civil disobedience (which is open, nonviolent, and submissive) relates to the duty of fair play, which establishes the obligation of obedience even to some unjust laws. The central feature of civil disobedience from the standpoint of this question is submission to arrest

12. For a discussion of the *Golden Rule*, see Albert S. Bigelow, *The Voyage of the Golden Rule* (New York: Doubleday, 1959) and excerpts in Lillian Schlissel, ed., *Conscience in America* (New York: Dutton, 1968), pp. 350–61. See also Bigelow, "Why I Am Sailing into the Pacific Bomb-Test Area," *Liberation* (Feb. 1958), reprinted in Staughton Lynd, ed., *Nonviolence in America: A Documentary History* (New York: Bobbs-Merrill, 1966), pp. 340–47 and in Bedau, *CD*, pp. 146–52. For the similar voyage of the *Phoenix*, see Earle Reynolds, *Forbidden Voyage* (New York: McKay, 1961) and excerpts in Schlissel, ibid., pp. 362–75.

and punishment. While some contend that the civil disobedient does not really reject his obligation to obey the law, based on fair play, because he accepts the penalty for his act, others argue that submission alone does not fulfill the obligation of obedience.

Although the issues are drastically oversimplified when submission is viewed as *the* justification for civil disobedience, Darnell Rucker makes such an argument: *"the justification* [of civil disobedience] rests on the individual agent's choice to submit to the coercive force of the law instead of acting against his interest or his conscience in accordance with the law."[13] Those who deny that an illegal act can be justified by the disobedient's acceptance of the legal consequences often use extreme examples to show the absurdity of the argument. These encompass acts that are quite different from civil disobedience, including, for example, the assassination of a president and turning in false fire alarms—presumably regardless of motivation so long as the actor accepts the legal consequences.[14] But to hold that submission is important in justifying civil disobedience is not to imply that it sanctions all forms of disobedience. In addition to conceptual points (such as the criterion of nonviolence which would exclude assassination from civil disobedience), one must emphasize that the material end, the consequences, and so forth are indispensable for justification. Furthermore, most civil disobedients do include such considerations rather than simply advancing submission as "their only justification," as Kennan seems to claim.

The issues in this debate, then, must be sharpened and re-

13. Darnell Rucker, "The Moral Grounds of Civil Disobedience," *Ethics* 76 (1965–66): 144. Italics mine.
14. See MacFarlane, "Justifying Political Disobedience," *Ethics* 79, no. 1 (Oct. 1968): 36, and George Kennan, *Democracy and the Student Left* (New York: Bantam, 1968), p. 16.

fined before any progress can be made, for submission to arrest and punishment may well mitigate certain charges even if it cannot be regarded as a sufficient justification for disobedience. A central issue is whether submission can rebut the charge that civil disobedience is unfair. In dealing with this issue, it is necessary to consider both the actor's intention and the balance of freedom and restrictions in the democratic state.

Unfair play is often defined so as to highlight the actor's intention and motive. Thus it is claimed that one acts unfairly in breaking the rule of a practice "with the intention of doing so for the benefit of oneself, when one knows (or has good reason to believe) that one's personal benefit is only made possible by the efforts and restraints, sacrifices and burdens, hardships and inconveniences of others."[15] If this is the proper description of unfair play, the civil disobedient's moral-political appeals stressing what is good for the state or society would stand positively against the charge that he is concerned only about his own personal advantage. Furthermore, submission adds to the act an element of personal sacrifice that may indicate the disobedient's bona fides, especially by demonstrating resolution and conscientiousness even in the wake of adverse circumstances. For this reason, H. B. Acton contends that "when disobedience is accompanied by submission to legal penalties the distinction between ambition and personal integrity is marked as closely as it can be."[16] Often, however, self-interest (e.g. avoiding being killed in war) may merge with genuine moral-political convictions about the injustice of the war, and in such instances imprisonment may seem preferable to induction on *both* grounds. Nevertheless, Acton's point holds: the act of submissive dis-

15. Lyons, *Utilitarianism,* p. 176.
16. H. B. Acton, "Political Justification," in Bedau, *CD,* p. 233.

obedience shows the most precise distinction between self-interest and conscientiousness, in ourselves as well as others.

A second and even more important consideration is the mutuality of freedom and restrictions between participants in a practice, which, following Hart, I made a fundamental element in the obligation to obey the law based on fair play. Some contend that the civil disobedient by the act of submission restricts his freedom, preserves the mutuality of restrictions, and thereby avoids the charge of unfair play. He "takes and pays, and thus affirms, rather than overrides, the duty of fair play."[17] He cannot be charged with "free riding" or "free loading." This point is sometimes combined with the argument that the civil disobedient contributes substantially to society in other ways, perhaps even excelling the efforts of most other citizens.[18] But neither argument is finally adequate for reasons that can be expounded in relation to two points: (1) a judgment of unfair play does not require that harmful effects, even increasing the burdens of others, be present, and (2) a problematical view of law seems to underlie many interpretations of civil disobedience as fulfilling the duty of fair play through submission.

The argument that submission does not counter the charge of unfair play does not depend on showing that disobedience increases the burdens of other citizens; if it did depend on this point, it would resemble the argument from consequences. Someone might contend: "If there is one thing which any act of disobedience inevitably does, it is to increase the burdens which fall on all the law-abiding citizens. If someone disobeys

17. Milton Konvitz, "Civil Disobedience and the Duty of Fair Play," Hook, *L & P*, p. 28. Rawls's failure to take account of the specific description of civil disobedience in his major essay in this symposium created some of the difficulties of interpretation; this failure is overcome in his later essay, "The Justification of Civil Disobedience," in Bedau, *CD*.

18. See Richard Brandt, "Utility and the Obligation to Obey the Law," Hook, *L & P*, pp. 48 ff.

the law even for what seems to be the best of reasons, he inevitably makes it harder—in some quite concrete sense—on
everyone else."[19] Of course, it is possible to construct cases
for which this claim holds. A child's refusal to give adequate
support to his parents when it came his turn to do so could
possibly create hardship for them. If the government had to
raise a definite amount of money by taxation, the failure of
some citizens to contribute their share would increase the
amount required of others.[20] A more realistic concrete example can be drawn from the draft. Because the Selective Service
system must provide a certain number of men for a certain
period, a draftee who refuses induction makes it necessary in
a very concrete way for someone else to be drafted and in-
ducted. Furthermore, it is possible to argue that one of the
consequences of civil disobedience, at least on a broad scale,
would be an increase in police protection, cleanup services,
and so forth, and those costs would have to be borne by tax-
payers. One might well level the charge of unfair play in all
of these cases, but not because of the harmful effects on the
practice nor merely because of the increased burdens of
others. While the latter is a sufficient condition for a judgment of unfair play, it is not a necessary condition. Thus, those
who insist that the charge of unfair play draws its plausibility
from analogies with such cases miss part of its significance, as
the following example indicates.

An automobile with six passengers has stalled. It could be
moved by five of the passengers, and none of them has a
legitimate reason for being excused from the labor although
all are tired. One decides to pretend to push in order to get

19. Wasserstrom's statement of an argument which he does not necessarily support, "Obligation to Obey the Law," *UCLA Law Review* 10
(May 1963): 804.
20. On the second example, cf. ibid.; on the first, cf. Brandt, "Utility
and the Obligation to Obey the Law," in Hook, *L & P*, p. 49.

the others to work. He in no way undermines the enterprise; indeed, if he did not push, or at least pretend to push, perhaps no one else would. It may well be that in failing to push, he increases the load each of the other participants has to bear. But that factor is not necessary to the charge that he is acting unfairly, for if he neither harms others by increasing their burdens nor undermines the activity itself, we can still accuse him of acting unfairly.[21] He benefits from a practice but does not shoulder its burdens. It is not necessary to show, for example, either that I damage a lawn by crossing it late at night or that I thereby increase the burdens of others for the judgment of unfair play to be legitimate. Furthermore, contribution to the practice in another way (such as driving the car or operating a lawn mower) may not be sufficient to rebut this charge.

Several of those who argue that submission justifies civil disobedience also adhere to a theory—perhaps indebted to Justice Holmes—that the law merely presents the citizen with a choice: to obey or to accept the legal penalties prescribed for disobeying. Darnell Rucker defends this view: "Law presents (or should present) us with a clear alternative: obey this law or suffer this penalty. As rational beings, we have a choice with respect to the law as well as an obligation to the structure of law." In a similar vein, Harris Wofford insists "that a free man should look on each law not as a command but as a question, for implicit in each law is the alternative of obedience or of respectful civil disobedience and full acceptance of the consequences."[22] From such a perspective, both obedience and submissive disobedience are *obligation-meeting* actions, although neither is *obligatory*.[23]

21. The example is from Lyons, *Utilitarianism*, pp. 128–31, and passim.
22. Darnell Rucker, "Moral Grounds of Civil Disobedience," p. 143. Harris Wofford, Jr., "Non-Violence and the Law: The Law Needs Help," in Bedau, *CD*, p. 66.
23. For this distinction, see A. I. Melden, *Rights and Right Conduct* (Oxford: Blackwell, 1959), pp. 9 ff.

This theory stresses what some label purely penal law, whose crux is the contention that some overt acts are not *mala in se* but *mala prohibita*.[24] Traffic laws provide good examples of acts that are mala prohibita. A red light is on, but no traffic is coming on the cross-street in the early morning hours. Am I obligated to stop or only to pay the penalty if I am caught? Natural law theorists often deny that running a red light is an act that is mala prohibita because "it is factually impossible for an overt act that is important enough to be made the content of law, taken in its actual circumstances, not to have some relation to the common good."[25]

The theory of purely penal law is faulty, but not for the reasons that natural law theorists adduce—that is, not because each *law* (by definition) is positively related to the common good. The difference between many theories of natural law and the position I defend is evident, for I contend that there can be a moral obligation to obey a law which is externally related to it. My position stresses the distinction between a legal system and a particular law. Within a relatively just system, there may be an obligation based on fair play to obey particular laws that are even inefficient, inane, and unjust. It is not necessary to show that such laws are essential to the functioning of the system in order to establish an obligation

24. But it is not to be confused with penal law or penal statutes since, as Thomas E. Davitt, S.J. indicates, it "does not refer primarily to the fact that laws have penalties. Its main concern, rather, is with the way these law *oblige*. According to this theory, a purely penal law, such as a pure food and drug law is said to be, obliges not to the observance of the law but to the payment of penalties inflicted after violation. Since such laws oblige merely to the payment of penalties, they are called 'purely penal.'" *The Elements of Law* (Boston: Little, Brown, 1959), p. 189; cf. Franz Böckle, *Fundamental Concepts of Moral Theology*, p. 64.

25. Davitt, *Elements of Law*, p. 191: "Hence, in the light of the means-end relation of overt acts in their circumstances to the public good, the theory of purely penal law is wholly unintelligible." Cf. Messner, *Social Ethics*, chap. 49, especially pp. 299–300.

to obey them, although such an argument is probably necessary for those theological positions which base political obligation upon the maintenance of order.

My position, on the contrary, emphasizes the relationship between citizens within a generally just system, and within that framework it is impossible to maintain the view of law as presenting a choice. One's fellow citizens have a right to expect that deference to the law will be rendered not only by submission but by obedience, for their general obedience *(not* disobedience accompanied by submission) has sustained the practice. Thus a specific mode of cooperation is required. The obligation is to obey the law; this is the exchange rate, for which submission is inadequate payment. Furthermore, without doubt law confronts a citizen with an emphasis on "obey" rather than "take the consequences." Rather than an equal alternative, the latter is in part a threat to secure the former. Thus, both from the standpoint of the law itself and from the standpoint of the broader system of relationships and obligations, one must reject the view of law as a question, which supports the idea that submission fulfills the obligation to obey the law.

Although submission, then, may not rebut the charge of unfair play, it does perform several significant functions in civil disobedience and its justification. First, it may indicate the depth and intensity of the disobedient's convictions about his objectives, for he is willing to subordinate and even to sacrifice personal advantage to their attainment. Although submission is not an infallible index, as I have already indicated, certainly conscientiousness is suggested, at least in part, by the firm adherence to convictions even when personal difficulty arises. But this appeal to conscience, like submission itself, cannot be regarded as *the* justification of civil disobedience. Of course, in one sense anyone has to do what he thinks is his duty after examining all the relevant factors, but civil disobedience is not justified merely by pointing to an inconsistency between the content of the law and one's own conscience. Moral justification, as Sidney Hook insists, "is a matter of reasons not conscience."[26] The end, circumstances, and consequences must be assessed and presented as reasons. While justification perhaps cannot really proceed without conscientiousness, sincerity, and integrity, certainly such factors are only necessary rather than sufficient conditions.

As I have suggested, elements of nonviolence and publicity converge in submission although they cannot be reduced to it. All three features, but especially submission, help to keep civil disobedience within the system, even if only on its boundary. Except when civil disobedience is used as a preliminary tactic of revolution, submission may indicate the actor's bona fides, his dedication to the principles underlying the present political order, and his willingness to remain within the system. Thus, this feature keeps at least some forms of civil disobedience from being identified with and justified in the same way as revolution, either violent or nonviolent.

Other arguments must be considered, the first one having to do with submission as offering and indicating respect for the law. Submission involves what Ramsey calls "*conscientious* conscientious objection," which shows deference for the conscience of the law and the order it represents as well as one's own conscience.[27] Like Martin Luther King, the civil disobedient often believes "that he who openly disobeys a

26. Hook, "Social Protest and Civil Disobedience," Paul Kurtz, *Moral Problems in Contemporary Society,* p. 165. Cf. H. B. Acton, "Political Justification," in Bedau, *CD,* pp. 227 f.

27. *Christian Ethics and the Sit-In,* p. 84. For a good discussion of some of these issues (including submission) in relation to the stages of moral development, see Lawrence Kohlberg, "Education for Justice: A Modern Statement of the Platonic View," in *Moral Education,* with an introduction by Nancy F. and Theodore R. Sizer (Cambridge, Mass.: Harvard University Press, 1970), pp. 57–83.

law, a law conscience tells him is unjust, and then willingly accepts the penalty, gives evidence thereby that he so respects that law that he belongs in jail until it is changed." King also contended that his disobedience could be sharply distinguished from that of the segregationist whose behavior would lead to anarchy; for, according to King, open and submissive disobedience of an allegedly unjust law "is in reality expressing the highest respect for law."[28] Such claims have been impugned on the grounds that they embody a very limited and even odd view of respect and disrespect. I shall ignore arguments which hold that respect for law is rendered by obedience to "higher laws" in order to concentrate on the more substantial questions of open and submissive disobedience. One criticism of King's view is that the difference between respect and disrespect is not coterminous with the boundary between open-submissive and clandestine-evasive disobedience, but rather must, at least to a certain extent, depend on the boundary between obedience and disobedience.

Furthermore, so the argument goes, there is a sense in which furtive and evasive disobedience may even show more respect for the law than civil disobedience, for it expresses "that aspect of respect linked up with heeding, giving serious attention to, believing that one has good reason not to run afoul of, and even fearing the thing respected" as when a boxer respects his opponent's left jab.[29] Such an argument, however, depends on a view of respect that is itself very limited and unhelpful, to say the least, when it is applied to the legal order. For respect involves more a recognition of *legiti-*

28. Martin Luther King, Jr., "The Time for Freedom Has Come," selection in Mulford Q. Sibley, ed., *The Quiet Battle* (Garden City, N.Y.: Doubleday, Anchor Book, 1963), p. 303. King, "Letter from Birmingham Jail," *Why We Can't Wait*, p. 84.

29. Gerald C. MacCallum, Jr., "Some Truths and Untruths about Civil Disobedience," *Political and Legal Obligation: Nomos* 12, ed. J. Roland Pennock and John W. Chapman, p. 393.

macy than of unbridled but threatening power. Hence, the critical question is whether civil disobedience is both compatible with and expressive of respect for the law, in the sense of respect for the legitimacy of the entire system.

Civil disobedience is not necessarily inconsistent with respect for the law, which can be manifested in a variety of ways, including the general habit of obedience that may characterize a person's whole life except for a rare act of civil disobedience based on conscience. One's whole biography, then, is a relevant context for a consideration of whether or not civil disobedience is inconsistent with respect for the law. Another aspect of this issue is whether or not the act of civil disobedience itself is one of respect for and deference to the law, especially through its characteristics of openness and submission. Can it be said, for example, that the "Phone Tax Rebellion" which involves the refusal, usually accompanied by a letter of explanation, to pay the 10 percent federal tax on the phone bill levied to help finance the war in Vietnam, is an act of respect for the law? There is no more of an attempt to avoid the consequences in this instance than there is in the refusal to pay a portion of one's income tax. Such actions can embody *both* disrespect and respect for the law—disrespect for a particular law by violating it, respect for law by paying its penalties and thus submitting to the system as a whole. Such a claim can be defended, in part, by recalling the distinction (so important in this study) between a particular law and the conduct it requires and the legal system as a whole within a broader political framework.

Up to this point I have mainly been interested in examining whether civil disobedience rebuts the charge of unfair play and, if it does not, whether it has other important functions in justification; but another question is equally significant: does fair play demand submission so that no other form of disobedience is justified within a relatively just democratic order? I have contended that civil disobedience, as traditionally conceived, is not exempt from the charge of unfair play simply because of submission; but now I would suggest that the demands of fairness seem to point in the direction of requiring submission, although, of course, this requirement, like that of obedience itself, is not absolute.

Because the questions of obedience-disobedience and submission-evasion are logically distinct, it is one thing to inquire into the justification of disobedience and another to examine the justification of evasion of legal penalties. Special problems appear in the latter, for if I cannot render what is required by a particular law, am I still under a moral claim to submit to legal penalties and, in effect, to the legal system as a whole? This question has been raised with particular vividness and poignancy by four members of the Catonsville Nine, including Daniel Berrigan, S.J., who in protest of the war in Vietnam and other matters, burned with napalm 378 records from the 1-A files of the draft board in Catonsville, Maryland, for which they were prosecuted and convicted. Their decision to go underground rather than accept their sentences departs from classic civil disobedience, and Daniel Berrigan has since eloquently called into question the "moral necessity of joining illegal action to legal consequences."[30] Labeling this a part of liberal mythology, he insists that it simply serves to support those in power. Thus, he and others became "fugitives from injustice" and "criminals for peace."

Such evasive actions can be viewed in different ways. First, they may simply be efforts to delay submission until it can be

---

30. Dick Adler, "A Priest Speaks from Underground," *New York Times*, Sunday, August 16, 1970, sec. 2, pp. 1, 3. On the trial, see Daniel Berrigan, *The Trial of the Catonsville Nine* and also the discussion of the Berrigans as well as the trial, Francine du Plessix Gray, *Divine Disobedience: Profiles in Catholic Radicalism* (New York: Knopf, 1970), pp. 45–228.

granted on the terms of the protesters, who want to derive the maximum political effect from arrest and punishment. (This seems to have been the intention of Philip Berrigan.) In such cases, resistance to arrest and punishment is more symbolic than actual. Second, evasion of legal penalties may actually indicate a transition to revolutionary activity, at least within a democratic context. According to Sidney Hook, the *democrat* can defend his act of disobedience

> only if he willingly accepts the punishment entailed by his defiance of the law, only if he does not seek to escape or subvert or physically resist it. If he engages in any kind of resistance to the punitive processes of the law which follows upon his sentence of legal guilt, he has in principle embarked upon a policy of revolutionary overthrow.[31]

This is not to say, of course, that evasive and revolutionary action can never be justified (as in Nazi Germany or in violation of the Fugitive Slave Act) but only that it can never be justified on democratic grounds within a functioning democracy. The justification of evasion is tantamount to the justification of revolutionary activity, not civil disobedience.

Although the questions of obedience-disobedience and submission-evasion are logically distinct, they are usually combined in practical experience. In fact, in trying to justify an act of disobedience it is impossible to abstract it from the various forms it takes; no general justification of disobedience can encompass both civil disobedience and revolution. While

---

31. Sidney Hook, *The Paradoxes of Freedom*, p. 117. "Occasionally it seems that, in his abhorrence for the war and for what he sees as political oppression in America, Daniel Berrigan is only a syllogism away from extreme physical, as distinct from measured moral rebellion" (*New York Times*, August 9, 1970, E7).

there are some similarities between the justification of civil disobedience (with submission as a major component) and the justification of revolution, there are situations in which civil disobedience is justified although revolution is not. Any attempt to justify revolution, beyond civil disobedience, will depend on certain assumptions about the condition of the existing political order.

As I indicated in chapter 1, nothing in the conceptual criterion of submission entails relinquishing legal efforts to avoid conviction. Thus a disobedient may appeal his case in courts while maintaining that his disobedience is morally justified, even if he is convicted. Often the rhetoric of protest is understandably confused on this score, as the trial of Dr. Benjamin Spock, the Reverend William Sloane Coffin, Jr., et al. illustrates. Many of their actions as cited in the trial involved the rhetoric of civil disobedience, including submission to punishment. Since no effort would be made to argue for their innocence, their submission, with the accompanying reasons for disobedience, would sear the American conscience, or at least embarrass the government. This plan changed, however; the men pleaded not guilty and made a rigorous defense.

The charge that they were inconsistent because they pleaded not guilty simply assumes a static view of confrontation between conscience and government. In this case, the government's conspiracy charge surely had little warrant. Furthermore, it is even possible to take a sinister view of the prosecution's intentions; rather than seeking a conviction, they may in the long run have been more interested in intimidating other vocal critics of the war in Vietnam who might also be subject to such broad charges as conspiracy.[32] Possibly

32. See Jessica Mitford, "Guilty as Charged by the Judge," *The Atlantic* 224, no. 2 (August 1969): 48 f., and *The Trial of Dr. Spock* (New York: Knopf, 1969). Cf. also Alan Dershowitz's review of the latter, *New York Times Book Review*, Sept. 14, 1969, pp. 3, 24 f.

some, if not all, of the defendents would have pleaded guilty to a different charge, as their earlier rhetoric suggested.[33]

Such shifts are to be expected in extremely fluid situations of confrontation between conscience and the government, where academic analysis sometimes breaks down. At any rate, what is ruled out in civil disobedience (conceptually and normatively) is not appeal to the legal system, but rather the *illegal evasion* of arrest and punishment. Although the civil disobedient submits to the legal system and its decisions, he is not required to submit to every penalty that might be exacted without exhausting his appeals. Of course, certain tactical considerations might require either appealing the decision or accepting the penalties without appeal, on the grounds that one or another action would provide the most publicity or the best forum for the cause or the appeal to the community's sense of injustice. Although I earlier suggested that appeal to the legal system does not preclude applying the term *civil disobedience* to an act, I am now suggesting some of the conditions under which such an appeal makes moral sense even within the rhetoric of submission and suffering. Finally, accepting legal penalties does not mean acknowledging that they are right and just, although it does mean acknowledging the state's right to impose them.

Submission may well be required by tactical considerations, in addition to the basic commitment to the system and the

33. Cf. Mitford, *Trial of Dr. Spock*. At one point Coffin said, "We have quite a decision to make . . . to decide whether to fight this indictment—the men at Yale Law School say we have a duty to fight an illegal indictment—or just to say, fine, we're guilty just like those boys you've been sending to jail, so send us to jail. My feeling would be to fight it, but there's a danger in getting so tangled up in legal complications that we never get a chance to make our moral point." Furthermore, he said, "Unchallenged, the precedent it would set might make it much too easy for the government to indict anybody for conspiracy, and this would diminish the possibilities of dissent and the exercise of the rights of conscience" (Fred C. Shapiro, "God and That Man at Yale," *New York Times Magazine*, March 3, 1968, p. 62).

demands of fairness, especially insofar as civil disobedience is directed toward changing a law or policy by communication rather than by coercion. Submission is important in the communication of ideas and convictions about moral-political matters primarily because it endows disobedience with a ceremonial quality. Disobedience can thus be a ritual that permits an individual to break, to a limited extent, the laws of his community while affirming the community itself. The civil disobedient may well say, "You can trust my collaborators and me, as our willingness to submit to arrest and punishment indicates." Trust is possible because the foundations of community are not being impugned, as they would be if the disobedients claimed to see more than a limited area in which there was a clash between ideals and reality, between values and practice. If this clash were total, or if the disobedient's view presented it as such, so that the whole community, its members and its structures, stood condemned by such ideals, the picture would change. The disobedience would now appear within a different frame of discourse, for it would insist not merely that the people's sense of justice had ignored some area or had not been cognizant of some faulty law or policy, but that their sense of justice was almost totally diseased.

Nonviolent, open, submissive disobedience, in contrast to political terrorism and bombings, offers a gesture of good faith, a signal that mutual trust is possible and desirable. Whether an individual chooses terrorism or civil disobedience will often depend, then, on his view of the social and political order as a whole in the light of ideality, and on his view of the capacity of the people to respond to new visions. Yet other factors are at work, as Staughton Lynd's arguments indicate. As a proponent of civil disobedience, he endorses the choice of open and submissive disobedience in order to communicate ideas and values. He thus denies that the Catonsville Nine or the Milwaukee Fourteen (who also destroyed Selective Service files) remained at the scene, inviting arrest, because of a legalistic belief in accepting penalties. For him the model of fair play that I have sketched would simply be inapplicable on the grounds that the "larger system of law and order" is unsound.[34] As Howard Zinn writes,

> If the social function of protest is to change the unjust conditions of society, then that protest cannot stop with a court decision or a jail sentence. If the protest is morally justified (whether it breaks a law or not) it is morally justified to the very end, even past the point where a court has imposed a penalty. If it stops at that point, with everyone saying cheerfully, as at a football match, "Well, we played a good game, we lost, and we will accept the verdict like sports"—then we are treating social protest as a game. It becomes a token, a gesture. How potent an effect can protest have if it stops dead in its tracks as soon as the very government it is criticizing decides about it?[35]

But for Lynd, openness and submission, as well as nonviolence, help to humanize the disobedient's actions and preserve "the spirit of love and mutual respect." A simple example Lynd draws from the Milwaukee action illustrates this point. Because they had seized keys from a cleaning woman, their first act after imprisonment was to send her flowers and candy in order to apologize for frightening her. Through this simple act—but more importantly through their openness, submission, and nonviolence (in relation to persons)—they "practiced disruption in a manner which kept the spirit of dialogue alive."[36] There is no dialogue with the laws (despite Socrates) but only with persons in their roles as fellow citizens, jurors, judges, legislators, and so forth. Often the reality of civil disobedience is far removed from such an analysis, which does, however, suggest some important features of some protest.

34. Staughton Lynd, "Letter from Jail: Telling Right from Wrong," *Delivered Into Resistance,* p. 15.
35. Zinn, *Disobedience and Democracy,* p. 30.
36. Lynd, "Leter from Jáil," pp. 16–17.

Many disputes about the effectiveness of civil disobedience revolve around submission and its functions. Arguing against even normal legal appeals, Carl Cohen insists that too many disobedients "underestimate the moral force of the self-sacrificial element in disobedient protest, and underestimate, therefore, the deleterious effect upon any civilly disobedient protest which would result from the evasion of the punishment normally meted out to those who knowingly break the law."[37]

It is not necessary to draw on some religious or metaphysical affirmation about the political efficacy of suffering in order to assert that the moral sense of the majority may make them reluctant to inflict punishment for disobedience committed on behalf of certain ends. This moral sense may function more negatively than positively, for although it may not impel the majority to initiate moral-political reforms that the protesters deem necessary, it may restrain them from opposing and defeating a proposal for which a minority is willing to suffer by accepting legal penalties.[38] Often, though, the issue will be decided less by the majority's moral sense than by its apathy. I shall concentrate on the mechanism of civil disobedience, the way it works, in the next section.

What factors besides worthy ends and submission affect the justification of civil disobedience? What else is significant in dealing with the claim to obedience on the basis of fair play? Because political obligation arises in the context I described earlier, certain moral prerequisites for justified resistance are established. Among the most important prerequisites is the exhaustion of established legal and political means for re-

37. Carl Cohen, "Law, Speech, and Disobedience," in Bedau, *CD*, p. 177. Cf. also his book, *Civil Disobedience: Conscience, Tactics, and the Law* (New York: Columbia University Press, 1971) which was published too late for consideration in this volume.

38. See Rawls, "The Justification of Civil Disobedience," in Bedau, *CD*, pp. 253–54.

dressing grievances. If legal devices are still open and resistance is undertaken, "either the dissenter is acting irresponsibly, or his policies are anarchical, or both." It appears
that this is part of what John Rawls suggests in stipulating
the condition that there must be not only a grave injustice
but also a "refusal more or less deliberate to correct it."[39]
For efforts to effect change by established legal and political
channels enable protesters to test whether the law or policy
or state of affairs is deliberately unjust. This prerequisite of
exhausting available channels is simply a further specification of what is involved in fair play, for unless he is a committed revolutionary, the dissenter should give the system
and his fellow citizens a fair chance to respond and make
amends.

Although the absence of legal recourse is not a sufficient
justification for disobedience, the presence of such recourse
may not mean that obedience is required, for the time factor
may well be critical. For example, court injunctions have
on occasion been very effective instruments for limiting social protest in the South since, unless they are disobeyed,
their disposition may consume a few years. The problem is,
of course, that "rights can be as effectively destroyed by restraining their exercise during the period of time it takes to
test a court order as by prohibiting their exercise altogether."[40]

The charge is sometimes made that civil disobedience is
"scarcely capable of being put in a form that is not contradictory," or that there is "no coherent political philosophy
whatever in terms of which civil disobedience could con-

39. Ibid., p. 249, and "Legal Obligation and the Duty of Fair Play,"
Hook, *L & P*, p. 15. The previous quotation is from Hugo Bedau, "On
Civil Disobedience," p. 661.
40. Taylor, "Civil Disobedience: Observations on the Strategies of Protest," in Bedau, *CD*, p. 103.

ceivably make sense, let alone find justification."[41] Such claims seem to involve two distinct but not totally separate criticisms. First, civil disobedience is necessarily an incoherent and internally inconsistent doctrine. Second, it cannot be generalized or made a rule of general observance without disastrous consequences. I shall focus on the second criticism, although some of my comments relate, at least indirectly, to the first one too.

This second criticism implies another moral prerequisite for justifying civil disobedience: it must pass the generalization test, which is often phrased as a question, "But what if everyone did that?" This test is connected with what Marcus Singer calls the Generalization Argument: "If everyone were to do that, the consequences would be disastrous (or undesirable); therefore, no one ought to do that." The Generalization Argument presupposes what Singer calls the Generalization Principle: "What is right (or wrong) for one person must be right (or wrong) for any similar person in similar circumstances."[42] By reducing a discussion of these two arguments to its bare essentials, at the risk of oversimplifying, I shall try to show that the Generalization Argument fails to demonstrate that civil disobedience can never be justified, that its force in some contexts is partially derived from the independent principle of fairness, and that the Generalization Principle has practical functions in limiting instances of civil disobedience.

The Generalization Argument forms an interesting link between our discussion of fair play and our later discussion

41. The first quotation is from Herbert J. Storing, "The Case Against Civil Disobedience," in *On Civil Disobedience: Essays Old and New,* ed. Robert A. Goldwin (Chicago: Rand McNally, 1969), p. 96; the second is from Will Herberg, "Dicta," *Virginia Law Weekly* 22, no. 12 (1969): 2.

42. Marcus Singer, *Generalization in Ethics* (New York: Knopf, 1961), pp. 4, 5. On the Generalization Principle, or the Principle of Universalizability, see R. M. Hare, *Freedom and Reason* (Oxford: Clarendon, 1963).

of the problems of order, although this link to some extent results from a confusion of hypothetical and empirical questions about disobedience. The empirical question is "What are its direct and indirect consequences?" While I shall return to this question later, I now want to examine the hypothetical question, "What if everyone did that?" which does not ask whether disobedience will generate disorder or set a bad example for others.

The generalization test is meaningless without a description of the act. We have to know what the civil disobedient is up to before we can assess the consequences of everyone doing that. Any discussion, therefore, will have to take account of several different features of civil disobedience, especially illegality, dependence on conscience, and the use of some force, as well as the other elements that I have stressed in this study. When illegality is emphasized, the question becomes "What if everyone violated the law?" But opponents of civil disobedience claim a victory too easily if they assume that lawlessness is generalized, for the civil disobedient's maxim may well be discriminate but not indiscriminate disobedience. There is no logical inconsistency in opposing indiscriminate disobedience and defending discriminate disobedience.[43] But even discrimination does not exhaust the act's description, for civil disobedience has certain other specifications: nonviolence, publicity, and submission to arrest and punishment. Thus the civil disobedient cannot be asked to justify all disobedience to law or all resistance to the state, but only the particular form in which he is engaged.

Another description of civil disobedience, according to some interpreters, includes the principle that each person

43. See Richard Wasserstrom, "Obligation to Obey the Law," *UCLA Law Review* 10 (1963): 792–93.

disobeys laws that he thinks are unjust.[44] But what if everyone violated laws which seemed unjust to his conscience? Would the consequences of such a general rule of action be desirable? Or, in the perspective of Kant, would a stable, functioning order be possible and could one will to live in such an order?[45] Any cogency of the test applied to this description of civil disobedience stems from the picture of anarchy it evokes: all men following their consciences at all times even if violence, disorder, etc. result. But the civil disobedient is not necessarily committed to absolute freedom of conscience, since all he has to affirm is that each person heed his conscience in disobeying the law in certain situations in a particular manner (publicly, nonviolently, submissively). One may hold that a society in which this is a common principle of action is possible, that its consequences would not be undesirable, and that one could will to live in it.

Other interpreters see other principles at work in civil disobedience, and thus describe the act quite differently. Harry Prosch argues that the civil disobedient's rule of ac-

44. I do not follow Richard Lichtman in drawing a sharp distinction between universalization of pure principle and the hypothetical consequences of a general practice (see Lichtman's article in *Civil Disobedience* [Center for the Study of Democratic Institutions, 1966], p. 14). My main reason for underplaying this distinction in my discussion is that one cannot generalize an act or ask what the consequences would be of everyone doing the same unless he can offer an accurate description of the act. This cannot be accomplished without considering the maxim or principle of much civil disobedience, for the maxim or principle states more precisely what the civil disobedient is up to.

45. Kant writes, "Some actions are so constituted that their maxim cannot even be *conceived* as a universal law of nature without contradiction, let alone be *willed* as what *ought* to become one. In the case of others we do not find this inner impossibility, but it is still impossible to *will* that their maxim should be raised to the universality of a law of nature, because such a will would contradict itself" (*Groundwork of the Metaphysic of Morals,* trans. H. J. Paton [New York: Harper and Row, Torchbook 1964], p. 91).

tion is that "it is right to use force in the attempt to nullify
or to change unjust laws" or "it is morally right to fight for
the right."[46] Such a maxim cannot become a "common principle of action." It is impossible to impose moral restrictions
such as nonviolence on actions like these because the commitment to the fight for right entails doing what is necessary
to win. Since the state of war and the moral state are mutual-
ly exclusive, the outcome can only be an "appeal to heaven."

Prosch's argument fails on several counts. He identifies
civil disobedience with the use of force (at least as a principle
of its conduct) and its underlying principle with the rightness
of using force for the right cause.[47] Such an interpretation
cannot withstand scrutiny, for while it may be applicable to
some forms of coercive and obstructive civil disobedience, it
is irrelevant to much persuasive, communicative civil disobedience. But, even more importantly, there is no logical
inconsistency between holding that one can justifiably engage in certain kinds of limited force for certain moral ends
and yet insisting that this force be *limited*. Although Prosch
seems to think that civil disobedience logically involves a
"holy war" in which all means are hallowed (except in those
few cases where persuasion is possible), it may have limits
and restrictions on its conduct which are closer to a "just
war" than to a "holy war" or crusade.

Even coercive civil disobedience is not force without limits;
some of its limits are given in its description—nonviolence,

46. "Limits to the Moral Claim in Civil Disobedience," *Ethics* 75, no. 2
(January 1965): 106, 109, and passim.
47. Prosch does begin by considering whether civil disobedience could
be viewed as a mode of moral persuasion. His answer seems to be negative
because of his view that actions (in contrast to words) really constitute a
military tactic, the use of force. Another facet of his argument is that the
consequences of persuasion by action are so uncertain as practically to
eliminate this appeal as an ethical justification (ibid., p. 106). But it is
hard to see how this fails to apply to speech as well. I shall return to the
question of force and persuasion later.

openness, and submission. At least as far as this act is concerned, overthrow of the government is not a necessary implication. Furthermore, recognition of the moral claims of others may be indicated in the submission to arrest and punishment. Thus, even in concentrating on coercive civil disobedience, one can deny that its principle is (necessarily) that force *without any limits* can be used for the right; its principle is more likely to be that force in specified forms can be used for the right. Prosch's argument is unconvincing because he takes only illegality and unlimited force as the defining characteristics of civil disobedience and ignores its other features.

It is interesting to examine cases of tax refusal (whether Thoreau's or more contemporary examples such as withholding portions of one's income tax or the federal telephone tax) because they raise special problems in relation to the generalization test. Some commentators insist that Thoreau's tax resistance (regardless of its aims and actual consequences) was "in its logic—that is, when thought of in terms of universalizing the principle on which he has acted—a revolutionary act, and any adequate appraisal of it must ultimately take this into account." Tax resistance is revolutionary in its logic, because "if it is widely practiced, it will bring any government to its knees."[48] It goes beyond most other acts of resistance, the argument has it, because it would deny to government its capacity to govern.

It does not appear to me, however, that such a case can be made about tax resistance as compared to other forms of civil disobedience, for many of them—if widely practiced—might have equally deleterious effects on the government or society (e.g. tying up draft boards, blocking traffic, locking government officials out of their offices). Perhaps all of them are revolutionary but not, I think, because of the generaliza-

48. Bedau, *CD*, p. 22.

tion test. Indeed, what I have argued about the proper description of the act to be generalized holds in this specific case too. Not only is the act submissive, but as Thoreau did not refuse to pay *all* his taxes (e.g. the highway tax), so most contemporary tax resisters simply withhold the portions of their taxes that might be used for purposes they oppose. Any impact is symbolic, and that feature too must be considered in determining whether tax refusal is revolutionary. Thus, I do not think one can argue that tax resistance is revolutionary without considering its other elements in a total context; it is too much to say that it would not be justified (given the generalization test) unless revolution were justified.

Such cases raise again the matter of the specificity of the maxim. How specific can one's description of the act be? Which factors can be included? In considering tax refusal in relation to the question "What if everyone did that?" some would answer "But not everyone will." According to this interpretation the principle of civil disobedience might be, "A dissenter is justified in tax resistance for certain ends and in certain ways when he is certain that others will not act on that principle." Singer would reply that such an answer is inappropriate, for the knowledge or belief that not everyone will do the same in a similar situation is not part of the circumstances of one's action.[49] His point is valid insofar as it is necessary to distinguish between empirical and hypothetical considerations, since the generalization test does not depend on empirical consequences, but it is not wholly satisfactory in handling the critical question of what one can include in the description of the act.

If the generalization test fails to establish that disobedience is always wrong and always unjustified, it still has other

49. Singer, *Generalization in Ethics,* p. 150. Contrast Wasserstrom's argument, "Obligation to Obey the Law," 793–97.

important functions, especially because it forcefully directs us to the claims of fairness and fair play. If an institution depends on the obedience of most participants who have submitted to it and who expect me to comply in turn since I have accepted its benefits, my disobedience is subject to the charge of unfair behavior. As Joel Feinberg writes,

> The real point of the question "What if everyone did the same?" is not utilitarian at all. When others inconvenience themselves or otherwise forgo personal advantage to vote or to detour around the lawn, it is *unfair* to them for me to abstain or to cross the lawn, even when my doing so is harmless.[50]

Thus, to ask the question "What if everyone did that?" is to ask whether I am making an unjustified exception of my behavior in the context of a practice that is relatively just and useful.

What Singer calls the generalization principle and what others call the principle of universalizability is also closely related to principles of justice; for the formal criterion of justice, which can be seen as a primary feature of the Kantian principle of universality, is to treat similar cases in a similar way.[51] Some philosophers argue that such a principle, which means acknowledging that anyone else in a similar situation would be right in acting as I am acting even if it contravenes my interests, is a formal condition for making moral judg-

50. Feinberg, "The Forms and Limits of Utilitarianism," *Philosophical Review*, 76 (1967): 373 (review of Lyons, *Utilitarianism*). Donald Evans writes, "The generalization-argument question does two jobs. Like the question, 'What if *most* people did X?' it may form part of a rule-utilitarian justification of a rule. But it also refers us to considerations concerning *fairness* or *rights*" ("Love, Situations, and Rules," in Outka and Ramsey, eds., *Norm and Context in Christian Ethics,* p. 395).

51. See Henry Sidgwick, *The Methods of Ethics,* 7th ed. (London: Macmillan, 1962), p. xx, and Chaïm Perelman, *Justice and the Problem of Argument,* trans. John Petrie (London: Routledge & Kegan Paul, 1963).

ments at all. Without considering its important features, I want to look at this principle's function in evaluating civil disobedience. In order to restrict and limit instances of civil disobedience, John Rawls suggests that the dissenter should engage in such acts only when he "is willing to affirm that everyone else similarly subjected to injustice has the right to protest in a similar way."[52] The dissenter should be suspicious of his own conduct if he would not be willing for others faced with what seems to be an equally worthy cause to engage in the same kind of act or willing to accept the empirical and hypothetical consequences of their disobedience.

This is, in effect, a practical function of the principle of universalizability. Various theological interpretations of resistance try to reduce the influence of distorted perspectives in other ways. Künneth, for example, appropriates from the Reformation tradition the requirement that the leaders of resistance be a group of office-bearers, while other theologians emphasize reflection in the context of the church. The principle of universalizability is useful in this practical way, for to have the civil disobedient ask whether he would be willing for others to act in a similar way under similar conditions for their own conscientiously held purposes may help him to grasp the significance of what he is doing.

Some critics and defenders of civil disobedience think that if civil disobedience can be defended in any situation it must be defended in all situations. Thus, Staughton Lynd supports the southern segregationist's nonviolent disobedience of recent civil rights legislation "on the ground that he may have something which I have not yet seen to point out to me about those laws."[53] This theme arises from Lynd's unbounded confidence in nonviolence, which leads him to over-

52. "The Justification of Civil Disobedience," Bedau, *CD*, p. 250.
53. "Civil Disobedience in Wartime," *Maine Law Review* 19 (1967): 49–54.

look other important considerations. As I have already contended, endorsement of one act of civil disobedience for a
certain end does not necessarily imply endorsement of all
such acts regardless of their ends and consequences. Although the southern segregationist is convinced of the rightness of his cause, one could argue that his action is unjustified because of the end he is seeking.

This brings us to the difference between justifying an act
and justifying an agent.[54] The point of such a distinction,
which is close to that drawn between moral rightness and
moral goodness, is that a person's conscientious moral reflection may lead him to commit civil disobedience although
his reasons for it are inadequate. He may even deserve our
moral praise although we condemn his action as wrong.
Furthermore, there is a difference between disobeying laws
that only affect the state and those defining the rights of
others. Civil disobedience concerned mainly with staking
out a relationship between governmental authority and the
individual's freedom (e.g. the flag salute cases) raises less
serious moral problems than civil disobedience attacking
laws that define the rights of others (e.g. trespass laws).[55] All
these factors must be considered in assessing and finally rejecting any claim that the principle of universalizability requires all civil disobedience to be approved if any is approved.

It is possible, then, to establish in relation to the claim of
fair play which engenders a prime facie obligation to obey
the law and the generalization argument and principle, the
fact that civil disobedience may be morally justified, but do

54. See Richard Lichtman's statement in *Civil Disobedience*, p. 16.
55. *West Virginia State Board of Education* v. *Barnette*, 319 US 624.
See *The Supreme Court on Church and State*, ed. Joseph Tussman (New
York: Oxford University Press, 1962), p. 144.

we say that the disobedient has the *right* or the *duty* to disobey? William Sloane Coffin doubts that "any man ever has the *right* to break the law, but . . . upon occasion every man has the *duty* to do so."[56] Several other interpreters of resistance, including Gunther Lewy, Bayard Rustin, and Martin Luther King, echo this opinion.[57] In spite of such an interpretation both categories, "right" and "duty," are applicable to different situations in a constitutional democracy. Where the conditions for political obligation based on fair play (and other moral principles) are simply lacking, one has a right to disobedience, although he perhaps should not exercise it. Thus, one might have a right to disobey the law as far as the principle of fairness is concerned (e.g. the constitution is unjust), although one might forego this right because of the great harm that would result. To establish a right of disobedience within the framework of this study, one has to determine that because of certain conditions the claim of fair play is not operative, or at least is not dominant. It might be overridden by other moral factors, since, as I have already suggested, some conduct is so immoral that it can never become morally obligatory even under the conditions required for fair play, although political obligation usually exists in relative independence of content.

When political obligation is overruled by other moral obligations, there may be not only a right but also a duty to disobey a particular law. For example, if an official directly demands that a person commit an act of inhumanity, whether in war or elsewhere, that person has a duty and not merely a right to disobey. Other laws may encourage or permit an un-

56. Charles E. Whittaker and William Sloane Coffin, Jr., *Law, Order and Civil Disobedience*, p. 30.

57. Cf. Bayard Rustin, in *Civil Disobedience*, p. 11; Martin Luther King, Jr., *Why We Can't Wait*, p. 82; Gunther Lewy, "Resistance to Tyranny," p. 594.

just state of affairs for a minority group. To establish an actual *duty* to engage in civil disobedience, perhaps of the indirect sort, to effect change, one must examine all facets of the situation (ends, means, consequences, etc.) in terms of relevant moral principles, and then conclude that, all things considered, the moral weight falls on civil disobedience as the required form of resistance.

FORMS AND MEANS OF RESISTANCE

A fundamental question is whether any restrictions should be placed upon the forms and means or conduct of civil disobedience. I have already contended that violence is excluded from civil disobedience although the boundaries between violence and nonviolence are not always clear; but nonviolence may not be the only moral restriction on its form or conduct.

It is impossible to follow interpreters such as Gandhi and King who tend to approve of all nonviolent action in principle and then simply extend this approbation to civil disobedience as one form of nonviolence. Such a view ignores too many other criteria for evaluation, occasionally by omitting the element of disobedience to law. Frequently the result is a confusion of nonviolent direct action and civil disobedience which is unacceptable because the latter has specific features, particularly illegality, which may decisively affect its justification.[58] Furthermore, the fact that an act is generally nonviolent does not preclude the possibility of deleterious consequences; but now the important question is whether "non-violence sums up the necessary *morality of means*" of civil disobedience apart from its consequences.[59]

58. Examples of this confusion can be seen in Harrop Freeman, "Civil Disobedience, Law and Democracy," *Law in Transition Quarterly* 3 (Winter 1966): 32; cf. Freeman's statement in *Civil Disobedience* (pp. 2–10) and Régamey, *Non-Violence and the Christian Conscience*.

59. Ramsey, *Christian Ethics and the Sit-In*, p. 86, n. 28.

For some Christian ethicists, nonviolence constitutes the complete morality of means. When the conduct is determined to be nonviolent, nothing else needs to be said about its form. For others, the kinds of means used in resistance are of little ethical significance as long as there is a probability of success, since all political means are ethically ambiguous. The main decisions are primarily technical and prudential rather than moral.[60] Defenders of this position sometimes argue that the difference between moral relations and force is so great that moral categories cannot be applied to the use of force.[61] Both approaches—the one making nonviolence the only consideration of form and the other concentrating solely on the consequences—are inadequate. Christian love requires both taking up resistance on behalf of one neighbor against another in a situation of conflicting claims and, at the same time, limiting the means of resistance, although not simply to nonviolence. Even if the distinction between nonviolence and violence is morally important, as I think it is, nonviolent acts including civil disobedience are subject to other restraints and limits that are usually discussed under the heading of "just war" theory, although they are applicable to any situation in which force is used. Ralph Potter writes,

> Rightly perceived, the criteria of the "just war doctrine" pertain to all situations in which the use of force must be contemplated as an immediate or remote possibility. . . . Whenever men think about the morally responsible and therefore politically purposeful use

60. See Künneth, *Die Vollmacht des Gewissens*, p. 171.
61. Prosch sees the effort to apply moral criteria to force as an effort of self-righteousness; "Limits to the Moral Claim in Civil Disobedience," *Ethics* 75 (January 1965): 110. Contrast the interview with Paul Ramsey in *Protest: Pacifism and Politics*, by James Finn (New York: Vintage, 1968), pp. 424–28.

of force, some analogue to the just war doctrine emerges, whether it be in non-Western cultures or in the Christian sub-culture.[62]

The "just war doctrine" offers a set of considerations for determining when war is justified, and analogous criteria must be employed in determining when civil disobedience is justified, although perhaps it is more accurate to suggest that civil disobedience is subject to the same general demands of morality as any other action rather than that it is illuminated by just war criteria.

However that may be, certainly the appropriate criteria for evaluating civil disobedience coincide to a great extent with traditional just war criteria such as just cause, good motives and intentions, exhaustion of normal procedures for resolving disputes, reasonable prospect of success, due proportion between probable good and bad consequences, and right means.[63] I have already considered some of these—such as just cause and exhaustion of normal channels—and I shall concentrate on the reasonable prospect of success and the test of proportion between probable good and bad effects in the concluding section. Now I am asking whether the means are morally blameless, and one of the most important points has to do with a restriction on the *direction* of force even in its nonviolent forms. A simple illustration from war will set the context: to attack an enemy's wife and children directly in order to get at him is never justified. Rather than asking simply whether violent or nonviolent force is used, one must inquire about the target of the force. As Paul Ramsey con-

---

62. Potter, *War and Moral Discourse*, pp. 49–50.

63. While Ramsey, in *Christian Ethics and the Sit-In*, uses just war criteria more clearly in relation to economic resistance, James Luther Adams uses them to discuss civil disobedience ("Civil Disobedience," pp. 302–11). My statement of the criteria is influenced by Adams and by Ralph Potter *(War and Moral Discourse)*.

tends, "the 'just conduct' of resistance is to be defined in terms of the limited *direction* of the resistance and not alone in terms of the nature of the weapons used."[64] This prohibition of direct attack on innocent persons or noncombatants depends on the distinction between primary and secondary, or direct and indirect, intentions and effects of actions.

Such a principle may not apply as clearly to civil disobedience as to certain other forms of nonviolent direct action such as economic boycott. But a few examples may indicate its relevance even to civil disobedience, in part because civil disobedience often is accompanied by other techniques, such as economic pressure in the sit-ins. When protestors tie up traffic during rush hour in a large city, they are using force directly against "innocents" who may be in no position to do anything about school conditions in Harlem or removing a superintendent of public instruction in Chicago. Joseph Farraher, S.J. argues that such acts are unjustified because obstruction was "used against persons not certainly guilty of wrong."[65] This is an indiscriminate use of force, which makes moral sense only if one assumes what George Kennan has aptly called "the principle of the total ubiquity of responsibility," or that worthy ends will justify any means. There may be equality of sin but there is also inequality of responsibility and guilt.[66] A counterargument might hold that the inconvenience caused by obstruction of traffic is not sufficient to warrant the label of attack and injury and that severe censure is thus inappropriate. But even if this counterargument is sustained, I would contend that such acts are

64. Ramsey, *Christian Ethics and the Sit-In*, p. 86, n. 28.
65. "The Natural Law and Conscience-Based Claims in Relation to Legitimate State Expectations," *The Hastings Law Journal* 17 (March 1966): 450.
66. Cf. Reinhold Niebuhr, *The Nature and Destiny of Man*, 1: 219–27.

difficult to justify on other grounds, including political effectiveness. The blocking of traffic on the Triborough Bridge during rush hour in order to direct attention to conditions in the slums was a failure, for this "admirable goal was deluged under criticisms of the potential dangers of tying up traffic and of the protest's implication that all New Yorkers, indiscriminately, were responsible for slum conditions."[67]

Certainly this principle raises some doubt about the moral viability of occupying a store in violation of trespass laws in order to force another autonomous store in the chain to alter its policies. Such action appears to be parallel to attacking a noncombatant to get at the combatant. I must emphasize that this principle does not mean that absolutely no injury or harm can befall noncombatant or nonresponsible persons; for even if they are not the appropriate objects of a direct use of force, they may nonetheless be affected by force that is primarily directed elsewhere. While such "fallout" is not prohibited, these secondary and indirect effects have to be weighed against the final good to be gained.

As in the application of just war criteria, there are numerous difficulties. Perhaps the most serious one is the definition and identification of the noncombatant, innocent, or "nonresponsible" party. This category does not imply that its members are any less subjectively and personally guilty than those against whom force may be appropriately directed. They may enthusiastically endorse the evil that has been perpetrated, and in this sense they may be as subjectively guilty as anyone else, but they are not "objectively at the point where some form of pressure needs to be exerted."[68]

67. Michael Lipsky, *Protest in City Politics: Rent Strikes, Housing and the Power of the Poor* (Chicago: Rand McNally, 1970), p. 192.

68. Ramsey, *Christian Ethics and the Sit-In*, p. 105.

The fact that this line between responsible and nonresponsible is often difficult to draw in practice does not undermine the principle itself.

Some contend that there are other means that cannot be justified, although they too are not excluded by the description of civil disobedience as nonviolent, public, submissive violation of law. These means, it is argued, are so outrageous as to be beyond the pale of justification even when they are allegedly hallowed by the most worthy cause. One example is especially conspicuous. In much civil disobedience in recent years, protesters have acted in ways that were designed to provoke retaliation. These provocative actions, such as spitting in an officer's face or shouting "fighting words," are often used not merely to provoke arrest and punishment (which would probably result from the act of disobedience itself) but rather to goad the representatives of the established order into an uncontrolled coercive and violent response, thus unmasking its hypocrisy and disclosing its true nature. The goal is to undermine the legitimacy of the dominant institutions by provoking the groups in control to respond in ways that cannot be reconciled with the fundamental values of the order.[69] It may well be, as Leslie J. MacFarlane maintains, that conduct such as the deliberate provocation of retaliation is "so vile . . . as to be unacceptable in any circumstances."[70] It is not accurate to assert, as some

69. Bruce Pech, "Radical Disobedience and its Justification," in Bedau, *CD*, p. 266; Robert L. Scott and Donald K. Smith describe the situation: "the confronter who prompts violence in the language or behavior of another has found his collaborator. 'Show us how ugly you really are,' he says, and the enemy with dogs and cattle prods, or police billies and mace, complies." "The Rhetoric of Confrontation," *The Quarterly Journal of Speech* 55, no. 1 (Feb. 1969): 8.

70. Leslie J. MacFarlane, "Disobedience and the Bomb," *Political Quarterly* 37 (1966): 366.

critics do, that nonviolence works, when it works, only by provoking such uncontrolled responses.[71] Furthermore, to rule out the *deliberate* provocation of retaliation is not to imply that any nonviolent act which arouses anger and hostility, and even provokes violent responses from bystanders or the police, is unjustified.

While the argument to this point is sufficient to establish that nonviolence is not the sole standard for evaluating the conduct and means of civil disobedience, it does not imply that nonviolence is unimportant from the moral standpoint. Some theologians argue that there is no intrinsic difference between nonviolence and violence, and that the distinction between them is accordingly less moral than pragmatic, since nonviolence, for example, can be combined with a greater respect for law and order than violence. The differences between them are in degree rather than in kind.[72] This position as defended by Reinhold Niebuhr and Paul Ramsey, among others, appears partly to be an overreaction to the equation of Christian love-in-resistance and nonviolence in much religious rhetoric. But it is not necessary to make such an equation or to ignore the coercive elements of nonviolence in order to make a significant *moral* distinction between nonviolent and violent acts, the latter by definition involving direct physical or mental harm. This moral distinction does not imply that nonviolence is always justified, or that civil disobedience is always justified because it is a form of nonviolence, or that violence is never justified. Nonviolent acts may be committed for unworthy causes, they may be indiscriminate, and they may have harmful consequences. Al-

71. Henry Pachter, "The Movement is the Message," *Dissent* 15, no. 1 (Jan.-Feb. 1968): 25.

72. Cf. Ramsey, *Christian Ethics and the Sit-Ins*, passim; Davis and Good, *Reinhold Niebuhr on Politics*, pp. 141; Robert Paul Wolff, "On Violence," *Journal of Philosophy* 66, no. 19 (Oct. 2, 1969): 615–16.

though nonviolence is not the distinctively Christian method to the exclusion of violence, surely it has a moral priority over violence in effecting social change. This priority derives from the fact that nonviolence preserves the other person for communication and community. Furthermore, in contrast to violence, it involves an "appeal to principle which the *opponent* is asked to acknowledge."[73]

I have focused the contrast between violence and nonviolence on the issue of direct injury to persons, but the matter of damage to property must also be considered, particularly because some interpreters would exclude (conceptually and/or morally) such actions as raids on Dow Chemical buildings. In February 1970 the East Coast Conspiracy to Save Lives vandalized General Electric Company files and draft board records in Philadelphia in order "to disrupt functioning of the machine of death and oppression."[74] It was not clearly an act of civil disobedience, for it involved, in addition to vandalism, secrecy and evasion of arrest for several days before the members of the group finally disclosed their identity to "be able to educate other people." There is little difference between this sort of conduct and terrorist bombings and destruction of property without the taking of human life. Furthermore, this act is distinguishable from those of both the Milwaukee Fourteen and the Catonsville Nine, who destroyed Selective Service System files openly and publicly with homemade napalm and then submitted to arrest.

On one level such conduct can be symbolic, as the Catonsville Nine claimed, although the judge could not understand why destruction of *one* file would not have been a sufficiently symbolic action. Beyond the argument that this destruction

73. John Smith , "The Inescapable Ambiguity of Nonviolence," *Philosophy East and West* 19, no. 2 (April 1969): 156.
74. *Washington Post*, Feb. 21, 1970, B2. Cf. my discussion in chapter 1.

of property is justified in order to show how our society values property in contrast to human life, some would contend that "some property has no right to exist," and that its destruction is therefore not an act of violence. But the argument that some property has no right to exist, presumably because it is connected with the betrayal of human ends, values, and needs, cannot be taken too far without encountering the difficult objection "Who decides?" Furthermore I want to stress that the distinction between injury to persons and to property cannot be absolute, for the two are often closely connected, as many protesters well recognize in their criticism of American economic involvement in other countries.

Even nonviolent disobedience often involves more than moral educational force and persuasion; frequently it is coercive. Some claim that acts of noncompliance cannot involve coercion and be considered civil disobedience, while others claim that although such acts are properly described as civil disobedience, they cannot be as easily justified as its persuasive forms. I argued in chapter 1 that the first claim is unwarranted. Coercion may be effected by the use of economic or physical or moral pressure (i.e. the opprobrium of the community), and its presence in civil disobedience cannot be denied by means of the simple distinction between resisting evil and resisting the evil-doer.[75] Never does one encounter disembodied evil. Coercion limits freedom of choice

75. Cf. Martin Luther King, Jr., *Stride Toward Freedom*, p. 84. Nevertheless this distinction does have a point which is expressed in Barbara Deming's argument: "We can put *more* pressure on the antagonist for whom we show human concern. It is precisely solicitude for his person *in combination with* a stubborn interference with his actions that can give us a very special degree of control (precisely in our acting both with love, if you will—in the sense that we respect his human rights—and truthfulness, in the sense that we act out fully our objections to his violating *our* rights)" (*Delivered Into Resistance*, p. 28). Author's italics.

so that even if the one coerced can be said to act voluntarily, his range of options is restricted and he feels constrained to choose a certain response. The robber's demand, "Hand over your wallet or I'll shoot," is thus coercive.

In recent years one particular form of coercive civil disobedience—nonviolent physical obstruction in the violation of some law—has become quite widespread: cases of blocking traffic, stopping troop trains, efforts to shut down induction centers, King's projected dislocation of northern cities, "liberation" of campus buildings, locking up deans of colleges and universities, and so forth, abound. One of the main advocates of such "nonviolent obstructive civil disobedience" is Staughton Lynd, who views it as a possible middle way "between Thoreauvian civil disobedience and Lockean revolution."[76] His approach, however, is internally inconsistent. On the one hand, he argues that history will vindicate those who have "sought to clog as best they could the American warmaking process in Vietnam." On the other hand, he contends that "nonviolent civil disobedience [including obstruction] is a valid, and should become a routine, form of democratic dialogue," because it remains "within the framework of democratic political philosophy."[77] Such statements are replete with difficulties. Even if physical confrontation (standing in front of another person as an obstacle or threat), restraint and coercion can be considered elements of a kind of dialogue, it is difficult to see how clogging the war machine (which is being operated by duly elected representatives) can be construed as a valid and possibly routine form of *democratic* dialogue. When a minority acts to thwart the results of an untrammeled democratic process, its action cannot easily be reconciled with

76. Staughton Lynd, "Civil Disobedience and Nonviolent Obstruction," *Humanist* 28, no. 3 (May/June 1968): 3.

77. Lynd, Letter to Editor, *New York Times,* Friday, Oct. 27, 1967, p. 44, and "Civil Disobedience and Nonviolent Obstruction," p. 3.

a democratic commitment. It is one thing to attempt to convince the public and elected officials in a democratic order, it is another to try to prevent them from carrying out policy decisions, as when several draft protesters blocked the entrance to national Selective Service headquarters in Washington in March 1970 in order to keep employees from getting to work. One spokesman, Arthur Waskow, said that their aim was "to stop the draft entirely, not just for a single day."[78] This aim was to be accomplished by nonviolent obstruction combined with efforts to engage draft employees in dialogue in order to convince them that they ought to resign. Others have argued that the destruction of 1A draft files by the Milwaukee Fourteen and the Catonsville Nine was "effective" because it delayed induction in those areas for as long as a year.

The argument that civil disobedience is revolutionary does not apply to all its forms, but it may apply to obstructive civil disobedience designed to impede the democratic process. Such disobedience can be justified, but only if revolution (nonviolent and perhaps violent) is justified. One of the main prerequisites for such justification is the absence of due process, but obviously other factors would also have to be present to justify the material end and the rejection of obligations, and to determine the probability of success and relative balance of good over bad consequences.

One possible counterargument that Lynd might make is implicit in some of his statements: nonviolent obstruction would not destroy the democratic process, even if it were widespread among both the Right and the Left. Even if the rejoinder that he is wrong on empirical grounds is not cogent—and I think that it is—the major argument really does not depend on predicting and assessing consequences, but rather on

78. *Washington Post*, March 21, 1970, B 1; cf. Feb. 10, 1970, A2.

showing that some actions are *inconsistent* with democratic commitment and processes.

The questions whether coercion must necessarily be involved in civil disobedience if it is to be successful, and whether it ought to be, raise significant issues in theological anthropology, as I suggested in chapter 1. On the basis of a realistic assessment of man and the possibilities of social change, Reinhold Niebuhr predicted early in the 1930s, in *Moral Man and Immoral Society:*

> The emancipation of the Negro race in America probably waits upon the adequate development of this kind of social and political strategy [nonviolent resistance].
> . . . the white race in America will not admit the Negro to equal rights if it is not forced to do so. Upon that point one may speak with a dogmatism which all history justifies.[79]

Niebuhr's realistic anthropology stands in striking contrast to Gandhi's and King's views of man, although there is some reason to think that King's shifting thought about civil disobedience and the possibilities of nonviolent resistance before his death were related to a growing realism about the means of effecting social change. Certainly King emphasized to a much greater extent than Niebuhr the efficacy of self-sacrificial love in history.[80] According to Niebuhr, when self-sacrificial love enters history, it is crucified.[81] Effective action in history thus depends on a realistic perspective. Niebuhr

79. *Moral Man and Immoral Society* (New York: Scribner's, 1932), pp. 252–53.

80. See Herbert W. Richardson, "Martin Luther King—Unsung Theologian," *New Theology No. 6,* ed. Martin E. Marty and Dean G. Peerman pp. 178–84.

81. Reinhold Niebuhr, "The Power and Weakness of God," *Discerning the Signs of the Times* (New York: Scribner's, 1949), pp. 142–43: "Powerless goodness ends upon the cross."

has also recognized that one cannot reduce politics to force and coercion, and he has manifested in recent years a greater appreciation for the pursuit of the common good. The position that I defended in chapter 2 likewise tries to hold conflict and cooperation, force and persuasion, in some creative balance in the context of the doctrine of God's relation to man. Political society can be viewed as neither impervious to redemption within history nor susceptible to full redemption.

Recognition of the place and necessity of force and even coercion in effecting social change does not only depend on theological-anthropological assumptions, for such assumptions are somewhat corroborated by empirical evidence. William L. Taylor's perceptive analysis of strategies of protest in the civil rights movement demonstrates that the greater relative effectiveness of the sit-ins over most other forms of protest stemmed from their multilevel approach. They were "simultaneous appeals to conscience, to law and to economic self-interest."[82] His point has been confirmed by several studies, including one of the impact of the sit-ins in Greensboro, N.C., where they were started in February 1960. The students hoped that their sit-ins and picketing would "arouse public opinion and thus force a change on the part of the variety stores." But this part of the strategy was relatively unimportant in the end, for the determinative factor was "the tremendous economic power put on the stores by the Negroes' boycott," along with the reluctance of whites to trade in these stores because of their fear of trouble.[83]

82. William L. Taylor, "Civil Disobedience: Observations on the Strategies of Protest," in Bedau, *CD*, p. 104.

83. Miles Wolff, *Lunch at the Five and Ten: The Greensboro Sit-Ins* (New York: Stein and Day, 1970), pp. 137, 173; cf. 174–75, 179; See also Merrill Proudfoot, *Diary of a Sit-In* (Chapel Hill: University of North Carolina Press, 1962), p. 185. William Robert Miller writes: "opponents were seldom if ever won over to the side of justice as a result of voluntary suffering or Christian love on the part of the demonstrators. The key

A very interesting study of the implications of theoretical and experimental examinations of attitude change for nonviolent action stresses the importance of coercion rather than persuasion or conversion. The authors' conclusions deserve thorough consideration:

> The application of attitude-change theory to the study of the effects of nonviolence does not leave one with a feeling of optimism. . . . attitudes or ideologies resist change through the effects of a variety of equilibrium maintaining mechanisms. Nonviolent actions often do not seem to have characteristics which guarantee the undermining of the resistance to change. However, there are two reasons for hope by the proponents of nonviolence. The first is that the theories might help in avoiding tactics which increase resistance to change. The second and more important one is the recognition that *under the proper conditions, coercion can ultimately lead to attitude change.* For this hope to be realized, the nonviolent agents of change need to know about the sources of the attitudes they wish to affect. They need to know the content of the beliefs brought to the protests by targets and by bystanders. They need to know the reference groups supporting the attitudes to be changed and also the reference groups or individuals who might soften the opposition to the goals and methods of the nonviolent protests. Neither of these two types of knowledge is easily acquired. Under these circumstances, *it is probably best for the protesters to concentrate on coercing behavior*

---

factor was economic leverage, and closely related to this was the merchants' desire for stability and civil order. A marginal factor of varying importance was the basic attitude of the white community: hostile, neutral, or sympathetic" (*Nonviolence: A Christian Interpretation* [New York: Association Press, 1964], p. 311).

change in a way which uses as little force as is possible to ensure the desired changes and to focus on changing attitudes only when the information needed to apply attitude-change theories is available.[84]

It is certainly an oversimplification to view most civil disobedience as being either persuasive or coercive rather than a mixture of these elements. In fact, both elements are often involved in relation to different audiences; for what is persuasive in relation to the reference publics (e.g. those groups to whose opinions and pressures the administration is sensitive) of the target (e.g. the mayor's office) may be very coercive in relation to the target (e.g. the reference publics of the mayor put pressure on him to respond in certain ways against his conviction and will). Michael Lipsky, in *Protest in City Politics,* provides a good theoretical as well as empirical interpretation of this process by examining protests by the relatively powerless in the rent strikes in New York City during 1963–65. Because the protesters had very little in the way of bargaining resources, they had to create them by protest that could activate third parties with the requisite power to shape the response of the targets. Indispensable in this whole process, of course, are the communications media. Lipsky's point was expressed to a great extent by E. A. Ross in a succinct formulation half a century ago:

Disobedience without violence wins, *if it wins,* not so much by touching the conscience of the masters as by exciting the sympathy of disinterested onlookers. The spectacle of men suffering for a principle *and not hitting back* is a moving one. It obliges the power holders to con-

84. Sidney I. Perloe, et al. "Attitudes and Nonviolent Action," *Nonviolent Direct Action. American Cases: Social-Psychological Analyses,* ed. A. Paul Hare and Herbert H. Blumberg (Cleveland: Corpus Publications, 1968), pp. 443–44. Italics mine.

descend to explain, to justify themselves. The weak get
a change of venue from the will of the stronger to the
court of public opinion, perhaps of world opinion.[85]

By virtue of being *action,* which nonetheless has all the
features that I have described, civil disobedience is always
more than mere persuasion. Furthermore, there is often an
element of moral coercion in the presentation of the end or
objective, for the civil disobedient not only says "Your failure
to alter this evil is blameworthy" but "You are responsible
for my suffering if you refuse to make these changes." Thus,
civil disobedience depends to a great extent upon creating a
sense of guilt about the disobedient's suffering as well as
about an objectionable law, policy, or state of affairs. It has
been aptly described as "moral jiu-jitsu" which causes the
opponent to "lose his moral balance."[86]

These comments can only be suggestive for moral reflection since the mechanism of nonviolence has yet to be
subjected to thorough and exhaustive scrutiny. The best
available studies tend to abstract social-psychological considerations from sociological, economic, and political matters,
and they also suffer from some of the maladies afflicting social
scientific research in general.[87] Some of the foremost prac-
titioners of civil disobedience and other forms of nonviolence
have contributed to its obfuscation by defining actions and
practices in moral, religious, or metaphysical terms often far
removed from their actual mechanisms.[88] A closely related

85. E. A. Ross, Introduction to *Non-Violent Coercion* by Clarence
Marsh Case (New York: Century, 1923). Author's italics.

86. Richard B. Gregg, *The Power of Nonviolence* (New York: Shocken
Books, 1969), p. 44. For another perspective, see the discussion of "creative
disorder" by Arthur I. Waskow, *From Race Riot to Sit-In: 1919 and the
1960s* (New York: Doubleday, Anchor Book, 1967), especially chapter 16.

87. See Hare and Blumberg, *Nonviolent Direct Action,* especially p. 22.

88. See Gandhi's definition of Swadeshi as discussed by Anthony de
Crespigny, "The Nature and Methods of Non-violent Coercion," *Political
Studies* 12, no. 2 (June 1964): 258.

tendency is to confuse moral reasons for preferring nonviolence as a method of protest with explanations of its mechanism: love may well be a strong moral reason for favoring
nonviolence but it may not explain how nonviolence works.
The contention that the principle which justifies an action
also explains its effects must be analyzed in each particular
case; and, as I have suggested, there are good grounds for
thinking that nonviolence is not merely "love begetting love",
in Sorokin's terms, but also, at least in many instances, a form
of coercion.[89] The moral reasons for favoring civil disobedience or other forms of nonviolence should not blind us to a
careful analysis of how it actually works in concrete cases.

Many interpreters agree that moral educative or persuasive
disobedience may have a very significant place *within* democratic political life, for it is "still in the area of debate, and is
a method of persuasion rather than a recourse to force. The
resister puts his plea into the arena of debate, and stakes
himself upon it: and if he invites the application of force to
his own person, he does not seek to apply it to the persons of
others."[90] I have already argued that one form of coercive
disobedience—obstruction to prevent officials from carrying
out policies—is not consistent with democratic commitment
and process. However, my analysis has suggested that most
civil disobedience and nonviolence work by some form of
coercion as well as persuasion, and some of these other forms
of coercion are expressed in normal political processes as well
as in civil disobedience. A good example is the exertion of
economic pressure, whether by threatening to withdraw funds
from a candidate or by boycotting a variety store.

89. See the selection from Sorokin's *The Ways and Power of Love:
Types, Factors, and Techniques of Moral Transformation,* reprinted in
Hare and Blumberg, *Nonviolent Direct Action,* pp. 342–45.
90. Ernest Barker, *Principles of Social and Political Theory* (London:
Oxford University Press, 1961), pp. 223 f.

Whether persuasive or moderately coercive, much civil disobedience may be seen as falling just within the boundaries of the democratic commitment and rule of law. While it should never be confused with normal political activity, it is often not so great an aberration as to be totally beyond the democratic realm. Democracy may need an occasional "prophetic shock minority"—in Jacques Maritain's phrase—to awaken its dormant conscience, perhaps because of the temporary cloture of other channels, the impossibility of securing funds for promulgating ideas, the time consumed by normal legal and political processes, and so forth.

Another area of profound debate is *indirect* disobedience, which involves a violation of an admittedly valid and just law in order to call attention to some goal or objective. Too often this type of disobedience is simply ignored (as by Rawls). One fundamental question is whether the only conditions under which it can be justified are also conditions that justify revolution. This claim is sometimes made on the grounds that indirect resistance is more revolutionary and antidemocratic than direct resistance. Thus, Joseph Farraher contends:

> Civil disobedience against admittedly just laws is not considered justified. Intent to put pressure on those who can and should correct injustices does not justify the use of illegal means. General civil disobedience is only justified where rebellion would be justified—only when it is necessary self-defense against tyrannical oppression.[91]

Abe Fortas, in *Concerning Dissent and Civil Disobedience*, makes a similar argument on moral and political grounds when he claims that civil disobedience is "never justified in our nation where the law being violated is not itself the focus

91. Farraher, "The Natural Law and Conscience-Based Claims," p. 451.

or target of the protest" (p. 63). Finally, Judge Wyzanksi calls for "delayed civil disobedience" after the example of Sir Thomas More: "each of us may bide his time until he personally is faced with an order requiring him as an individual to do a wrongful act."[92]

Three factors should be considered in response to such arguments. First, while there is much merit in Wyzanski's argument, he and others tend to view the civil disobedient as being primarily concerned with extricating himself from involvement in such an evil as the demand to kill civilians in Vietnam rather than interested in eliminating a policy which leads to the slaughter of civilians.[93] The civil disobedient is most often engaged in moral-political protest. Second, indirect disobedience is no more revolutionary than direct disobedience as long as it meets the conditions about submission, nonobstruction, and so forth that I have sketched in this chapter. Third, in many instances there is no law specifically related to the evil that is being protested. While direct disobedience is the refusal to obey a demand to engage in or refrain from some form of conduct, indirect disobedience is most often aimed at policies or social conditions rather than at particular laws. I mentioned several examples in chapter 1, but others can be given. The unilateralist in Great Britain objected to a policy, although he violated a law in protest of nuclear armament just as the crew of the *Golden Rule* did in their protest of nuclear testing by the United States. A group protesting against Dow Chemical may stand for ten hours blocking a sidewalk in violation of a town ordinance. Or civil disobedients may try to call attention to de facto school segregation or to environmental crises in the hope that these will become matters of public decision and governmental policy

92. Charles E. Wyzanski, Jr., "On Civil Disobedience," *The Atlantic* 221, no. 2 (February 1968): 60; also in Bedau, *CD,* pp. 194–200.

93. This is particularly true of George Kennan's interpretation in *Democracy and the Student Left,* pp. 147–48.

and be rectified instead of remaining the consequences of a series of private actions. In such cases, the law that is violated is not the object of protest, but direct disobedience is impossible.

While this fact alone does not justify indirect resistance, it becomes very important when it is coupled with the other conditions for justifying civil disobedience I have presented in this chapter, for the feature of *indirectness* does not necessarily render disobedience unjustifiable. Certainly, however, indirect disobedience is not as easily justified as direct, ceteris paribus, although justifying circumstances short of revolution do exist. The assessment of consequences is especially significant in indirect disobedience, which appears to pose a greater threat to the legal order and to be less effective than direct disobedience, particularly in the communication of ideas. Both points are related since they stem, to a great extent, from the frequently tenuous connection between the act of disobedience and the objective. This tenuous connection makes the disobedience appear more arbitrary and hence less respectful of the system of law, and it also makes the communication of ideas and persuasion even more difficult than in direct disobedience.

Often the connection between the law that is violated or the act of disobedience and the cause is *symbolic,* as when the Baltimore Four in October 1967 splattered 600 draft records with blood as "a symbol of reconciliation," of "life and purification," or when the Catonsville Nine destroyed draft records with homemade napalm.[94] Both groups attempted to communicate certain judgments about American society, its institutions and practices. In such instances the symbolic connection may be evident to the protesters but obscure or even misleading to their audience. Thus, burning

94. See Daniel Berrigan, *The Trial of the Catonsville Nine,* pp. 43–44, and passim. It is interesting to note how the participants construed the symbolic meaning of the action in quite different ways.

a draft card which symbolizes the Selective Service system may either suggest that one views the system as reprehensible or that the war for which the system provides men is unjust. A careful examination of the way the actions will probably be interpreted is indispensable to the justification of civil disobedience, particularly of an indirect sort, as Carl Cohen argues:

> In most cases of indirect civil disobedience the relation between the object of protest and the law or policy disobeyed is far from arbitrary. Some symbolic relation between the two will usually be sought to make the protest effective. This symbolic relation may spring from the *location* of the disobedient act (e.g., trespass in the Selective Service office or on the site of segregated construction work), or from the *time* of the disobedience (e.g., deliberately blocking traffic on the anniversary of some fateful event), or from the *nature* of the disobedient act (e.g. setting one's self afire to protest the indiscriminate burning of women and children by one's government), or the like. In some measure the relation between the act of indirect disobedience and the object of protest must be purely conventional—established only for the purpose of that protest. In any case it is essential for the success of the protest that these relations, symbolic and conventional, be widely understood by members of the community in which the protest takes place. Such relations, and their being generally understood, are necessary conditions of the justifiability of indirect civil disobedience. But by no means are they sufficient for justification.[95]

It has been suggested that Christian tax refusal, for ex-

95. Carl Cohen, "Civil Disobedience and the Law," *Rutgers Law Review* 21, no. 1 (Fall 1966): 5.

ample, cannot be judged in such terms, for it really takes
place in an eschatological rather than a historical perspective. Thus, it is a prophetic sign-act, like Jeremiah's pur-
chase of a choice piece of land while Jerusalem was under
siege, and as such it is not subject to traditional canons of
rationality and prudence. Such an argument, which could
be made in relation to either direct or indirect disobedience,
ignores one critical point: even the prophet's sign-act is a
form of communication, and thus can be judged according
to the connection between the act and what is symbolized
and according to its capacity to convey certain ideas or evoke
certain responses.[96]

In recent years much civil disobedience, whether Christian or non-Christian, has been aimed at expressing, representing, and altering consciousness while also changing
policies and laws. This is close to the educative function of
civil disobedience, but many participants and proponents
stress symbols, images, and metaphors instead of the presentation of ideas. They assume that statement of a moral-
political argument against a law, policy, or state of affairs
will not move people to action. They see the source of the
difficulty not primarily in terms of faulty reasoning or misdirected policy but rather in terms of consciousness, for the
reasoning and policy making take place within a certain kind
of consciousness. Thus, it is necessary to alter that consciousness through dramatic use of images and symbols that strike
the imagination—which can be described as "reasoning in
metaphors."[97] Consequently, much civil disobedience is, and

96. Melvin Schmidt seems to qualify his argument that such prophetic
sign-acts cannot be judged in traditional terms when he admits that "Tax
refusers have an immensely important message to convey to our world."
"Tax Refusal as Conscientious Objection to War," *The Mennonite
Quarterly Review* 43, no. 3 (July 1969): 246.

97. David V. Erdman, "Coleridge as Editorial Writer," in *Power and
Consciousness,* ed. Conor Cruise O'Brien and William Dean Vanech
(New York: New York University Press, 1969), p. 197.

is expressed in the context of, revolutionary or guerrilla theatre, with an emphasis on the revolution of consciousness. God's words to Job in Robert Frost's "A Masque of Reason" express this orientation:

> Society can never think things out
> It must see them acted out by actors
> Devoted actors at a sacrifice—
> The ablest actors I can lay my hands on.[98]

Whether the action is pouring blood on draft files, burning draft files with napalm, or portraying the murder of Vietnamese women and children with the appropriate costumes and effects before governmental officials, we can see this emphasis on the alteration of imagination and consciousness rather than persuasion or coercion. Indeed, what is sought is close to conversion. One of the most interesting and significant dramatic or theatrical protests was staged by the Vietnam Veterans Against the War (April 1971), who mounted a series of actions aimed at altering the consciousness of the American people about the Vietnam War. Their actions included smashing toy guns, returning medals and awards, and staging, on the steps of the Capitol, mock search-and- destroy missions with women being "shot" by soldiers. If these actions accomplished their ends, they were effective as part of a larger strategy, and their effectiveness resulted from several contextual elements, including the credentials of the actors.

Although this kind of civil disobedience is based on a sound recognition of the importance of imagination and consciousness, it raises other questions, mainly from the standpoint of strategy and tactics. Often the play or the drama becomes the central object of attention, almost an end in itself. Referring to James Forman's disruption of church

98. *A Masque of Reason* (New York: Henry Holt, 1945), p. 12.

services to demand reparations for blacks, and other incidents, Robert Brustein contends that

> the incidents have been staged for the newspaper reporters and television cameras and should, therefore, be more properly evaluated by aesthetic than by political criteria, according to the quality of the dialogue, costumes, acting, and direction. . . . And what may have been originally stimulated by a desire to dramatize a cause for the sake of curing an injustice now often seems like theatre for its own sake, destructive in its aim, negative in its effect, performed with no particular end in mind.[99]

Even when the drama does not become an end in itself, such approaches may reflect the assumption that changing conduct or institutional patterns is either impossible or insignificant unless there are basic changes in consciousness. Certainly effective action will consider both conduct and consciousness, but, as suggested earlier, available evidence indicates that coerced changes in conduct may lead individuals to changed values and attitudes. Some of this concentration on consciousness may indicate that the old shibboleth, "Law can't change morality," has been revived in a new form.

I have emphasized the faulty assumption of some defenders of this kind of civil disobedience that consciousness is the only avenue of change, as well as the danger that the drama will become an end in itself, but I should reiterate that the effects of any such dramatic civil disobedience are usually quite unpredictable, as the Baltimore Four discovered when they poured blood on the draft files.[100] Already my analysis

99. *Revolution as Theatre* (New York: Liveright, 1971), pp. 18, 22.

100. See Francine du Plessix Gray, *Divine Disobedience*, p. 123. For a fuller discussion of imagination and politics and also the unpredictable effects of dramatic politics, see Conor Cruise O'Brien, "Imagination and Politics," and "Politics as Drama as Politics," in O'Brien and Vanech, *Power and Consciousness*, pp. 203–28.

of indirect disobedience and symbolic communication has raised the central topic of the next section: the prediction and evaluation of consequences.

CONSEQUENCES: POLITICAL CHANGE AND THE THREAT OF DISORDER

While Martin Luther King stressed that "one has a moral responsibility to disobey unjust laws," other factors, including the assessment of consequences, are indispensable for justifying civil disobedience. It is necessary to emphasize this point, for, as I have indicated, a person might be able to establish that he has a right to disobey a particular law but not that it is right for him to exercise that right because of other features of the situation, including probable consequences. Although political change and disorder are not the only possible important effects, they are among the most widely and fervently debated. Disagreements about such topics usually are rooted as much in factual differences (What will happen?) as in moral differences (Are the probable effects good or bad? What is the net gain or loss?). Since such factual differences are shaped, at least in part, by theological and anthropological perspectives, the views of God's purposes for man, human sin, and the necessity for order that I developed briefly in chapter 2 are important for my assessment of the consequences of civil disobedience.

Some theologians assert that the probability of successful, effective action is irrelevant to moral evaluation in certain areas, including political resistance. Thus, Karl Barth argues that the demand for a country to fight in a war is "quite unconditional," and—as seen from a distinctively Christian perspective—"is independent of the success or failure of the enterprise, and therefore of the strength of one's own forces in comparison with those of the enemy."[101] Other theologians such as Walter Künneth emphasize that the probability of success is a necessary presupposition of the "ethical possibility" of political resistance, although they refuse to recognize an "ethical justification."[102]

From my perspective, the possibility and probability of successful action are important to justifying most civil disobedience, although such considerations are not sufficient, as I have already suggested. Dietrich Bonhoeffer rightly stressed the ethical significance of success:

> Though success can never justify an evil deed or the use of questionable means, it is not an ethically neutral thing. . . . To ignore the ethical significance of success is to betray a superficial acquaintance with history and a defective sense of responsibility. . . . The ultimate question the man of responsibility asks is not, How can I extricate myself heroically from the affair? but, How is the coming generation to live? . . . Prudence and folly are not ethical *adiaphora*.[103]

The primary element of success for my purposes is political effectiveness: will the act probably be effective in attaining objectives in the political order? My discussion of this question will not be complete, although I have already referred at various points to tactical matters and to the conditions under which civil disobedience might be effective, e.g. the

101. *Church Dogmatics*, vol. 3, pt. 4, p. 463. His discussion of the abortive July 20, 1944 attempt on Hitler's life is more ambiguous on this question of success (see pp. 449–50).

102. See Künneth, *Politik*, pp. 220–27; *Die Vollmacht des Gewissens*, pp. 84, 173.

103. Bonhoeffer, *Letters and Papers from Prison*, ed. Eberhard Bethge and trans. Reginald H. Fuller (New York: Macmillan, 1962), pp. 20–22, 26.

necessity of a close relation between means and the object of protest, and the necessity of combining coercion with persuasion in many contexts.

Although it is very difficult to determine the probability of success at the time of an act, this task cannot be ignored, at least from the standpoint of an "ethic of responsibility" in contrast to an "ethic of intention or ultimate values." Matters are usually not very clear even for a *post factum* analysis, especially because of the convergence of independent as well as related factors and forces with civil disobedience itself. Civil disobedience is seldom an isolated incident of protest but is usually combined with sundry other activities in a broader strategy or movement, although there may be no central direction or organization. A cogent argument can be constructed to show that nonviolent direct action, including civil disobedience, was very important in the passage of the Civil Rights Act of 1964, for such action interacted with numerous other forces—often in quite accidental ways—to stimulate public concern and congressional and presidential action.[104] Another example is civil disobedience in protest of nuclear testing. In *The Quiet Battle,* Mulford Sibley contends that, although the voyages of the *Golden Rule* and the *Phoenix* into nuclear testing areas (and related actions such as invading missile bases and boarding submarines under construction) "did not result in the abandonment of testing at the time, they did have considerable success in arousing opinion and probably helped prepare the way for the nuclear testing moratorium of 1958–61" (p. 307).

It is difficult to be more precise than this in such discussions of causation even in relation to more limited problems in more limited areas. For example, in New York in the early

104. See Robert Dahl, *Pluralist Democracy in the United States: Conflict and Consent* (Chicago: Rand McNally, 1967), pp. 416–28, especially p. 420.

1960s, several citizens refused to take shelter during the compulsory air raid drills, and it is likely that the necessity of having to arrest several citizens each time led to the cancellation of the tests. Nevertheless, this civil disobedience operated not in a vacuum but in relation to numerous other factors and forces, and it is impossible to weigh the impact of each element separately. Even in a simple and somewhat trivial matter such as protesting the increase in bus fares from twenty-five to forty cents in Washington, D.C., it is difficult to gauge the effectiveness of the act of civil disobedience committed by boarding a bus, paying only the earlier rate, and then being arrested.[105] In one sense, it should be clear when this act is unsuccessful, that is, unproductive of a return to the earlier rate; but in another sense, its long-term effects may be more positive—for example, the bus company might be unwilling to raise the rates again under similar conditions because it has reason to expect strong protest if it does.

In recent years, much of the debate about civil disobedience's political effectiveness has been conducted under the broader rubrics of nonviolence and violence and their relative efficacy. For example, in the 1950s and early 1960s nonviolent protest in South Africa kept open some channels of communication between the oppressed and the oppressors, but it made little tangible progress, and indeed may have exacerbated the situation. In Kenya, however, violence was used and political change effected, although the hostility between the various parties may have increased as a result.[106]

105. *Washington Post*, July 11, 1970, A4.
106. Leo Kuper, *Passive Resistance in South Africa*, p. 94. Edward Feit tries to show how the failures of passive resistance in South Africa can be explained "in terms other than the odds themselves." *African Opposition in South Africa: The Failure of Passive Resistance* (Stanford, Calif.: Stanford University, The Hoover Institution on War, Revolution and Peace, 1967), p. vii, and passim.

These contrasting examples are taken from nondemocratic contexts, and the argument would take a somewhat different form in a functioning democracy. Thus, although nonviolence may keep disobedience within the existing order (if on its fringes), a relevant question is whether or not one sacrifices political effectiveness in order to remain democratic.

Of course, it is also necessary to have a broad view of relevant factors for predicting and evaluating the effects of one's action: whether evaluating the actions of active resisters like John Brown and Dietrich Bonhoeffer or civil disobedients like Henry David Thoreau and Daniel Berrigan, one has to consider their "probable symbolic and emotional consequences."[107] The difficulty of making such predictions and assessments is obvious, but they must be made, particularly because they keep one's vision from being limited to the tangible effects that are immediately evident within a very narrow segment of history.

Besides immediate changes of policy, there is another important objective of much civil disobedience. The aims of the Catonsville Nine included halting the machine of death, saving lives, communicating with the people, and raising an outcry.[108] With respect to some of these aims—except for communicating the horrors of the war to the people and delaying the inductions of some men from one area—their action must be viewed as unsuccessful, unless at some future point it stimulates reference publics or third parties beween the government and protesters to effect the desired changes. But in Daniel Berrigan's refusal to surrender and serve his

107. Edward Madden, *Civil Disobedience and Moral Law in Nineteenth-Century American Philosophy* (Seattle: University of Washington Press, paperbound, 1970), p. 82.

108. Daniel Berrigan, *The Trial of the Catonsville Nine*, pp. 30, 34–35, 48, 59, 74, 103–04, 111.

sentence, the objective of building "communities of resistance" became dominant.[109] By persuading several people to share his plight and to take risks on his behalf, he hoped to create or bring to attention a kind of solidarity. Perhaps then these formerly hesitant persons would recognize and extend their own solidarity through more concerted and effective action toward major objectives. The value of such an approach has long been stressed by Saul Alinsky, who sees protest and confrontation as vehicles for building organization.[110]

Certainly civil disobedience as part of a protest movement must be called into question if and when it appears to be counterproductive on any of these levels. Persistence at such a point may be an expression of self-righteousness rather than political wisdom. In the 1960s a favorite term for this counterproductivity was *backlash. How* a group or movement attains its ends and avoids a disastrous backlash is a *political* question to be handled by political prudence, but *that* it chooses the most efficient means (within moral limits) and counts the cost is a *moral* demand.

Because it is necessary to count the cost of civil disobedience, the problem of political effectiveness can be resolved only when it is conjoined with the whole range of direct and indirect effects for others and the society as a whole. The responsible civil disobedient recognizes the irony of history, and thus views the test as "not the magnitude of the benefit sought, but the net worth of the anticipated benefit over its

109. *Newsweek,* August 24, 1970, p. 37. See also Philip Nobile, "The Priest Who Stayed Out in the Cold," *New York Times Magazine,* June 28, 1970, p. 40.
110. See Charles E. Silberman, *Crisis in Black and White* (New York: Random House, 1964), chap. 10; Michael Lipsky writes, "the cohesion of relatively powerless groups may be strengthened by militant, ideological leadership which questions the rules of the game and challenges their legitimacy" (*Protest in City Politics,* p. 165).

probable costs."[111] However, a person might object to this procedure on the grounds that his act is a purely personal, conscientious protest since he, for instance, refuses to take part in the war in Vietnam on nonreligious but nonetheless moral grounds. Because Congress has unjustly discriminated against his position, he must disobey the induction order.[112] While it is likely that his act will not have deleterious effects on the body politic, this is a factual matter which has to be determined from case to case. It is impossible to assume that a personal protest will not have broader, political ramifications. A civil disobedient who refuses to consider such possible and probable effects is behaving irresponsibly, for such a *Gesinnungsethik* as Thoreau's politics of the upright man is morally inadequate. Although it is not necessary that consequences be the dominant consideration, they are always morally relevant. As Sidney Hook suggests,

> The judgment of the character and legitimacy of acts of civil disobedience must, in the end, depend not so much on whether the acts are nonviolent or not but on the consequences of those acts on the community. A nonviolent or passive act of disobedience which will result in starving a city or in deprivation of essential care may be much worse and less tolerable, from a democratic point of view, than a flurry of transient violence.[113]

Although some civil disobedience may pose a substantial threat to order and the rule of law, it is difficult to delineate

111. Keeton, "The Morality of Civil Disobedience," *Texas Law Review* 43, no. 4 (March 1965): 521. Cf. Kent Greenawalt, "A Contextual Approach to Disobedience," in Pennock and Chapman, eds., *Political and Legal Obligation: Nomos 12*, pp. 332–69.

112. Prior to the Supreme Court decision in *Welsh* v. *United States*, 90 S. Ct. 1792 (1970).

113. Hook, *The Paradoxes of Freedom*, p. 120.

precisely and accurately its nature and scope. Arguments on this point, just as those on political effectiveness, arise as much from divergent interpretations of the facts as from divergent moral values. Because much of civil disobedience's threat to order stems from its openness, many critics have charged that this characteristic is more a vice than a virtue.[114] While such a charge overlooks the respect that openness and its accompanying virtue, submission, may pay to the legal system, it does stress that public disobedience is ambiguous.

Some defenders of civil disobedience insist that open and submissive disobedience actually strengthens rather than weakens the legal system, for it makes the law increasingly sensitive to the demands of human conscience and buttresses the system as a whole because it does not involve an evasion of legal penalties.[115] Furthermore, submission sets a "limit on the example of disobedience."[116] While it is very difficult to provide empirical evidence for such interpretations, it is equally difficult to find empirical support for much of the opposition to civil disobedience. As a result, the arguments against it usually consist of simple enumerations of "possible" undesirable consequences, as though they necessarily and self-evidently flowed from civil disobedience. The so-called wedge argument is often implicit. Thus, Charles E. Whittaker, former associate justice of the U.S. Supreme Court, writes, "it can hardly be denied that a large part of our current rash and rapid spread of lawlessness has derived from planned and organized mass disrespect for, and defiance

114. Louis Waldman, "Civil Rights—Yes: Civil Disobedience—No," in Bedau, CD, p. 109.

115. Harrop Freeman, "Moral Preemption Part I: The Case for the Disobedient," The Hastings Law Journal 17 (March 1966): 437; H. L. A. Hart, "Legal and Moral Obligation," in Melden, Essays in Moral Philosophy, p. 105; Martin Luther King, Jr., Why We Can't Wait, pp. 83–84.

116. Greenawalt, "A Contextual Approach to Disobedience," p. 361.

of, the law and the courts."[117] Such lists almost always include riots and mob violence in addition to general lawlessness. That these are *possible* direct and indirect effects of civil disobedience is enough to urge great caution, particularly because of the importance of maintaining order; but it is necessary to ask whether they are also *probable* effects of civil disobedience and, if so, under what conditions.

Assumptions about men and society in general, and these men and this society in particular, shape one's response to the view that civil disobedience is a wedge for lawlessness in the structure of order. Howard Zinn, in *Disobedience and Democracy*, argues that the domino theory does not apply to civil disobedience, for "society's tendency is to maintain what has been" (p. 16). From such a perspective, he minimizes the possible harmful effects of civil disobedience on the fabric of order. Other observers discern an "empirically observable tendency" for disobedience to spread from worthy to unworthy objectives and hence to increase disorder.[118] Certainly in recent years not only bad but trivial objectives have rarely lacked backers who were ready and eager to wear the badge of civil disobedience. The experience of a genuine moral dilemma about seeking one's objectives by disobeying the law seems to have been almost extinguished, perhaps because the sense of an obligation to obey the law has atrophied. While numerous factors have undoubtedly contributed to the weakening of the feeling of political obligation, surely among the most important ones are the failures of the democratic system to achieve some of its ideals.

117. Charles E. Whittaker, "The Effects of Planned, Mass Disobedience of Our Laws," *F.B.I. Law Enforcement Bulletin*, Sept. 1966, p. 10. See the stress on the unplanned and irrational consequences of civil disobedience by William H. Marnell, "Civil Disobedience and the Majority of One," *Religion and the Public Order, No. Five*, ed. Donald A. Giannella (Ithaca, N.Y.: Cornell University Press, 1969), pp. 138–39.

118. Hook, "Social Protest and Civil Disobedience," in Kurtz, *Moral Problems in Contemporary Society*, p. 165.

Perhaps the major source of concern and dispute is whether nonviolent disobedience contributes to violent crimes. This question cannot simply be answered by showing the plausibility of the connection between these two kinds of action on the grounds that both are forms of disobedience, for one is violent and the other is nonviolent. Furthermore, the available data indicate that black communities have fewer violent crimes during direct action campaigns than usual. Some commentators think that the reason is that "[s]uch emotional expression, when it occurs in a framework of community organization may reduce the need for aggressive outbursts of a violent sort, thus reducing the incidence of such crimes."[119] These data, however, provide evidence only of the effects *during* the time of protest, not after the protest. Nevertheless, studies of long-range effects preclude any assertion that civil disobedience undermines the habits of observance of laws and other social expectations. One study of approximately three hundred young black protesters indeed suggests less antisocial or criminal behavior among civil disobedients than the population at large. Among this group there were "virtually no manifestations of delinquency or anti-social behavior, no school drop-outs, and no known illegitimate pregnancies."[120] It is also possible that *effective* civil disobedience of a nonrevolutionary sort may give the disobedient a stake in the system so that he is less likely to violate other laws. These points concern the effects of civil disobedience on the protesters, especially their habits of law observance; some of my other points concern its effects on those not involved in the protest and on the system as a whole.

119. Frederic Solomon, et al., "Civil Rights Activity and Reduction in Crime Among Negroes," *Archives of General Psychiatry* 12 (March, 1965): 236.

120. *To Establish Justice, To Insure Domestic Tranquility,* The Final Report of the National Commission on the Causes and Prevention of Violence (New York: Bantam, 1970), p. 85.

An equally pressing question has to do with violence that is more closely related to moral-political opposition to laws, policies, and general social conditions, as are some rioting and terrorist activities. Such violence may be only inadequately described as "politically purposive" since much "rioting is a spontaneous outburst of group violence characterized by excitement mixed with rage," and since it is often difficult to identify political purposes and aims.[121] Certainly much planned violence, in contrast to spontaneous violence, is "politically purposive." Furthermore, there is a difference beween violent crimes such as murdering the manager of a store for a few dollars and destruction of property and life in outrage over oppression. Even if there is no evidence for a causal relation between civil disobedience and the former, it is at least possible that one can establish a connection between civil disobedience and violence that is politically purposive or that is an expression of outrage over oppression.[122] If such a connection exists—and the evidence is inconclusive—it probably stems not from the *escalation* of protest—for example, from civil disobedience to planned terrorism—but more likely from the *frustration* of protest. As Hannah Arendt argues in *On Violence,* violence, conceived as the polar opposite of power, may well result from the absence or diminution of power—the frustration of the faculty of action. Ralph Conant expresses the point cogently:

121. Ralph W. Conant, "Rioting, Insurrection and Civil Disobedience," *The American Scholar* 37, no. 3 (Summer 1968): 420.

122. See *Report of the National Advisory Commission on Civil Disorders* (New York: Bantam, 1968), pp. 204–05, for an ambiguous statement, since it may merely claim that some groups engaging in civil disobedience turned their backs on nonviolence and resorted to violence. The National Commission on the Causes and Prevention of Violence concluded, by a seven to six margin, that even nonviolent civil disobedience is an underlying cause of disorder. See *Washington Post,* Dec. 9, 1969, A1 & A4, and *To Establish Justice, To Ensure Domestic Tranquility,* pp. 74–77.

While all riots stem from conflicts in society similar to those that inspire civil disobedience, they ordinarily do not develop directly from specific acts of civil disobedience. Yet repeated failures of civil disobedience to achieve sought-after goals can and often do result in frustrations that provide fertile ground for the violent outbursts we call riots.[123]

Few consequences attributed to civil disobedience and related actions are as salient and as dramatic as rioting, but others may be even more momentous in the long run. While not all forms of civil disobedience involve force and coercion, so much political "debate" in recent years has been conducted by force and coercion instead of rational, moral-political persuasion that it is possible to point to "a loss of civility in the conduct of public controversies in the United States."[124] Nowhere is this loss of civility more evident than in the use of disruptive tactics to prevent speakers from presenting opposing ideas. While I have emphasized the possible value of civil disobedience as a form of speech-action in communicating ideas when other channels are closed, certainly it would be disastrous for democracy if such speech-actions (even of the noncoercive, nonobstructive sort) were to become the dominant or exclusive mode of discourse. Perhaps it would even mean that democracy had already ceased to exist as an effective order.

Paradoxical though it may be, there is a real sense in which the decline of civility and other secondary virtues such as tolerance, fair play, and compromise is in fact the result of an intensified respect for the morality of the primary virtues of ends and purposes, which are now frequently construed in

123. Conant, "Rioting, Insurrection and Civil Disobedience," p. 420.
124. Francis Allen, "Civil Disobedience and the Legal Order," pt. 1, *University of Cincinnati Law Review* 36, no. 1 (Winter 1967): 34.

absolute and ultimate ways and extended to broader areas of human experience. Thus, Alexander Bickel responds to the question "What is happening to morality today?" by suggesting that "one answer, not too far off the mark, is that it threatens to engulf us."[125] Accompanying this exalted morality of absolute ends are a bifurcation of the world of politics into absolute good and evil and a tendency to see one's opponents in demonic terms—an example of what Peter Berger has called "selective humanism." Furthermore, one of its characteristic traits is an arrogant self-righteousness which refuses to give opposing view-points a hearing (by definition "evil") or to compromise (by definition "selling-out"). It is not necessary to estimate the extent of such tendencies in order to note their presence and to see that they may be connected with widespread uses of civil disobedience (and more drastic measures) for effecting social change. Such a connection is one of mutual interaction: these attitudes were partially fostered by the frequent use of civil disobedience and other dramatic protest methods, while they certainly encourage such protest.

Another danger of civil disobedience is generally overlooked—perhaps because it too is not as dramatic as disorder, backlash, or even the decline of civility. Michael Lipsky concludes that "the opportunity to protest deflects attention away from the systemic inability of *relatively powerless* groups to engage in politics of any kind."[126] Without ques-

125. Alexander Bickel, "What is Happening to Morality Today?" *Yale Alumni Magazine* 33, no. 2 (November 1969): 59. In the same issue, in an article entitled "Morality, Violence and Student Protest," Kenneth Keniston suggests that the "problem is not the presence of the ethical impulse, but the absence of the qualities needed to humanize it" (p. 58).

126. Lipsky, *Protest in City Politics*, p. ix. If power is defined in terms of the capacity to affect the results of the policy-making process, groups may be relatively powerless in some areas but influential in others. Perhaps, for example, most groups are relatively powerless in the area of foreign policy.

tioning Lipsky's point, I would contend that for the *relatively powerful* groups, protest activities, including civil disobedience, may deflect attention from the system's amenability to their influence in and through the established channels, and that the symbolic and emotional rewards of protest (e.g. experience of crisis and confrontation, publicity, sense of community) may be accepted as substitutes for tangible rewards, including desirable changes in policies. Thus it is possible that civil disobedience may divert activity which could make the democratic process more humane and effective. It may even constitute a self-fulfilling prophecy: we go outside established political channels because they appear to be unresponsive, and by so doing, we deprive them of resources that could make them responsive. Arnold Kaufman offers such an argument:

> Civil disobedience tends to be counterproductive—not so much because bad public reaction is generated, though this may occasionally be the case, but because it wastes energies and resources that are better spent making American democracy work.[127]

His point is well taken, although frequently civil disobedience is in fact less an alternative to political action within the system than only one form of such action (certainly on the outer boundaries of the system) which may persuade the people and officials of the moral and political viability of some laws and policies. Surely, however, this danger of counterproductivity must be included in the calculations of responsible civil disobedience, although the weight one gives to it will depend on one's view of the amenability and flexibility of the system.

127. Kaufman, "Opposition Politics is More Important," *Dissent* 15, no. 1 (Jan.-Feb. 1968): 23.

Recognition of the duty of fair play within the democratic context, with its concomitants of having exhausted all available remedies, and so forth, puts the burden of justification on the civil disobedient. Such a burden may well lead to a fitting concentration on what is possible within the system rather than an eagerness to experiment with extralegal activities. Thus, sometimes deontological considerations (such as fair play) can lead to a discovery of new ways to attain goals within the system.

My interest in civil disobedience as a technique of moral-political protest has involved an emphasis on groups and movements rather than individuals, although I have drawn occasional examples from individual conduct. Certainly the most interesting examples for analyzing civil disobedience from Gandhi to King, from the sit-ins to draft protests, have involved group activity. A consideration of the consequences is more urgent and pressing in mass civil disobedience for several reasons. Not only are the consequences likely to be extensive, but also there are particular difficulties, which Gandhi clearly recognized, in conducting mass civil disobedience or any other form of nonviolence.[128] Furthermore, as I have already indicated, *indirect* disobedience is more risky than direct disobedience from the standpoint of misinterpretation, counterproductivity, and disorder. For this reason, and for others, it is more difficult (although not impossible) to justify.

128. Sibley writes, "Mass civil disobedience, other things being equal, is usually closer to the pole of revolution than its individual form" (*The Obligation to Disobey: Conscience and the Law*, p. 82). Nevertheless, the importance of mass civil disobedience can be seen particularly in James Luther Adams's discussion of the connection beween civil disobedience and "voluntary associations," that "serve as mediators of sensitivity, of expanding conceptions of justice and mercy, of new prickings of conscience, which are transmitted from minority groups to the community at large" ("Civil Disobedience: Its Occasions and Limits," *Political and Legal Obligation: Nomos* 12, p. 327).

Although a calculation of consequences is required in order to avoid burning a house down to roast a pig, as in Charles Lamb's story, there is no single, accurate scale for weighing the effects of disobedience. Ernest Barker stresses this point:

> The weighing itself will differ according to time and place; and the decision will depend on the degree of stability of law and order existing in a given country at a given period. The common love of use and wont, the strength of convention, the habit of tradition, are sometimes a sufficient guarantee of the stability of law and order; and where and when that guarantee is present, the electric disturbance of a new idea, pressed to the point of resistance, may serve to correct men's tendency to settle down on the lees of custom.[129]

Calculation is thus clearly involved, but the lack of a clear calculus means that any decision about resistance is always uncertain, and therefore can only be a venture and a dare (*Wagnis*). It is an act of civic courage. Nothing in my framework of civil disobedience denies either this point or that the situations in which such action is undertaken are usually so emotion-packed as to render objectivity even less possible. While calculation and resultant uncertainty are particularly evident in predicting and assessing consequences, they also appear in justifying the cause, rejecting obligations, and determining means.

Dietrich Bonhoeffer rightly stresses that

> Disobedience can never be anything but a concrete decision in a single particular case. ... The refusal of obedience in the case of a particular historical and political decision of government must therefore, like this decision

129. Barker, *Principles of Social and Political Theory*, pp. 224–25.

itself, be a venture undertaken on one's own responsibility. A historical decision cannot be entirely resolved
into ethical terms; there remains a residuum, the venture of action.[130]

But acceptance of this point does not mean that we can
simply discard the procedures and principles for justifying
resistance. The impossibility of certainty and the necessity
of Wagnis should not lead to a denigration and rejection of
such procedures and principles, which have a significant
place and function so long as they are open to criticism and
reformulation. They constitute a framework within which
the discussion and evaluation of civil disobedience can
proceed.

I have made no attempt, however, to establish a code of the
necessary and sufficient conditions of justified civil disobedience, for such an endeavor would be futile. Rather I have
tried to sketch a tentative framework (whose primary element
is a theory of political obligation in a relatively just constitutional democracy) which will illuminate the conditions
under which civil disobedience can be justified within such
a context. Margaret Macdonald's remarks about the limits of
social contract theory remind us that it is impossible to develop a closed system which will enable us to deduce exactly
what we ought to do: "[i]t does not follow that this [the contract metaphor] is the sole criterion of political obedience,
still less that having derived all political obligations from a
social contract or a general will we can accept them all
happily and go to sleep. As rational and responsible citizens
we can never hope to know once and for all what our political
duties are. And so we can never go to sleep."[131]

130. Bonhoeffer, *Ethics,* pp. 307–08.
131. Margaret Macdonald, "The Language of Political Theory," in
Flew, *Logic and Language,* 1st ser., p. 194.

INDEX

Acton, H. B.: his concept of submissive disobedience, 175–76

Adams, James Luther: on early Christian civil disobedience, 26n49; his use of "just war" criteria, 204n63; on relation of voluntary associations to civil disobedience, 240n128

Adler, Mortimer J.: his concept of civil disobedience, 32n67, 34

Agapism. *See* Love, concept of

Alinsky, Saul, 231

Allen, J. W., 116

Althaus, Paul, 79

Aquinas, Thomas, 79; his concept of natural law, 54 and n26, 56; on political obligation, 60–63

Arendt, Hannah: her concept of obedience and command, 42n21; on essence of the state, 45–46; *On Violence,* 236

Augustine: his concept of natural law, 54n26, 56

Austin, John: positivism of, 57, 65

Backlash, 231

Baltimore Four: civil disobedience of, 221, 225

Barker, Ernest: on consequences of civil disobedience, 241

Barmen declaration, 117n10

Barth, Karl, 78, 79, 94, 95, 103, 150; his concept of political ethics, 77n65, 83–84, 86–87; his philosophy vs. Wolf's, 116 and

n9; his concept of justification of resistance, 166; on war, 226–27

Bartsch, Hans-Werner: on Christian love, 118, 119n13

Bay, Christian: on civil disobedience related to political life, xi–xii; on civil disobedience related to concept of illegality, 5; on early Christian civil disobedience, 26

Bedau, Hugo, 8; on justification of obedience and disobedience, x, 11n21; on direct resistance, 33n69

Bellah, Robert: "Civil Religion in America," 130 and n41

Benn, S. I.: on political obligation, 43n5, 111; *The Principles of Social and Political Thought,* 111

Bentham, Jeremy: positivism of, 65

Berger, Peter, 238

Berlin, Isaiah, 144n65; on political obligation, 44

Berrigan, Daniel: on religion related to civil disobedience, 25n47; civil disobedience of, 184, 185n31, 230–31

Berrigan, Philip, 185

Bickel, Alexander: on present-day morality, 238

Birmingham, Ala.: King's actions in, 31

Black Muslims: civil disobedience of, 21

243

litical obligation, 159; on justification of civil disobedience,
181, 232; on defenses of disobedience, 185

Indirect disobedience, 32–34, 219–
22 passim, 240
Internal Revenue Service: resistance to, 8, 196–97
Intuitionism, 52n24, 53

Jehovah's Witnesses: civil disobedience of, 21
John XXIII, Pope: on natural
law, 54n26; on civil authorities,
103n110
"Just war" theory: related to civil
disobedience, 203–06

Kant, Immanuel: his principle of
universality, 194 and n45, 198
Käsemann, Ernst, 115; his concept of essence of the state,
119n13
Kaufman, Arnold: on counterproductivity of civil disobedience, 239
Keeton, Morris: on civil disobedience related to legality, 37
Kelsen, Hans, 57
Keniston, Kenneth, on present-
day morality, 238n125
Kennan, George, 174, 205, 220n93
Kenya: consequence of violence in,
229
King, Martin Luther, ix, 9, 38, 211,
213, 240; his concept of civil disobedience, 1, 3, 26, 30–31, 34,
181–82, 201, 202, 226; his Montgomery bus boycott, 6, 30; "Letter from Birmingham Jail," 34;
on political vs. moral obligations, 56
Künneth, Walter, 79, 92, 95, 116n7;
his concept of Christian political
ethics, 82–83, 102; his concept of

justification of resistance, 165–
66 and n2, 227 and n1

Ladd, John: on political obligation, 149n71
Laslett, Peter: on political obligation, 44
Laws and policies, moral evaluation of: civil disobedience related to, 5–39, 202–42; obligation of obedience factor of,
42–50, 100–10, 149–64; concepts
of, 112–20; justification requirements for disobedience of, 165–
73. See also Love, concept of;
Natural law; Positive law; Social contract theory
Lehmann, Paul, 79n68; Ethics in
a Christian Context, 88
Lewy, Gunther, 210
Lichtman, Richard, 194n44; on
civil disobedience related to
morality, 24
Lipset, Seymour M.: on revolution in democracy, 154
Lipsky, Michael: Protest in City
Politics, 216; on value of unified
protest, 231n110; on consequences of civil disobedience,
238
Locke, John: on tacit consent, 125
Love, concept of (agapism): Ramsey's interpretation of, 88, 90–
93, 119n14; Fletcher's interpretation of, 98–99; Wolf's interpretation of, 114–15; obligation related to, 121–23, 128; fair play
related to, 128–29; resistance related to, 203; self-sacrificial, 213
and n81, 214n83
Luther, Martin, 116 and n7
Lynd, Staughton: his concept of
civil disobedience, 188–89, 199–
200, 211, 212